GENTLEMEN UNDER THE ELMS

Gentlemen Under the Elms

Published by Brown Alumni Monthly

by Jay Barry

We are grateful to the following for the illustrations in this book: Michael St. A. Boyer, *Brown Alumni Monthly*, *Brown Jug*, Brown Photo Lab, Brown Theatre Arts Photo File, Imogen Cunningham, John Forasté, John Hay Library Archives, Betty Kraus Hartline, Uosis Juodvalkis, *Providence Journal* Library, *Providence Journal* Rotogravure Sunday Supplement, Hugh Smyser, Esther Dick Snell, Celia Robinson Stillwell, Theresa Taft, Marge Tomas, Professor Vincent Tomas, Professor Don B. Wilmeth.

Designed by Gilbert Associates
and printed by Union Printing Company

Contents

Preface

This book is dedicated to my wife, Ella, a nice gal to spend the rest of my days with, and to the three young people who made our marriage complete – Kathy, Jay B., and Bill.

On a cold January day in 1980, George D. Flynn, Jr., a gregarious Harvard alumnus, invited Senior Vice President Richard J. Ramsden and me to lunch at the Hope Club. A gentleman of the old school with a penchant for extolling the various virtues of his Alma Mater, George soon started reciting the long list of books written about Harvard professors and by Harvard professors. Dick Ramsden listened with polite interest for some time, then turned to me and said, "Jay, I'd better free you up for a year to write a book about some of *Brown's* famous old professors."

President Swearer gave the project his blessing, stipulating that any professor deceased or retired would be fair game. By December of 1980 I had been granted a leave of absence from the *Brown Alumni Monthly*, was settled into comfortable quarters in Wilbour Hall at the corner of George and Prospect Streets, and had urged a vintage 1930 typewriter into action.

My plan was to select ten or twelve interesting and colorful professors who were prominent in their chosen fields and then write a profile about each that would represent them fairly and evoke pleasant memories among the Brown University family. I planned also to weave into the stories, whenever possible, some of the mores and traditions of the University. The selection process was long and sometimes painful. For reasons of time and space, some highly interesting professors had to be left out of this book. The process was also frustrating in the sense that there were no women professors to include. If another book of this sort is written a decade or so from now, this problem, fortunately, will no longer exist. My final choice of the eleven professors found here was based on my feel for the University after spending close to forty years in and around her hallowed halls, refined by countless conversations with members of the faculty and administration whose opinions in this area I particularly respect. Especially helpful during this stage of the project was W. Chesley "Chet" Worthington '23, my first boss on the BAM and a walking encyclopedia of Brown University history.

Working on *Gentlemen Under the Elms* was a thoroughly enjoyable experience from beginning to end, the end being a two-month search in the photo archives of the John Hay Library, the *Providence Journal*, and other dusty locations to pull together the variety of pictures needed for the layout of each chapter. As you browse through these pages, I hope you will allow your mind to wander back for a few moments to your days on College Hill, to the friends you made, the fun you had, and, particularly, to your favorite professors among those legendary Gentlemen Under the Elms.

In closing, I would like to express my appreciation to a few special people. First, President Swearer and Vice President Ramsden for their solid support in getting this project started and their continued interest in the months that followed. – I was at least twice blessed in having Margaret "Peg" Bishop as my secretary during the writing of the book. She is one of those superbly organized people who anticipates your next need before you think of it yourself. – Among the talents needed to bring a book into condition to withstand the scrutiny of knowing readers is an editor, a man who can spot and correct the awkwardness of construction, the cliches, the windiness of style, and the other failings of writers. My thanks here go to Robert M. Rhodes, editor of the *Brown Alumni Monthly* and a three-time winner of the Sibley Award, symbolic of the best college magazine in the United States.

The designers of this handsome book are Joseph Gilbert and his wife, Melissa Moger Gilbert '71, an extremely talented young couple who treated *Gentlemen Under the Elms* with tender loving care and never seemed to tire of my endless phone calls and constant visits to their office during the final months before publication. – This book is printed by Union Printing Company of West Warwick, Rhode Island, a new company with old fashioned ideas on how to put quality and craftsmanship into their work. Denny Glass is the man behind the success of this firm. – My thanks also go to four friends who took the time to look at some of the chapters and offer suggestions: Elmer M. Blistein '42, professor of English; David H. Scott '32, a former non-fiction editor at Harper and McGraw Hill; Richard A. Parker, professor emeritus of Egyptology; and Martha Mitchell, head archivist at the John Hay Library, a woman who knows more of the important facts (and some not so important!) about Brown University than anyone I've ever met. – Another who was helpful in the closing months is Joseph O. Mehr, librarian of the *Providence Journal-Bulletin*, who graciously opened his picture files to our use. – Finally, a thank-you to Alice Fuller, widow of Rufus C. Fuller, Jr. '19, for suggesting the title of this book.

J.B.

Chapter 1 🍂
Few have borne more titles
or worn more hats

Some years ago when the *Brown Daily Herald* ran a trivia quiz, one of the questions read: "What man served as dean of both Brown and Pembroke?" Rumor has it that the BDH received a call that afternoon. "On that trivia quiz," the voice said, "the man who was dean of Brown and Pembroke is Robert W. Kenny of the class of 1925. And," the caller continued, a touch of mischief now in his voice, "I want you to know that he did one hell of a job." The caller was Robert W. "Pat" Kenny. And he's one hell of a guy.

In case anyone wants to challenge that statement, keep in mind that when Dean Kenny left Brown to go back into the service in 1951 he was the subject, believe it or not, of a long and loving editorial in the *Brown Daily Herald*. Then there was the time that Professor Kenny was voted "favorite professor" by the students at Pembroke. He didn't get that vote on his well-trimmed mustache alone.

Perhaps, though, the most obvious example of the respect and affection in which Kenny is held by his former students came in the spring of 1980 when the *Brown Alumni Monthly* turned the still dapper Kenny into a "cover boy" as part of a lengthy article in which the long-time professor-administrator spoke with complete candor on a wide variety of subjects concerning the University. Within a month of the publication of this story, Pat Kenny had received more than 100 letters and phone calls from former students, many of whom hadn't been in touch with him since their days in his classroom.

"If you're going to be on the cover of the *Brown Alumni Monthly*, then you're going to have to put up with fan mail," one former student wrote. "I was a freshman in your English 48 class in the spring of 1970," the letter continued. "Not a very happy or tranquil spring, you'll recall. But it was brightened by all those wonderful stories – not just about Smollett, Pope, and Fielding – but about Wriston, Keeney, and Faunce, too. Most of us that sad spring thought history had begun only a couple of weeks before, and it was the healthiest of joys to listen to someone with a somewhat longer and not always so deadly a view of history."

Another alumnus wrote about the days when Dean Kenny would speak in Chapel. "Your talks were always interesting and usually sprinkled with humor. I especially recall one of the stories you told of a fox hunt and the term 'tally ho,' which you described as English for 'There goes the son of a bitch.'"

One writer, commenting on Kenny's charisma, compared him to Clark Gable, noting that he was respected by the male students in his classes and loved by the females. "It wouldn't be kind of me to reject such a compliment," Kenny chuckled.

Robert Webb Kenny's association with Brown University is one of the longest and richest on record, with forty-nine of his first fifty-six years since graduation being spent as a faculty member, administrator, and neighbor. In addition to being an inspirational teacher of English, he was also regarded as a wise counselor and tutor of students and colleagues alike.

With the advent of World War II, Professor Kenny began what was also to be a distinguished career in the military. He attained the rank of field captain in the 43rd Infantry Division, participated in the Pacific campaigns, and rose to the rank of lieutenant colonel in command of a field artillery battalion. He received the Bronze Star with Oak Leaf Cluster and remained in the Army Reserve until 1960, when he retired as a brigadier general and commanding officer of the 76th Division.

A Phi Beta Kappa graduate of Brown, Pat Kenny received his master's degree in 1926 and his Ph.D. in English in 1934, both from Brown. He was an assistant professor of English at his Alma Mater until 1945, became dean of students in 1946, and then served as dean of the college from 1947 to 1951, the year he was named to a full professorship. In an unusual move – one that was picked up by all the wire services – he was named dean of Pembroke College in 1961 during the illness of Nancy Duke Lewis.

In 1975, on the fiftieth anniversary of Pat Kenny's graduation, the University conferred an honorary degree on this favorite son. The citation read, in part: "Few men have borne more titles, worn more hats, than you. Twice a dean, first at Brown and then at Pembroke, you administered those two colleges with wisdom, compassion, and an administrator's most essential ingredient – a gentle but perceptive wit."

The honorary degree citation might also have mentioned that few alumni have a better grasp of the recent history of Brown University or are better able to weave the story of those years with more charm than Pat Kenny.

The Kenny family originally came from Brandon, a once Protestant enclave in the heart of Roman Catholic Ireland. Pat Kenny was born in Somerville, Massachusetts, on February 10, 1902. At the turn of the century, Somerville was similar to most other suburbs of Boston. Early nineteenth-century homes, fronted by

wide lawns and white picket fences, dominated the town. Each afternoon, paper boys lazily bicycled along the elm-shaded streets to deliver their wares. There was a band concert in the park every Sunday night during the summer months. In short, it was a comfortable New England town. Too comfortable, thought the senior member of the Kenny family.

"My father was afraid that my upbringing was too provincial," Pat says. "He had broken away from home early in life to fight in the Spanish-American War, and then he had gone to France with the 26th Infantry Division during World War I. I remember his stories about the flamboyant Teddy Roosevelt and his Rough Riders and how in the public mind they dominated that war in Cuba. I also remember my father quoting Mr. Dooley, a fictitious bar-room philosopher created by Peter Finley Dunne. Speaking of Roosevelt's history of the Rough Riders, Mr. Dooley says, 'Tis a very fine book, but the title is all wrong. It should have been called *Alone in Cuba*.'

"Well, the bottom line is that my father wanted me to get away from home and to realize that, after all, the country was at least somewhat civilized west of Worcester. So he pulled me out of Somerville High and sent me to Mercersburg Academy in Mercersburg, Pennsylvania."

At that time, Mercersburg Academy, like Lawrenceville, was a feeder for Princeton. But Pat Kenny didn't want to go to Princeton. He also didn't want to go to Dartmouth, despite (or perhaps because of) a very strong selling job by his brother and a cousin. It finally came down to Brown or Harvard. It would be nice to report that his decision as to which of these two centers of higher learning he would attend came after long hours of deep meditation. It also would be wrong. Pat recalls the circumstances surrounding the decision.

"I passed up Harvard because Somerville was so close to Cambridge that I would have been expected home for Sunday dinner. Brown was just far enough away so that I could go home if I wanted to or find a convenient excuse not to go home."

When Robert W. Kenny entered Brown in the fall of 1921 he became part of a college community that the Brown student of today would hardly recognize. Take tuition, for example. Where in 1981-82 a student paid $7,120 a year in tuition, the annual charge for a year of instruction at Brown in 1921 was $250. Enrollment has also jumped – from 1,310 sixty years ago to 6,851 today. The University of Kenny's day didn't house all of its undergraduates. Hope College, Slater, and Caswell were the only buildings used exclusively as dormitories. Students were also housed on the top floors of Maxcy and University Hall. But a good percentage of the student body lived in rooming houses where, for a moderate fee, they had comfortable quarters plus two meals a day. Gardner House, the now lovely mansion at 106 George Street, was a rooming house in the 1920s.

"Across from Gardner House, on the south side of George Street about where the Refectory is now, was a cluster of eighteenth-century homes," Kenny says. "These had been used for rooming houses for years, and while on the outside they looked quaint and historically significant, long years of student abuse had made a pretty grim mess. When it became time to build the Wriston Quadrangle, these three or four houses were demolished. There was considerable outcry at this turn of events, an outcry which was not softened by President Wriston's exuberance when he declared that this was the greatest slum clearance since Sherman burned Atlanta. It is claimed that this remark brought the Providence Preservation Commission into being. If so, it served a purpose."

Even venerable University Hall served a different purpose at the time Kenny entered Brown. It then housed the English department, the Departments of History and Classics, the controller's office, physical plant, the mail room, the telephone switchboard, four classrooms – plus the fourth floor as a dorm. The administration building was Van Wickle Hall, located then at the corner of Prospect Street and College Hill, where the Rockefeller Library now stands.

Pat Kenny has had personal contact with seven of Brown's presidents, including the man who was at the helm when he entered college – William Herbert Perry Faunce. A liberal, at least by the standards of the 1920s, Faunce frequently found himself at odds with reactionary Baptists because of the positions he took on evolution and science. Faunce was a very eloquent Baptist preacher, but like many great orators he fell into the old cliché trap. The late Ben Brown, former director of Sock and Buskin, often imitated Faunce opening the

President William Herbert Perry Faunce '80.

college year at Chapel in Sayles Hall with the same lead every year: "Today, Brown University throws wide its venerable gates to usher in another freshman class."

A learned theologian, Prexy Faunce was extremely close to his Bible. One day, a member of the class of 1925 learned just how close. The smart aleck in question thought he could disrupt the tri-weekly Chapel service by sneaking into Sayles Hall earlier in the morning and hiding the Bible, which traditionally was left on the podium. According to Pat, who remembers the situation clearly, when the president stood up to speak and found the Bible missing he didn't even blink an eye. He just started reciting Psalm after Psalm after Psalm. In fact, Faunce warmed up so well to his task that he went well beyond the regular fifteen-minute service, completely disrupting the 10 o'clock classes. There is no evidence that the president and his Bible were ever separated again.

Whether deserved or not, Prexy Faunce earned a reputation for being absent-minded. Pat Kenny carries with him a number of stories to illustrate the point.

"There were some who felt that Prexy usd this absent-minded thing as a device. Personally, I think his reputation here was well deserved. In the early 1920s,

Faunce was wont to ride horseback, frequently hiring a horse from a stable then located on East Manning Street. He was walking down to the stable one afternoon and up comes Dr. Beasley, a dentist who was located near the tunnel. The two gentlemen greeted each other and Dr. Beasley said: 'Dr. Faunce, I didn't know that you rode. I have a horse down here which, because of my practice, I can't exercise every day. So, any time you come down and my horse hasn't been exercised, feel free to use him.' 'That's very kind of you, Dr. Beasley.' Well, a couple of weeks later they met again at about the same spot. This time Faunce was coming up Manning Street and Beasley was going down. 'How are you, Dr. Beasley?' 'I'm fine. And how are you, Dr. Faunce?' 'Well, I've just had a splendid ride. A very dear friend of mine has given me the use of his horse.'

"Then there is the story Watson Smith, class of 1919, likes to tell. He had just walked through the Van Wickle Gates on the Friday afternoon of his 5th reunion when he spotted Dr. Faunce. Smith introduced himself and the two men strolled leisurely toward University Hall. Faunce then broke away, saying he had to mail a letter at the Faculty Mail Room, which was then in U.H. Smith continued on his way, passing between University Hall and Slater, and as he reached the Middle Campus he bumped into Dr. Faunce again. 'It's good to see so many of my old boys back again for reunion,' Faunce said. 'I've just been talking to Watson Smith.'

"And yet, Faunce was capable of putting in the needle when the situation called for it. One day as he was walking home from his office in Van Wickle Hall, he passed Sayles Hall in time to hear the late Jim Adams holding forth with his economics class. Jim was a vigorous sort of person, and his voice roared like a cannon. It was said that Jim didn't need a telephone. He could call a colleague across campus merely by opening his window. A few days later, Prexy Faunce met Jim Adams on campus. 'Professor Adams,' the president said, 'I passed by the other day and heard you delivering with particular vehemence your discussions on economics. It was most effective. But tell me, Mr. Adams, what do you do when you want to *emphasize* a point?'"

Pat Kenny went through college during an exciting period. The Jazz Age, they called it. It was the age of the hip flask, bathtub gin, and speakeasies. It was the first era of the sports hero, men such as Ruth, Dempsey, Grange, Tilden, and Jones. Social values were changing, perhaps more quickly than at any time in our history, and the changes were depicted in the stories of Scott Fitzgerald and the cartoons of John Held, Jr. And nowhere was this change more evident than in the colleges.

"Despite the picture the press has painted of the Roaring '20s, I know I didn't drink bathtub gin every night," says Kenny. "Not even every *second* night. As a matter of fact, if you had money, enough of it, you could get pretty good liquor – thanks to those slick rum-runners which played hide and seek with the Coast Guard boats just off the coast.

"You could even have your alcohol tested if you were at Brown at that time. Some members of our chemistry department would test alcohol for its potency and purity. Glad to do it. There was only one rub. The price was high because they wanted a *pint* of alcohol in order to make the test. If truth be known, all they really needed was an eyedropper full. As I look back in the benevolence of my old age, I'll assume that the chemists just wanted to be sure!"

The students' handbooks at Pembroke in the early 1920s told the young ladies that hats must be worn when on the Brown campus and that "knickers and gymnasium bloomers shall not be worn in the classroom or at chapel, unless concealed." Strangely, there were more rules and regulations for the male students, especially freshmen. The year young Pat Kenny entered college, freshmen could not smoke on campus, wear galoshes unbuttoned, or don a straw hat before Memorial Day. The first-year men also couldn't walk down the left side of College Street until the eve of Memorial Day, when the freshman beanies were burned. These rules were traditional, but were enforced by the sophomore class.

Kenny recalls one rule that is long forgotten, and has every right to be. The students' handbook of 1920-21 says: "Members of the faculty should everywhere be treated with the utmost consideration. In the classroom, by observing decorum and respect; in doorways, by giving them precedence; in meeting them, by saluting courteously with the right hand."

By the 1925-26 academic year, that policy had been liberalized. No longer did the students' handbook

"Petting Parties" of "Love Hungry" Girls Shock College Boys

Astonishing Things the Society Buds Do at Brown University Dances Bring Sharp Scoldings in the College Newspaper

The Campus at Brown University.

The Masked Ball—by Icart. Usually the Attentions, If Any, Were Expected to Come from the Escort—Not from the Ladies as the Brown College Boys Complain.

"The modern social bud drinks, not too much, often, but enough. She smokes unguardedly, swears considerably, and tells 'dirty' stories. All in all, she is a most frivolous, passionate, sensation-seeking little thing."

IN those words the Brown Daily Herald, college newspaper of Brown University, at Providence, Rhode Island, characterizes the Providence girls who come up to the college to dance. This editorial, published recently, has stirred up a tempest in Providence; started tongues wagging, and finally has resulted in the police authorities saying that if conditions at Brown parties are as bad as reported they will not hesitate to have police stationed in Brown Union at the next dance.

The question, seething all over Providence now, is "what are they doing up a Brown dances?" What have Providence girls, members of the very best families, said and done, which has set the young college men to writing such sharp editorials and causing the police to promise action?

"These girls are popularizing indecency," said one of the editors of the Brown Daily Herald, the college newspaper.

"These girls are going fast; so fast they don't know when to stop," remarked another editor of the same newspaper.

"I have known the girls as sub debs; I have known them as little girls. They were sweet and innocent and grave, as little girls should be, just five or six years ago," explained one of the associate editors of the Brown Daily Herald. "I knew them then and I know them now. Gee, what a change."

"I saw a debutante I had known almost from childhood, arrive here one evening for a dance clad in short socks, bare knees, knee-high skirts and a glad smile. And the smile afforded her about as much covering as the rest of what she put on."

"What do these love-hungry do?" is the question asked, again.

To which came the answer:

"Everything." Which, in detail, leads to many explanations.

"A little while ago," explained one Brown man, "the first need for reform at our dances came to me when I saw a debutante I had known almost from childhood, arrive here one evening for a dance clad in short socks, bare knees, knee-high skirts and a glad smile. And the smile afforded her about as much covering as the rest of what she put on.

"That evening I met a girl who seemed to me about as nice as a girl could be. I hadn't noticed her dancing. In fact, I had been busy with arrangements that evening, and had not danced much myself. So I do not know whether this particular girl danced vulgarly, like all the rest, or not. But, along toward the end of things, she and I walked out upon the campus. Now, frankly, between you and me, I was pretty smitten with this particular little lady. Felt about her, don't you know, like a real guy feels about the girl he could imagine himself married to. Thought she was too nice to touch, almost; you know the grave sort of love affair a man always has once in his lifetime.

"Well, we walked a bit, and I guess I didn't say much, for a while. I felt plenty—respectfully—just the same. And, as we turned the corner of one of the buildings here she grasped my hand. Hers was trembling. 'Love and let love is my motto, dearie,' said this seraph of my dreams; 'come, we're losing a lot of time getting started.' That girl thought I was dead slow,' the youngster explained. "She didn't know that, just then, I imagined the great love of my life was just entering the door."

The youngster who told this story blushed, embarrassed. He continued, with sorrow in his voice, "I felt awfully sorry about this girl. She seemed so nice. It was cruel the way she got down from the pedestal I had built for her, there on the Brown campus, in the moonlight.

"It wasn't long after this that a group of fellows and myself were comparing some notes of our different young lady guests, in a dormitory, one night. There were souvenirs of the last dance, shown, before the talk was over.

"Say," explained one of the fellows, "in the old pure days, before prohibition, a corset steel used to be a prized souvenir of a dance, but what's taken its place now?"

"'You tell us,' somebody suggested.

"'The satin garter.' And the fellow opened his top drawer. Inside were seven round garters.' You know, not the kind she usually keeps her socks up with, but the kind a woman wears when she doesn't wear the usual things—ahem—which keeps her stockings up. Get the idea?

"Well, we checked up on one girl who came here to Brown to dance, and we found that she had left a whole regiment of little silk round garters behind her, blue and red, and what she called her 'pash' garters—this last was an orchid color. The young imp never wore one of these garters herself; her socks were of the below the knee type and she fastened them otherwise, but she carried a whole dry goods line in her corsage, and took a garter out to give to a fellow as a souvenir whenever she thought him her kind.

"'Here, Jimmy, my best to you,' she would say to whichever fellow it happened to be, 'all warm next my heart.' And another garter would part from the collection.

"But say," and the undergraduate who was telling the story, asked a question. "Say, I used to hear that, in the old days, at the old style kind of dances, fellows used to call girls who came with firm corsets on 'old ironsides.' Well, after I've supported all too clinging waists through the Camel Walk for a whole evening, I could wish for old ironsides back again. For, do you know what certain girls of our very best Providence families do now, at Providence dances, particularly dances at hotels?

"They check their corsets. Word of honor. I had it from a checking boy in a hotel downtown, when I took a girl to a little dance there, private at that; a girl who comes regularly to our proms here."

"'Corsets checked—what are you giving us?' I said to the boy.

"'Regularly,' he answered back. 'There's over a hundred pairs of corsets 'parked' here to-night. The ladies are dancing, you know. Oh, yes, sir; they checks their corsets regularly, and, often, he carries them home for them, in his topcoat pocket.'

"Well, that's just one of the cute little tricks of Providence buds who come to Brown to dance.

"And as we turned the corner of one of the buildings here she grasped my hand. Hers was trembling. 'Love and let love is my motto, dearie.'"

"We found that she had left a whole regiment of little silk round garters behind her, blue and red, and what she called her 'pash' garters—this last was an orchid color."

William W. Hall, Editor of the Brown Daily Herald.

Marshall H. Carroll, Chairman of Dance Committee.

"But there are others. Now, here goes, for what the girls themselves would call 'pash stuff,' but which you can call what you like. First, let me explain. These girls have got the idea that a girl and a man can't have a good time at all unless dangerous emotions are played with. They, somewhere, from some perverted source, have heard that no man really enjoys a girl's company unless all the emotions are called into requisition. That is why, perhaps, that the lively girl in Providence is such a little sensualist.

"They're blase, all right, and their motto seems to be, 'pretend a passion if you have it not.' Therefore, it's an ordinary trick with them to work a fellow up to a pitch, and then place a hot hand over his, a hand which trembles like a leaf in a high wind. You look at the poor little fool, and feel sorry she is so worked up. Perhaps you may touch her, and find that her whole body is tense, and that, really, she is as cool as a hill wind. She just pretends to be excited because she has heard that is what appeals to you. And she has got to be such a little actress that she can simulate all the outward signs, while, like a vivisectionist, underneath, she is watching her effect on you.

"But these young Providence girls, who have offended in the vulgarity of their dancing here at Brown, have all the implements of their wiles down to a science. For instance, I could name you an innocent looking enough girl here, a member of one of the oldest families, who wears a charming little vanity bag suspended from her dainty wrist, whenever she comes up here to dance. But does that bag contain the lozenges, the perfume, the dainty lace handkerchief, which it used to contain, in the days of her grandmother's? It does not. What do you think's in it? Crammed, jammed, with cigarettes, which the young minx has to smoke, once in so often, even at a college dance. And if she cannot steal her smoke conveniently anywhere else, she goes into a telephone booth, for smoke she must. If she didn't smoke, she would be ashamed of herself. For she would feel that, somehow, she wasn't really smart.

"There's another little, touching weapon of the fair Providence debutante, which nobody should forget. Ever see that quaint locket, around a little white neck, which you are sure contains the miniature of dear, dead grandmama? Ever admire the fair maid who wears the locket, for her delicious, delightful, granddaughterly devotion?

"Shades of the dear old lady! It's not gramma's picture she's toting about with her. Just watch little Miss Debutante get into action. One snap of the cute little spring, in the cute little locket, and you get a perfect cigarette holder which the young miss proceeds to equip with a weed from her vanity case. Oh, she goes ready for action, does this ultra modern Providence girl who comes to dance at Brown.

"Which is just a few of their tricks. For there are more than a few not mentionable in society more or less impolite. But time, and open eyes, will show the observer a thing or two. The girls are popularizing indecency. Their dancing of the reprehensible Camel Walk is justified because they say, everybody's doing it. Petting parties follow the dance, when girls heavily doused with what they call their "pash perfume" dash madly about the streets of Providence in machines with youths in tuxedos, and everybody thinks they're happy. It makes you wonder what the next generation will find to amuse themselves with, if the sated, blase, frivolous little girls of to-day, are to be their mothers.

"Oh yes, sir; they checks their corsets regularly, and often he carries them home for them, in his topcoat pocket."

"But, do you know, I think a lot of these girls are preparing for themselves a nice, ultimate retreat in the old maids' home. One thing I know, I would never marry a girl who had Camel Walked a whole season with fellows indiscriminately. And, another phase of the whole business, the girls who do these things are the most popular girls in town. The girls who do not do them, hardly ever get asked anywhere. They are wall-flowers, all right, and stay-at-homes. Yet the fellows at Brown, right enough, have some pretty strong comments to make on the girls they have kissed, a few hours before, when the last dance has been danced, and the last petting party brought to an end. It's just as the editorial in the Herald pointed out."

Parts of that editorial, from the issue of January 20, follows: "The Modern age of girls and young men is intensely immoral, and immoral, seemingly, without the pressure of circumstances. At whose door we may lay the fault, we cannot tell. Is it the result of what we call the emancipation of women, with its concomitant freedom from chaperonage, increased intimacy between the sexes in adolescence, and a more tolerant viewpoint towards all things unclean in life? This seems the only logical forbear of the present state. And are the girls causing it now, or the men? Each sex will lay the blame on the the heads, or passions of the other, and perhaps both sexes are equally at fault.

"Whosesoever fault it may be (and that is not such an important question, since both sexes are equally immoral), the whole character of the social relations among young people is lamentable. The modern dances are disgusting—the 'toddle', and its variations and vibrations; the 'shimmy', and its brazen pandering to the animal senses, and the worst offspring of jazz—the 'Camel Walk.' There is but one idea predominant in these dances, one that we will leave unnamed.

"It is not only in dancing that this immorality appears. The modern social bud drinks, not too much, often, but enough. She smokes unguardedly, swears considerably, and tells 'dirty' stories. All in all, she is a most frivolous, passionate, sensation-seeking little thing.

"True, men may be just as bad in many ways. But it is a mark of our society, and has been for ages, however wrongly, that the man need not have any particular restraint. Things, however, have gone beyond the line for a great many of us. Many of the men in college are disgusted at what they see of girls who should be clean and pure, and should, but cannot, make good wives and mothers—girls who were well born and well educated, as far as material markings go.

"There is something fundamentally wrong in the point of view of these dilletante Bohemians. Their eyes are bent purely upon pleasure of any kind, gained in any way. What the outcome will be, we cannot foretell. We can say, however, that the control of business, of the arts, of all that is worth while, will not belong to the members of these degenerating families of the old stock."

specify which hand should be used in giving the salute.

Undergraduates, of course, feel that all rules are made to be broken. When Hegeman Hall was built in 1926, the ladies' men wanted rooms on the ground floor, especially the choice rooms overlooking the alley between Hegeman and St. Stephen's Church. A man in one of these rooms could just open his window and his girl friend could step in without running the risk of being seen entering through the front door on Thayer Street. As Kenny recalls the situation, it was "perfectly amazing" how many Pembrokers, of *all* faiths, signed out to attend services at St. Stephen's Church in the month immediately after Hegeman was constructed.

Dancing was one of the most popular social activities at the colleges in the early 1920s. Collegiate dancing at Brown was done in Sayles Hall or at the fraternity houses that surrounded the campus. After Alumnae Hall was dedicated in October of 1927, that became the "in" place for a dance. Tradition called for the men to wear white tie and tails and the young ladies to wear long gowns. But this was the Roaring '20s – and traditions were crumbling. In a blistering two-column editorial in January of 1921, the *Brown Daily Herald* took issue with some of these changes.

"The modern age of girls and young men is intensely immoral," the editorial said. "The modern dances are disgusting – the 'Toddle' and its variations and vibrations; the 'shimmy' and its brazen pandering to the animal senses; and the worst offspring of Jazz, the 'Camel Walk.' There is but one idea predominate in these dances, one that we will leave unmentioned."

Somehow, this editorial found its way to the attention of someone at the *Boston Sunday Advertiser*, a newspaper that believed it was always more fun to embellish the truth than to adhere to it. The result was predictable: a full-page spread a few weeks later with a banner headline – "Petting Parties of Love Hungry Girls Shock College Boys" – superimposed over a pen-and-ink drawing of the Front Campus. Adding spice to the article were five cartoons with captions supposedly based on interviews with Brown undergraduates. Things like: "I saw a debutante I had known almost from childhood arrive here one evening clad in short socks, bare knees, knee-high skirt, and a glad smile. And the smile afforded her about as much covering as the rest of what she put on."

Pat Kenny recalls the newspaper article, which was still being talked about when he entered Brown a few months after its publication.

"Let's say that there was no great enthusiasm for the story in the administration building," Kenny says. "I understand, however, that its immediate effect was to increase attendance at the Brown dances – by the mothers of the debutantes and other chaperones.

"They wrote about nice young girls removing pictures of their grandmothers and grandfathers from their lockets and replacing them with cigarette holders 'which the young miss proceeds to equip with a weed from her vanity case.' They also said that certain girls from some of the finest families in Providence were checking their corsets at Sayles Hall before starting to dance."

Off-campus dancing was also popular with the college set, especially at Rhodes-on-the-Pawtuxet and at the Arcadia Ballroom downtown on Washington Street next to the old Dreyfus Hotel. If you asked a non-college woman to dance, she would usually say: "How do you want to dance – varsity or cake?" Varsity was the old, slow drag, while cake referred to the newer, more vigorous dances.

For formal dances, the students usually imported dates from Radcliffe, Wheaton, Mount Holyoke, or Vassar. "Brown men then liked to pretend that they looked down their noses at Pembrokers," Pat Kenny says. "Which reminds me of a cartoon my classmate, Sid Perelman, did for the *Brown Jug*, our humor magazine, in which he showed a girl looking ruefully at herself in a tall mirror. The caption read: 'The only test a Pembroker can't pass.'

"In 1922, the Junior Prom was held in the Biltmore Hotel, which had been open only a few weeks. The hotel was as glamorous then in its youth as it is now in its middle age. Well, along about 11 p.m. it became obvious that there were very few people dancing in the Ballroom. A senior member of the faculty called over the chairman and said, 'Look, you've got a Grand March at midnght. Where are the people?' Well, most of the people were in the rooms on the fifteenth and sixteenth floors. The students had brought imports as dates and had put them up in rooms on those two floors, ostensibly to be near the dance floor. So, the chairman got his committee together and they all went downstairs and started pounding on doors. By midnight they had a quorum! But the Junior Prom went back to Sayles Hall the next spring, where the portraits of Baptist clergymen and former presidents looked down somberly on everyone."

Another favorite spot of the college set was the Green Lantern Tea Room, which was downtown opposite the Union Trust Building. Working there as a bouncer was Quent Reynolds, a member of the class of 1924. A prominent writer after graduation, Quent became a national figure during World War II with his first-hand stories filed from London during the blitz and from other hot spots of activity.

"They didn't serve any liquor at the Green Lantern," Kenny recalls. "But sometimes the college boys would get themselves gassed up and then go to the Green Lantern. Occasionally I was among this group. And Quent, or 'Red' as we called him, would come up to me and say, 'Pat, you really don't want to stay tonight, do you?' He'd put his big arm around me and walk me to the door. And I'd say, 'No, Red, I really don't want to stay.'"

When this story appeared in the *Brown Alumni Monthly* in the spring of 1980, Ernest J. Woelfel '23 wrote to add a new twist to the yarn. He seemed genuinely pleased that for the "first time ever" he was able to have the last word with Pat Kenny. Mr. Woelfel's letter read, in part:

Red and I roomed together at the Delta House and were looking for an opportunity to make a little extra money. One day while downtown we noticed the Green Lantern Tea Room. It was owned by a woman who was not doing too well financially. We talked to her and suggested that she allow us to be co-managers, and that we would try to interest our fellow students in patronizing the place. She agreed to give it a try, and this is what happened: My job was to work out front and handle the money. Red was to run the kitchen with the woman. The Delta House had a pretty good musical group – piano, violin, saxaphone, and drums. We persuaded them to come to the Tea Room and play, and we would pay them with either food, liquor, or money. Here I have to differ with Pat's story about the Green Lantern Tea Room and liquor. We used to buy alcohol by the gallon, and also vials of gin, Scotch, bourbon, and rum, so we could make any drink. That was Red's department.

Well, needless to say, with a little advertising around the fraternity houses and the campus, the Green Lantern Tea Room was a huge success, until one day Red and I received a little note from Dean Randall that he would like to see us in his office at a certain time on a certain date. Going down the hill Red said, "We'll deny everything," and I said, "No, we

will just stand there and listen and then tell the truth." What actually happened was that Randall greeted us with a smile as we stood shaking. All he said was, "I understand you two young men are associated in a very successful business down town. However, I am going to give you a choice which you must decide right now. You will have to give up the Green Lantern Tea Room or Brown University." That was the end of our association with that venture. I could go on telling you a great many things about Red, as he was a remarkable person.

The high point of the above story came years later during one of my frequent meetings with Red at Toots Shor's in New York. Red said, "Erney, I have a confession to make to you. I have always felt guilty about cheating you during our partnership at the Green Lantern Tea Room." My answer was, "How in the hell could you cheat me when I handled all the money and divided up the profits?" "Well," he said, "there is one thing that you didn't share in – my association with the woman who owned the place."

There was only one burlesque house in Providence in the early 1920s. Called The Sink, it was located on the south side of Westminster Street, up about one block from Grace Church. According to Kenny, who admits "an occasional" trip to The Sink, the aficionados of burlesque never paid much attention to the shows

May, 1924   PROM NUMBER   25 Cents

on Monday and Tuesday evenings because those were the prescribed nights for the police and members of the licensing commission to put in an appearance. Reportedly, the actresses wore more clothes on those two nights than they would wear on the street. However, by the end of the week the number of Brown students and other citizens attuned to the finer things of life picked up considerably.

"The show was made up of crude jokes and slapstick, but there was no disrobing," Kenny recalls. "Oh, some of the young ladies might display the opulence of nature, but they wore tights and you seldom even saw a bare leg."

The Sink became a second-run movie house and was eventually torn down. But it did play a role, if only a minor one, in the education of Brown students for quite a few years.

The College had a show of its own in the Kenny undergraduate years that, for a while, managed to stay one step ahead of the college censor. Called the Saint Patrick's Day Minstrel, the event was held on the second floor of Rockefeller Hall (now Faunce House), directly above what is now called the Airport Lounge. The Sock and Buskin performances also were held there. The minstrel was a take-off on vaudeville, with the jokes more border line than blue. In 1925, President Faunce wrote to the chairman of the minstrel and said that he would like to address the seniors at that annual show. Let Pat Kenny pick it up here:

"I was chosen to escort Prexy from his house on Hope Street to Rockefeller Hall. As I brought him into the wings to await the conclusion of the first act, a student in a dress suit, cane, and derby hat (painted gold) was on stage getting off a line that went something like this: 'You know, fellas, King Solomon had a rather "eunuch" way of managing his harem.' Faunce turned to me. 'Mr. Kenny, is this to be the general tone of this evening's entertainment?' I quickly explained that we had borrowed one or two acts from a vaudeville house downtown. Whether Prexy Faunce bought this, I'll never know.

"It was a moot point. The following year, after Percy Marks, a former English instructor at Brown, had written a book, *Martha*, the Saint Patrick's Day Minstrel

featured some of the larger members of the football team in a chorus line singing 'Red Hot Martha, Pull Your Bloomers Down.' Well, the final curtain on the popular old minstrel show also came down that year, on an edict from the administration."

The author of *Martha* was the same Percy Marks who brought the University national attention it didn't want during Pat Kenny's junior year. There is an irony here, in that through most of his Brown career (1921-24), the slight, scholarly looking Marks was the sort of instructor you could meet and easily forget.

All that changed in February of 1924 when his novel, *The Plastic Age*, hit the book stores. The free-swinging satire of the pomposity of formal education shocked the nation's mothers (the strange point that everyone forgets is that the book was dedicated to *his* mother), became an overnight best seller, and rocketed Marks to fame – a situation he did not find painful.

Although considered extremely risqué in its day (the book prompted a 1927 movie starring Clara Bow, the "It Girl"), *The Plastic Age* is tame by today's standards. There is little to titillate in the story of Hugh Carver, a student of high Calvinistic principles but low Calvinistic tolerance, whose chief collegiate concern is that if he "goes all the way" with Cynthia he will be doomed forever. However, the book did paint a fairly accurate picture of college life after World War I, when social relationships between the sexes were more free and easy than they were in the years immediately after the turn of the century.

Pat Kenny took a course with Percy Marks and remembers him well. "He had his affectations," Kenny recalls. "For example, he would wear a Navy pea coat in the winter. Same coat day after day after day. Someone asked him why and he said that the University didn't pay him enough to buy an overcoat. Yet, Percy Marks went to a manicurist once a week. With the money he would have saved by clipping his own nails he'd have been able to afford an overcoat.

"But Percy was a rebel. He frequently took strong positions on safe issues, such as when he described himself as an adversary of 'uninspired administrative offices, stupid professors, and alumni with false ideals.' Well, sure, who isn't an adversary of these things? *The Plastic Age* was an amalgam of his experiences at the three places he had taught – MIT, Dartmouth, and Brown – not just of his Brown days. Not knowing this, the general public thought that Brown University had turned into a hotbed of free love and the letters came pouring in. *The Plastic Age* was the 'cause célèbre' on the campus in the spring of 1924."

When Marks was not appointed to a fourth one-year term, the press assumed that he had been fired for writing his controversial book, a theory that persists today. As Kenny points out, the truth is that the University had voted in December 1923 not to reappoint Marks, several months before the book was published, and had so informed the instructor.

Until late in his freshman year, Mrs. Kenny's son was known as Bob. This situation changed quickly one night, under somewhat unusual circumstances.

"The area [on Angell Street] now used by the *Brown Daily Herald* once housed a telephone exchange," Kenny says. "The night shift got off at 10 o'clock, and it was customary for the girls to call the fraternity houses to see if, by chance, they could stir up a late date.

"One night this girl called the Beta Theta Pi house asking for Bob. Someone yelled up the stairs, 'Bob, you're wanted on the phone,' and I dashed down and had a long, and somewhat pleasant, conversation with the young lady – even though it was quickly apparent that I wasn't the 'Bob' she wanted. It turned out that the object of the call, a senior named Bob, had developed a rather comfortable relationship with this gal and was more than slightly miffed that I didn't put him on the phone. When it came time for fraternity initiation, this Bob paddled my rear pretty good and said, 'Now, Kenny, if you're going to live in this frat I want you to get a new nickname.' Under the circumstances, it seemed the proper thing to do. And so, I did."

Why the nickname "Pat"? If Kenny is being honest – and who has ever known a dean who wasn't honest? – "Pat" was selected because an Irishman who answered to the name of Pat Moran managed the Cincinnati Reds to the National League pennant that year and then to victory over the Chicago White Sox in the World Series. "The war was over, most of the soldiers were back, and this was an exciting World Series," Pat says. "That was the year the White Sox became known as the Black Sox when they threw the series. At any rate, Pat Moran was one of my boyhood heroes – don't ask me why at this point – and so I borrowed his nickname."

According to Pat, Brown had a fine teaching faculty when he was a student. Many of the men were recruited during the era of President Benjamin Andrews, who had a natural talent for seeking out and hiring good teachers. The group included Theodore Collier in history, an excellent lecturer; Albert G. Harkness, a Latin scholar; Ben Clough, who taught English and then transferred to the classics department; Johnny Greene, in Latin and Greek civilization; Courtney Langdon, whose course in Dante (it was called his "hell course") was a masterpiece; and Tom Crosby, the founder and long-time director of Sock and Buskin.

"Tom Crosby was a great coach of actors," Kenny says. "He was also the man through whom I first met Nathan Wallenstein Weinstein of the class of 1924, better known later as Nathaniel West.

"I didn't know West real well, but I did become privy to a bizarre incident involving this man. It all started with Tom Crosby's course on the English drama. In the first semester, he went from the Restoration to the end of the eighteenth century. By the second semester, Tom was into the nineteenth century, and, it seemed to us, was fated to stay there, even though the class looked forward to his discussion of the modern dramatists, such as Shaw, Yeats, Dunsany, and O'Neill. Tom's battery began to run down every spring, and if he came to class with his finger in a book we knew that instead of a lecture, which he did exceptionally well, we were going to get a reading, which could be very dull.

"The attention span during Crosby's readings was not very long. Nathan 'Pep' Weinstein would sit in the back of the room and shuffle his feet, a fact not lost on Tom Crosby. Pep didn't bother to read the assignments either. And he flunked the course.

"Just before this I had received a letter from Crosby asking if I'd be his paid assistant during my senior year, reading the hour tests and things. Well, I was glad for the money – and why not? On this particular day I came over to Tom's office in University Hall to discuss the matter. The door to his room was open and there was an altercation going on. I got out of earshot but stayed in the hallway. A little later Pep Weinstein came out. Tears were streaming down his face, but he was smiling. Tom had crossed out the 'E' and written in a 'D,' this at a time when it was a very rare thing at Brown to change a grade. This enabled Pep to graduate. I'm the only man who has a copy of that marked-up transcript.

"What isn't generally known is that Pep Weinstein graduated after only two years at Brown and two *phony* years on somebody else's credits at Tufts. I have the record on this. There was a man named Nathan Weinstein – same name – who was a better than average student at Tufts. After two years, this Weinstein transferred to Harvard Dental. Meanwhile, Pep decided that he didn't like it at Tufts. He heard about his namesake, apparently some lights went on in his mind, and he decided to drop out of Tufts before the first semester mid-terms so that there would be absolutely nothing on his record. Then, Pep applied for admission to Brown as a transfer student, asking the University officials to write to Tufts for his transcript. The result was that Tufts sent the transcript of the only Weinstein it had on its records and our Pep was admitted as a member of the junior class – with all his science courses out of the way!"

Another professor whom Pat remembers well is Edmund Loughnan, a member of the French department who arrived at Brown in the late 1920s. One of Pat's favorite stories concerns an incident that occurred in Loughnan's class around 1930.

At that time, students could not cut classes the two days prior to a vacation. One year there were eight students from New York City who wanted to catch the 12 o'clock train from Providence to get a jump on their Christmas vacation. The only rub was that they had an 11 o'clock class with Professor Loughnan in Marston Hall.

As the story goes, the New York delegation selected one of its most articulate members to speak to the professor and explain that an early dismissal of the class that day would be greatly appreciated. Loughnan was in sympathy with the request and said that he would tell them when to go.

"Well," Pat says, "the class droned on with nobody paying too much attention. All the suitcases were stacked in the hall and the taxi cabs had pulled up outside Marston. And still the class went on. The boys put their eyes on their spokesman, who raised his hand. 'Professor?' 'Yes.' 'Remember I spoke to you about letting us out a bit early today?' 'Yes, you did. And, gentlemen, in my best Parisian French I've wished you a Merry Christmas and dismissed the class *three* times.'"

Late in the spring of his senior year, Kenny applied

for – and received – an appointment as an assistant in English at Brown. His salary was $750 for a ten-month year. Then for the next two years it was "up the road a piece" to Northeastern as an assistant professor of English. By the fall of 1928 he was back at Brown, this time as instructor in English. As he looks back on it now, the working conditions were good, the associations were pleasant, but the living was *not* easy.

As an example, Pat likes to cite an incident that took place on a warm spring afternoon in 1929. The story involves Charles Brackett, who then lived in the Corliss-Brackett House at the corner of Angell and Prospect Streets, now the home of the Brown admission office. (Brackett later gained fame in Hollywood when he teamed with Billy Wilder to write the screenplays for a series of popular films, including *Ninotchka* [1939], with Greta Garbo and Melvyn Douglas; *Lost Weekend* [1945], starring Ray Milland; and *Sunset Boulevard* [1950], featuring Gloria Swanson and William Holden. The Brackett-Wilder team won Oscars for both *Lost Weekend* and *Sunset Boulevard*.)

"Jack Reid, an assistant professor of English, was friendly with Brackett," Pat Kenny says, "and he accepted an invitation for the two of us to join him for cocktails. When we arrived, Charlie suggested a game of backgammon while waiting for his wife to return from some errand. Finally, when she returned and the butler wheeled in the portable bar, the game stopped, and Charlie whipped out his checkbook and wrote me a check for $30. I was acutely embarrassed and felt compelled to tell him the truth – namely that if I had lost, I could not have paid. How could I when I was supporting a wife on a salary of $2,000 a year?

"When I was an undergraduate, I thought the members of the English department had a pretty good life," he says. "Only later did I discover that most of them had independent income, or that their wives did. *I married for love*."

The love of Pat's life was Gertrude Brady of Providence. The couple was married March 24, 1928, and spent fifty-one years together before her death in London in 1979 at the start of a brief holiday. The Kenny clan includes two children, Robert, Jr. '55 and Susan.

Pat Kenny's first year as a regular member of the Brown faculty was the last year of President Faunce's administration. In ill health for several years, Faunce retired in June 1929 and died the following year.

For some time prior to his retirement, Faunce felt that the Brown Charter should be changed by the

president of Brown – a compromise candidate if there ever was one."

Many alumni were disappointed that a man of Chafee's national reputation had been passed over in favor of Barbour. Walter G. Everett of the class of 1885, professor of philosophy at Brown and acting president of the College in 1912-13, voiced the opinion of a large segment of the alumni in a letter to Chafee on July 27, 1929. He wrote, in part:

It was an academic crime – the word is not too strong – that you were not selected for the presidency. We are in need of an educator of real power from outside to study the whole educational situation and to inaugurate a policy. We have none founded on principle, as you doubtless know, but have grown from pressure and pulls and these have largely come from those who have little interest in or understanding of our real needs.

You have the scholarship and the courage that are needed. And you could have appealed to the generous idealism of youth. You could have helped wonderfully in setting the boys to thinking on vital problems. As it is, we shall have only conservative and perhaps reactionary attitudes. Peace, harmony, and commonplace ideas will prevail.

The late Alfred H. Gurney '07, former alumni secretary of the University and a classmate of Zach Chafee's, once told me that the decision to appoint Barbour as president ranked as one of Brown's greatest blunders. As an example of Barbour's lack of vision, he told of the time in 1930 when John D. Rockefeller, Jr. '97 offered to pay for an addition to Rockefeller Hall if the University would then name the entire building in honor of Faunce. According to Gurney, who was then Barbour's secretary, Rockefeller sent Barbour a blank check along with the suggestion that the University look around to see what other construction was needed, get it done, and then fill in the appropriate amount. Gurney saw this as a golden opportunity for Brown to make major improvements in its plant at low Depression construction costs. Barbour saw things differently. He filled in the check with only the amount needed to cover the addition to Rockefeller Hall, saying that to do more would surely offend Mr. Rockefeller. Never again did John D. Rockefeller, Jr., offer to help the University in any major way.

Pat Kenny agrees that the choice of Barbour as president did not move Brown forward: "While Barbour was president of Colgate Rochester, Eastman had given that school a great deal of money, and the hope was that some of this would rub off on Brown after Barbour's

Rhode Island legislature so that the University would no longer have to have a Baptist clergyman for president. He actively promoted this cause, and the change was put through in 1926.

For a short while, it looked as though the University would strike gold in its search for a new president. The leading candidate was Dr. Zechariah Chafee '07, professor of law at Harvard and a nationally known defender of freedom of speech, press, and assembly. Professor Kenny recalls the situation:

"The recent Charter change didn't sit too well with some Baptists, who still played a dominant part in the running of the University. This group was able to block the appointment of Zach Chafee, who was by far the most attractive candidate. The general feeling was that maybe Brown had better give them one more Baptist clergyman as president.

"At that time, Clarence Augustus Barbour, of the class of 1888, was president of Colgate Rochester Theological Seminary. He was also on the committee to select Brown's new leader. As the story goes, the committee was fumbling around with the selection process one day and not getting anywhere. Then, according to legend, Mr. Barbour had to leave the meeting to go to the men's room. When he returned he was election as president in October of 1929. But then came the Depression – and that was that. Personally, Mr. Barbour was the best-hearted man in the world. Unfortunately, however, his contributions to Brown were not significant. His presidency was a period of stagnation."

It's interesting to speculate on Brown's long-range future had Chafee been elected president in 1929 at age 43. Under those circumstances, would there ever have been a Henry Wriston at Brown? Probably not. History sometimes moves in strange ways.

The dean of Pembroke when Pat was a young professor was Margaret Shove Morriss, who took great pride in the fact that she was a birthright member of the Society of Friends. A woman of strong conviction and a great drive for action, Dean Morriss acquired the nickname, applied affectionately by most, of "Peggy Push," derived from Margaret Shove. The Women's College came alive under her direction (1923-1950), drawing students from across the United States and Europe rather than just from the East Coast, becoming more selective in admissions, and gaining a national reputation. She was a fervent advocate of a strong role for women in both the academic and the national life. More than fifty years before Women's Liberation had been heard of she was asserting the soundest ideals of the movement. Dean Morriss often told her friends that she had taught the people of Brown two things: that Morriss was spelled with two "S's" and that there were women on the campus. Pat Kenny likes to tell a story involving the dean.

"Dean Morriss thought it appropriate to bring guest speakers to the Pembroke campus just as often as possible. A large, majestic woman, she would don her robe for these occasions and make her introductions as impressive as possible. One day, she invited the head nurse at the Rhode Island Hospital. The dean gave this woman a long, and laudatory, introduction, paused briefly and then said: 'Now, ladies, I give you a representative of the oldest woman's profession in the world.' Poor Dean Morriss never could understand what all the laughter was about. And no one dared to tell her."

Dean Morriss and Pat Kenny were neighbors on Bowen Street in the 1930s and became close friends. Pat was appreciative of this friendship following an incident that took place on the opening day of classes in 1934.

At that point in Brown's history, all classes for Pembrokers were held on the women's campus. Occasionally, if only one woman signed up for a course, the University would let her sit in with the men rather than assume the cost of setting up a separate section. Pat Kenny was teaching an English course in a room on one side of the front corridor in Sayles Hall. A course in economics was being taught across the way.

Pat's class was just getting started when there was a knock on the door. A Pembroke student stuck her head in and said, "Will you be having labor problems here?"

"As I recall," Pat says, "I looked at her for a moment and then said, 'God forbid, sister!' Well, all the boys started to laugh, the student became embarrassed, and she headed right for the administration building at Pembroke to make a complaint.

"The next morning Dean Morriss and I met on Bowen Street and proceeded to walk to work together. It didn't take very long for her to bring up the incident of the previous morning. Miss Morriss could be difficult to live with when she was angry, and I rather expected a reprimand. It didn't come. Instead, she glanced at me as we walked along, and with the faint trace of a smile on her lips, said, 'Pat Kenny, you shouldn't be so sexy.'"

The most popular course on the Pembroke campus in the 1930s was Kenny's English 51 section, which met in Pembroke Hall. A specialist in seventeenth- and eighteenth-century literature, Kenny's course covered the period from the return of Charles II to the start of the Romantic movement. You either signed up early for this course or you didn't sit in. The popularity of Mr. Kenny with the Pembrokers was made official in the spring of 1934 when the class of 1934 named him "Favorite Professor of the Year" in Spring Day exercises. My cousin, the late Lucille Barry Burdge, a member of this class, frequently spoke about Kenny's charisma. She was especially impressed with his ability in a one-on-one conversation to make the student feel that she was the most important member of the class.

Another former Pembroker who has fond memories of Professor Kenny is Ruth Hussey Longenecker '33 of Carlsbad, California, who starred in such films as *Marie Antoinette, H. M. Pulham Esquire,* and *The Philadelphia*

Dean Margaret Shove Morriss of Pembroke.

Story, for which she was nominated as best supporting actress in 1940. "Professor Kenny was a favorite with his students because, I think, he enjoyed teaching them – sparking their interest, opening doors," she writes. "There were no dozers in his classes because we didn't want to miss anything he said, and besides he might rap our knuckles if we did.

"I got an 'E' on the first paper I turned in because there were fourteen mispellings. I asked him if this was a class in English or spelling. It did no good. Though he was witty, debonair, and charming, he was a task master, too. No extension of time to get a paper in. I know. I tried.

"Freshman English in Mr. Kenny's class was such a joy that I decided to take another course with him, British Poetry, and guess what? I still have the notes I took in class and also have enjoyed reading poetry ever since. Pat Kenny enriched our thoughts and our lives. We loved him then, and still do."

From all accounts, Pat Kenny's classes were never dull. Writing from her home in Scarborough, New York, Rosa Rieser Schlossbach '33 recalls that each

meeting with Professor Kenny was "stimulating and fun" and adds: "His manner was easy going, and his criticisms of our work were apt and helpful, never cruel or denigrating. Perhaps the greatest thing was that he took the trouble to know each of us as individuals. We never had the feeling that we were just a roomful of faces."

The presidency of Clarence Barbour lasted only through 1936, when he became ill and was replaced by Acting President James P. Adams. In February of 1937, Brown had its eleventh president, Henry Merritt Wriston, who had been serving as president of Lawrence College in Appleton, Wisconsin. For the first time in its history, the University had a president who was not a Baptist minister.

"There was an air of excitement on the campus just before and after Wriston's arrival," Pat Kenny says. "His early speeches were crackling with vigor and you just sensed that something was going to happen. It did, very soon."

One of Wriston's first moves was to secure a grant from Henry Ford for the restoration of the interior of University Hall to its orginal design. When the work was finished, U.H. became what it is today – strictly an administration building, and one of the finest examples of colonial architecture on any college campus.

Pat Kenny was even more impressed with some of the academic moves Wriston made. "Before Wriston's arrival, any time there was a vacancy in the English department, the chairman would crawl to the Harvard Yard as fast as he could and pick up somebody from their graduate school. Wriston put an immediate end to this sort of thing. He had a wider view of how to build up a staff of quality and balance.

"When Wriston was hired, Brown was a college badly in need of shaking-up. Henry did the shaking, and enjoyed every minute of it. He had the advantage of being an outsider with no friends on the campus and no commitments to anyone. He was completely free to make the moves that had to be made, so long as he was willing to fight the entrenched faculty chairmen and the members of the Corporation who had been running the College for many years. You could see some power struggles shaping up. They were inevitable. There was static in the air those early Wriston years."

Four years after Wriston's arrival, Pat Kenny left with the 43rd Division for service in World War II. He didn't return until 1946. A captain in a National Guard unit when he was called into service, he came out of the Army a lieutenant colonel. After taking his basic training at Fort Blanding, Florida, his unit participated in the Louisiana maneuvers, where the physical or mental incompetents were weeded out, and then sailed for the Pacific in the fall of 1942.

Between 1942 and 1946, Pat saw combat service in a variety of campaigns leading to the defeat of Japan. He was in the late stages of the Guadalcanal campaign, participated in the Russell Islands occupation, fought in the battles of New Georgia, New Guinea, and Luzon, and then was for a short time part of the occupation force in Japan.

For his "exceptionally meritorious conduct" in performing his duties as an artillery liaison officer in the battle for New Georgia between July 4 and August 5 of 1943, Major Kenny was awarded the Bronze Star. The key to this battle was the capture of Munda Air Field. While the fighting was in progress, Pat maintained a continuous liaison between his artillery battalion battery and the infantry troops at the front lines. It was his responsibility to see that the howitzer fire was directed where it would do the most amount of damage to enemy installations.

"It was rather a grim battle, this fight for Munda Air Field," he says. "The scary thing was that we had no maps on Guadalcanal or New Georgia that amounted to anything. We did have air folders, which showed nothing more than the rain forests, or jungles. In the close jungle fighting, it was often necessary to drop shells within 100 yards of the American troops, and there was always the danger that if proper liaison wasn't maintained our own boys might be hit by *our* fire."

To this day, Pat Kenny has little sympathy for those who feel that the atomic bomb should not have been dropped on Japan. "If the battles for individual islands such as New Georgia were bloody and extremely costly in American lives – and they were – storming the shores on the main islands of Japan would have been a real blood bath. The main invasion was scheduled for November 1, 1945, and I can tell you that there wasn't one man in our outfit who wasn't overjoyed when the bomb was dropped and the Japanese surrendered.

Unfortunately, when you go to war you go from a moral world to an immoral world – and you make the best of it."

When Lieutenant Colonel Kenny returned from the Pacific to Brown University in the spring semester of 1946 he had another fight on his hands. Professor William Hastings, who was then chairman of the department, had put Kenny back teaching English I, the basic composition course. Fortunately, for harmony in the English department, the situation didn't last too long.

"Sam Arnold called me one afternoon and said, 'Pat, what does it mean when a soldier has lost eighty-four days under the 104th Article of War?' Sam was dean of the College then and was obviously confronted with a problem he wasn't equipped to handle. 'Well, Sam,' I said, 'for one thing you don't want him as a student at Brown. This is one of the punitive articles. If a man gets V.D., for example, and loses eighty-four days of duty, he has to make that up at the end of his three-year enlistment.' Sam thanked me for my help and then said, 'You know, there is a great deal of information we need in this area what with the veterans flooding the campus. Maybe you'd better come over and see me.' So, I went to his office – and within a week I was dean of students.

"Neither Sam nor Wriston seemed to have any clear idea of the mentality of the returning GI. They didn't always like what I said, but they knew very well that I said it clearly and in a way that the veterans were used to hearing – 'yes' or 'no.' Sam was inclined to tell the students that he would think the matter over and would they please come back next Thursday. Well, most of the veterans didn't want to come back next Thursday. They wanted an answer right away. Of course, you make some mistakes operating as I did. No two ways about that. I did have one assistant, a chap named [Joseph K.] Sonntag, who handled student activities. He was the only dean I've ever known who kept the Providence Society Blue Book on his desk."

There were approximately 4,400 undergraduate men at Brown in most of the immediate post-war years. Some were right out of high school, but most were veterans in their mid-to-late twenties. It was an engaging mix and the results were positive. Kenny feels that there was a beat and a drive to campus life between 1946 and 1951 that didn't exist before and hasn't existed since. He served as dean of the College through this period, having been promoted in the summer of 1947.

Pat Kenny was one dean who wasn't hard to find. His second-floor office in University Hall was open for business at 8:30 every morning on a first-come, first-served basis. You never had to have an appointment to see the dean in those days. If you sat outside his office long enough, you saw him. The veterans didn't want their hands held and they didn't feel the need for counseling, except on the technical matters of their education. Pat didn't have office hours on Saturday – but he remained on call for emergencies.

"I had to go downtown many a Saturday night and pull some of the boys out of the clink," Pat says. "These guys worked hard Monday through Friday and then they played hard on Saturday nights. The lieutenant at the desk and I were good friends. He'd call and say, 'I think I've got enough of your boys down here to justify a trip downtown, dean.'

"The lieutenant would separate the students for me. Those who came in with a lot of guff, the mouthy type, he'd put in the slammer. And they stayed there until the next day. The others he crowded off to one side until I got there. Those boys were usually released in my custody. One night the lieutenant said to me, 'Dean, you look like a *reasonably* bright man. Isn't there an easier way you can make a living?'"

While he was dean, Pat was frequently called upon by President Wriston to travel with him on the Brown Club circuit. One of Wriston's favorite swings would start at the Brown Club in New York and then include stops in Philadelphia, Baltimore, and Washington. Dean Kenny remembers these trips well.

"At each of these club meetings I'd be given ten minutes to talk on the state of the University. Then Wriston took on the state of the world. I can remember somewhere in my ten minutes one night I pulled a crack that got a good laugh. The next day while riding from New York to Philly on the train, Wriston turned to me and said, 'Pat, I think I'll tell that story tonight. I can work that into my speech.'

"Wriston had a set pattern for delivering speeches when he went on these Brown Club tours. First, he would write out his talk, and then he would read it in New York on his opening night. After working on the talk conscientiously while traveling from New York to Philadelphia, Wriston would speak only from notes the second night. By the time he was ready to tackle Baltimore and Washington, Wriston had the talk committed to memory. That's when he was at his best. People would sit there at these meetings and marvel that this man could so easily talk off the top of his head.

The 1950 Senior Class Dinner. First row, from left: Pat Kenny, Class President John Scott, President Wriston. Standing, from left: Vice President Bruce Bigelow, Dinner Chairman Tom Quinn, Provost Sam Arnold.

But it really wasn't easy at all.

"An audience excited Wriston," Kenny says. "He would look around and pick out the dullest dolt he could see in the audience and he'd make it his business to wake that son-of-a-bitch up. He'd glance right at him whenever he made a key point or a gesture. What a woman with beautiful legs or big breasts is to some men, an audience was to Wriston. He'd sit down after a major talk emotionally drained. Then he'd go right to bed. Of course, this was the best part of the evening for me. I'd have a chance to sit around with a few of my old pals and lift a glass or two.

"Another thing about Henry Wriston was that he had tremendous drive. Traveling with him for a week at a time gave me an idea of just how much drive he had. He was always taking notes and then he'd be on the phone to his secretary. These were not notes for his talks. By then he'd have all those set. These might be notes on things he'd use six months later. His brain was working all the time.

"Whether you liked him or not, Wriston was a great president for Brown. The right man at the right time. Personally, I didn't like the man. There was nothing kindly about him. He had wit but no humor. There is a humaneness in humor that you didn't get in Wriston's razor-sharp wit. Also, he was somewhat less than pleased when the joke was on him. In the late 1930s, Wriston had a brick addition put on the north end of the John Hay Library. Shortly after that, Bill Edwards of the class of 1919 commented on this to a small group he was dining with at the University Club. 'It was said of Caesar that he found Rome brick and left it marble,' he said, borrowing from the section on Dryden in Johnson's *Life of the English Poets*, 'while Wriston found the John Hay Library marble and left it brick.' Naturally, the remark got back to Wriston. For some time there was a marked coolness when the two men met.

"The funny thing is that I can say on the one hand that I personally didn't like Wriston and then admit on the other hand that he was the greatest president Brown ever had. He shook this place up."

In Wriston's day, Chapel was held Monday through Thursday at noon and was compulsory. The monitors who took attendance didn't care what you were doing in your Sayles Hall seat – sleeping, reading the *Brown Daily Herald*, or playing the football pool (and on any given day you would find a little bit of each going on) – if a body was there, you were marked present.

But there was no sleeping when Wriston spoke at

Chapel. On these occasions – and they were frequent – the students remained wide awake, and the front seats to the left and right of the podium were filled with administrators, not because any of them *had* to be there but because listening to Henry Wriston give a speech was an experience. He was certainly one of the finest orators we had ever heard.

In this connection, an interesting incident took place in 1956 when Dan Morrissey '56 and I were at the RCA Victor studios in Camden, New Jersey, to make the LP record, *Wriston and Brown*. We had stepped into the hallway while the engineer did a playback on a section we had just recorded. The only other person in the area was a painter, who was sitting on the floor munching an apple during his lunch break. As the voice of Wriston came booming through the speakers leading into the hallway, the painter cocked an ear and showed an interest. "Tell me," he said, "is that Franklin Roosevelt you guys are recording?"

Kenny feels that one of Wriston's major disappointments in life was not being asked to do anything of great importance during World War II. "He was a Republican, a McKinley high-tariff Republican. He talked about liberalism in education, but he voted the straight Republican ticket. And he made snotty remarks about Roosevelt all the time. Then when the war came, Mr. Roosevelt and his administration decided that they could win it without Henry.

"During the Eisenhower years, Wriston was involved in foreign-policy matters to some extent. He and the Secretary of State, John Foster Dulles, were great pals. Once in a while I would hear him pick up the phone and say, 'Good morning, Foster.' But I have the strong feeling that Wriston never got as close to the federal government as he would have liked. And I think this was too bad. He had great talent in that area."

The war years were particularly frustrating for Wriston. There were plenty of bodies on the campus, but most of them were in uniform – either members of the Navy V-12 or Army ASTP programs. These bodies paid only for the math and physical sciences part of Wriston's salary budget. During the 1943-44 academic year, there were only about 250 civilian students on the campus. Meanwhile, Wriston had a philosophy department, an English department, a classics department, and a history department to pay. According to Kenny, Wriston was not displeased when a professor or instructor in one of these departments was drafted and left the payroll.

Pat Kenny, left, with Secretary Howard Curtis and Professor Phil Bray.

From observing the Brown president closely, Pat Kenny feels that Wriston's chief frustration was that things usually didn't get done fast enough to suit him. He also liked to be completely in charge of everything that concerned Brown, and he liked to know exactly what was going on at the college.

"One afternoon Wriston came into my office and started asking me, while still in full stride, who my faculty spy was," Kenny says. 'If it's all right with you, I think I'll get along without a faculty spy,' I told him. He said, 'Well, when I was at Lawrence College I got me a bright young woman in the English department who gave me the general feel about the faculty.' Wriston didn't want to be surprised."

The two men Wriston leaned on most heavily were Provost Sam Arnold '13 and Vice President Bruce Bigelow '24. For a while during World War II, Arnold played a vital role in recruiting scientists to build the atomic bomb, doing his recruiting all across the country.

"I think Wriston was close to both Sam and Bruce," Kenny says. "But then he had every right to be. At first he felt that Sam was something of a postponer. Well, Sam *was* a great deferrer. But I recall Wriston once telling me that while he was on an alumni tour he was surprised to find out how fond of Sam Arnold alumni were, and also of how well Sam performed in his relationship with them. As for Bruce Bigelow – well, Wriston was smart. He knew that in Bruce he had a gem, a man of personality and charm who could talk to alumni, students, and heads of other colleges. In a sense, he was Wriston's trouble-shooter. He went around putting the bricks back in the wall after Wriston

had kicked them out. Bruce would have made a fine college president, here or anywhere else. He was as charming and bright a man as I've ever known."

In his desire not to "waste" time, Wriston ran his faculty meetings with alacrity and dispatch. Some meetings lasted as few as twenty-five minutes – and things were accomplished. This, Kenny, says, is because those meetings were planned as a regimental commander would plan a major campaign with his staff. If something unexpected came up, either Sam Arnold or Pat Kenny would quickly suggest that it certainly needed more study and that it would be the number-one item on the next agenda.

There were several faculty members at that time who could talk a subject to death, and usually did. If there was an issue that Wriston wanted defeated, he would call on any one or two of these men who he felt would speak in *favor* of the motion. They would talk on and on and on, killing the chances of the motion with their own verbosity. When everyone was bored silly, Wriston would flash a pre-arranged signal to Arnold or Kenny and one of them would call the question. Inevitably the motion would be killed, just as Wriston had expected.

Wriston was not the sort of man who would "pal around" with anyone. You'd never catch him in a bull session with his colleagues, on any subject. It just wasn't his style. He wasn't a club-oriented person. Usually he would beat a path back and forth to his home at 55 Power Street during the noon hour.

"To the best of my knowledge, Wriston never took a drink," Kenny says. "He also didn't smoke. When he returned to Brown to receive The Susan Colver Rosenberger Medal [the highest honor the Brown faculty can confer] in June 1976, we were chatting and I asked him about his health. 'I'm feeling pretty good,' he said, 'although my doctor tells me that it might be a good thing for me to take a small glass of brandy after dinner.' 'Mr. Wriston,' I replied, 'I've been doing that for years.'"

By 1951, Pat Kenny had been recalled into the Army. He did a term at the Strategic Intelligence School, was sent to Heidelburg, and returned to the English department in 1953. One afternoon in 1961, Pat received a call from Barnaby C. Keeney, who was then president of Brown.

"Barney was always direct and to the point," Pat says. "He told me that Nancy Duke Lewis, the lovely lady who was then dean of Pembroke, was ill. A temporary replacement was needed and Barney didn't want to choose between Lois Bigelow, Bruce's widow, and Eva Mooar [who were both assistant deans]. 'Pat,' he said, 'I'm going to send you up there. You can't do a hell of a lot of harm in one year.'"

Kenny was much closer to Brown's new president than he had been to Wriston. There were bonds between the men – the military (Kenney had a distinguished World War II record), enjoyment of a good story, and the late afternoon dry martini.

"Barney was a damn good president," Kenny says. "He also had a very warm heart, although he did a hell of a job concealing this fact. But I know personally that if any faculty member was in the hospital, for example, Barney was on the phone to the man's wife asking if she needed money or any other kind of help."

When Pat Kenny left Brown in 1951 to attend Strategic Intelligence School in Washington, D.C., Keeney left to work for the CIA. One day Pat was approached by a CIA agent he knew slightly.

"This man sidled up to me during a coffee break," Kenny says. "There was some small talk and then he said: 'I understand you're from Brown. Do you know this Keeney?' I assured him that I knew Barney quite well. 'What kind of a kook is he?' the man persisted. 'I don't know the point of your question,' I said, 'but Barney Keeney is a thoroughly intelligent man.'

"Well, it seems that Barney had done something out of line and there was a note in his box one Friday afternoon saying that the boss wanted to see him Monday morning. I guess Barney knew they were going to throw the book at him, so he went to some joke shop in Washington and he bought himself a rubber dagger. On Monday morning, bright and early, he walked into the office of the boss, right up to the edge of the desk, arms at his sides, and he took his bawling out. Then as he turned around to leave the boss could see that Barney had stuck this rubber dagger tightly in between his arm and his side, which as he walked out presented from the viewpoint of the boss the perfect picture of the stab in the back."

During the Keeney presidency (1955-66), enrollment increased almost a third, up from 3,581 to 4,632, the faculty doubled in size (492 to 911) and was substantially better paid, and the operating budget climbed from $8,700,000 in 1955 to $23,900,000 a decade later. "Barney had a profound influence on this college we love," Kenny says. "I think Brown history will be very kind to Barnaby Keeney."

As retirement age approaches, there are some who tend to slacken the pace. Not Pat Kenny. If anything, like an old cavalryman, he quickened his gait. Pat served as chairman of Brown's Bicentennial celebration in 1964-65, and between 1964-1971 was a member of the board of directors of the Associated Alumni. He became a trustee of the Providence Public Library and of the Rhode Island School of Design, and for nineteen years, between 1955 and 1974, he was executive director and secretary of the Rhode Island Foundation, one of the nation's oldest charitable community trusts. During this period, Pat stimulated the growth of the organization's distributions to local, non-profit institutions from $104,475 in 1955 to the record amount of $762,897 the year he left.

When Bob Hope came to Brown in June 1968 to receive an honorary degree, the choice of selecting the official escort was relatively simple. "Pat Kenny is a natural for the job," said Howard S. Curtis, secretary of the University. No one disagreed. It seemed an ideal parlay, the association of Kenny, the decorated military man, and Hope, who had devoted a major share of his time to visiting military bases around the world.

Kenny had met Hope once before, when the comedian came to Aitape in New Guinea during Christmas week of 1944, just prior to the invasion of Luzon. Obviously, Hope did not remember Kenny when they met at Brown twenty-four years later, but it didn't take the two men long to develop a comfortable relationship. One of the first moves recommended by the official escort was a visit to Hope College, Brown's ancient dormitory. "Wow," Hope exclaimed, as the cameras clicked, "just wait until Crosby hears about this."

There was one somber moment for Hope that June morning, when he learned that the commissioning of graduates from the Naval and ROTC units at Brown had been divorced from their previous status as an element in the Commencement exercises on the Green, because the administration feared student protests over the war in Vietnam. Shifted indoors to Sayles Hall, the ceremonies were already in progress when Bob Hope, alerted to the situation by Pat Kenny, made his entrance. Kenny recalls the moment:

"As Bob Hope was escorted down the center aisle, he passed through an audience of some 800 graduates, alumni, parents,, and friends – all standing and wildly applauding. It was an emotional scene, and I'll have to confess that it brought goose bumps to me. When

Hope spoke, the silence in Sayles Hall was broken only by the occasional creaking of those old benches and chairs that we all remember so well. I don't recall precisely what he said that day. The words aren't important anymore. What is important is that Bob Hope had turned what had been a bitter-sweet experience for those graduates into a day that they will never forget."

Perhaps the most important element in the Pat Kenny story is his versatility. Andrew J. Sabol '41, professor of English at Brown, touches on this point:

"I was fortunate to know Pat Kenny not only when I was an undergraduate in a course dealing with the eighteenth-century English satirists, but later – and for several decades – as a colleague in the English department. The wide diversity of his skills and talents was ever impressive, and is still so. As an administrator, both as post-war dean of the College and later as acting dean of Pembroke College, he ran a tight and ever seaworthy ship. As lecturer on his neo-classical greats, he could paint in masterful ways such subjects as the grand tour of Europe as undertaken by the young English aristocrats of the eighteenth century.

"As scholar, he showed again and again his historical approaches to the subjects which came into his purview, and his published works include informative articles on the famous tall ships of the past century, their crews, and their voyages, often as seen through surviving logs. His edition of *The New England Journal* by John B. Williams, of Salem, Massachusetts, describ-ing his journey to New Zealand in the late 1800s, shows Kenny at his best.

"For the department and the University alike, he presided again and again as grand master of ceremonies over various ritual activities, arranging conferences, and supervising special occasions such as the Bicentennial of 1964-65. He has a splendid 'occasional' sense. As a charismatic personality whose wit, joined together with that of his colleagues, I. J. Kapstein, R. G. Noyes, and G. K. Anderson, made the department a very friendly place where colleagueship – that which has departed from virtually every department in recent years – truly meant something, Pat Kenny graced our department – as he graced the University."

Now, as Pat Kenny cautiously approaches old age, he is wearing still another hat: curator of historic Gardner House on the Brown campus. From there, he makes the very informal morning meetings of the "10 o'clock Scholars" at the Faculty Club, a group of colleagues who indulge in great debate over such diverse subjects as the economy, the Brown hockey team, and the Boston Red Sox. "We're harmless," Pat says. "We *talk* about the problems but we don't solve them." There is a summer house in Middletown, Rhode Island, that needs his care, and, finally, there is time for writing. Three books now carry his name.

"I haven't made the best seller list yet," Pat Kenny says. "But the effort hasn't been completely wasted. At least it kept me out of the pool halls."

Kenny escorts Bob Hope at the 1968 Commencement.

Chapter 2 ✍
A sixth-grade dropout who became a favorite professor

Phil Taft was a man who enjoyed the finer things in life. He possessed the purist's appreciation for an around-the-horn double play, relished rendering a sea chanty in a soft tenor voice while in the privacy of the shower, and acquired a well-honed – and sometimes profitable – skill at seven-card stud.

This short, wiry professor of economics with the rumpled casual look and the shock of white hair hanging down on his forehead was a distinguished member of the Brown faculty from 1937 to 1968 and was one of the most widely known and highly respected labor historians of all time.

A sixth-grade dropout who didn't earn his college degree until he was thirty, Phil Taft possessed a combination of talents rarely found in one person. His interests were broad, his intellectual curiosity almost insatiable. He read voraciously – at any hour of the day or night – and was a connoisseur of classical literature, drama, and biography. He loved the theatre and was not above playing the role of critic for the benefit of his colleagues on College Hill. At age fifty-eight, he decided it was time to learn how to play the piano, and so he did, though at times he and the piano were not in close harmony. An incurable insomniac who often awoke at 4 or 5 a.m., he used those early morning hours to master the vocabulary necessary for a reading knowledge of several foreign languages. And he knew

labor law so thoroughly that, on occasion, judges would privately seek his advice when they were dealing with cases in the labor field.

By his nature, Professor Taft was not the sort of man who could escape controversy. He brought an unadorned and straightforward style to the academic world. He spoke with pungency and humor and, occasionally, with full-flowing profanity. Taft loved few things better than a spirited discussion or a no-holds-barred argument. He never left angry; others sometimes did. In his early days at Brown, some of the conservative students of the 1930s thought of him as a radical. Near the end of Taft's career, many of the activist undergraduates of the late 1960s considered him a conservative. Phil Taft hadn't changed; the times and the students had.

Phil Taft brought electricity to the classroom. "I wanted to be paid a professor's salary, but I never wanted any special privileges because I was a professor," he once said. "The janitor is just as good as I am. We have different skills, and I'm paid better. That's the only difference." During the student unrest of the late 1960s and early 1970s when professors and administrators at many colleges were in full retreat, Professor Taft attracted national headlines by stating that the universities "had failed the only real test they've ever been confronted with," adding, "I was never anti-student, but I'm convinced that if it had been factory boys who had been rioting, they would not have been treated so gingerly."

Phil Taft believed in the labor movement and felt that only through a detailed knowledge of its past could the movement prosper in the future. Many of his closest friends were in positions of power in various unions. Yet, the feisty professor wasn't above taking a poke at labor if he felt a blow was in order. In January 1946, for example, he told the American Economics Association that unions should establish an appeal tribunal as a safeguard against arbitrary leadership. And in the late 1960s, after the *New York Herald-Tribune* had folded, he lashed out at the printers union in that city, terming its action "self-defeating" and predicting that a continued abuse of power would also drive the book and jobbing printers out of the city and into Connecticut.

Even as a department chairman, Taft forced some of his colleagues to take sides. Although he admitted that he disliked the red tape and the detail involved with a departmental chairmanship (he was chairman of economics from 1949 to 1953), Taft made the most of his period of leadership. Acting with boldness that alternately left his colleagues startled, smugly satisfied, or angry (depending on where they stood on the issues), Chairman Taft radically changed both the make-up and the image of the economics department. He did it by setting himself up as an equal opportunity employer and bringing to the department younger faculty without regard to their religious affiliation or ethnic background.

At age fifty-one, after he had given up the departmental chairmanship, and at a time in life when some men are entering the winding-down phase of their careers, Phil Taft was just starting his major work as a scholar. He acquired a love for archives (he was soon tabbed the "archival sleuth") and dug through material in libraries, public buildings, or trade union storage files in many parts of the country. His writing kept pace with his research, to the point where he spent some time at his typewriter every day of the week. Altogether, he published fifteen books and some eighty-five articles on the labor movement. Both schol-

ars and union leaders recognize his works as the principal source of information on the growth of American labor. And in one field – the study of the American Federation of Labor from the time of its founding under Samuel Gompers – the Brown professor gained international acclaim.

A number of Professor Taft's books were translated into Japanese, Spanish, German, and Portuguese, for distribution overseas by the United States Information Service. Four of Taft's works were in the reference library at the White House during the presidency of John F. Kennedy.

The transition to retirement came and went for Phil Taft (he called this his "much ado about nothing" period) without any appreciable change in his life style. The bespectacled professor continued to rise early, jog, write, and travel to a number of campuses for lectures and research. In 1974-75, he worked with the United States Department of Labor in planning and producing the *Bicentennial History of the American Worker*. Also in 1975, he was appointed a consultant to the American Labor History Series, which was broadcast in 1978 and 1979 by Boston TV station WGBH and the Public Broadcasting System. And only seven months before his death, Taft was awarded a Guggenheim Fellowship to continue his work on the history of labor in Alabama. He was seventy-four at the time, one of the oldest men ever to receive a Guggenheim.

When he died on November 17, 1976, Professor Taft was eulogized by Senators, Congressmen, and other national leaders – but especially by the leaders of organized labor. In a letter to the dying Taft in September of 1976, AFL-CIO President George Meany wrote of "the debt the labor movement owes you as one of the nation's outstanding scholars and interpreters of labor affairs" and added: "Generations of students will continue to benefit from your scholarship and understanding of the economic, social, and human aspect of the world of work."

Philip Taft was born in Syracuse, New York, on March 22, 1902. His father died when Taft was a small boy, and the family moved a number of times before settling in New York City in 1905. The growing-up years were not happy ones for Phil Taft. His mother, an unskilled woman, did daily housework for others and was seldom at home. Taft found himself farmed out to relatives, who thought he was undisciplined and unruly – and he agreed that he was. Shortly before his death, Phil recalled those days in an interview with

Margot Honig for the Oral History Research Office of Columbia University.

"I was very unhappy living where I was," he said. "I don't mean every day. I played with other children occasionally. It's difficult to describe. I guess it was a cumulative experience. I probably had a fight with my mother one day. And then, I simply left."

Phil Taft was thirteen (and very small for his age) when he left home. He had progressed through the sixth grade, and no further. For a while, his new home was a youth hostel for newsboys on New York's West Side, where he paid 20 cents a night for a cot. He washed dishes, shined shoes, was an errand boy, and did other odd jobs to earn enough money for an occasional sandwich and a glass of milk.

He and other youngsters from the hostel also found time to hang around on the street corners and in the parks. Phil Taft was furthering his education, but not in the formal fashion. All the boys at the hostel had two things in common – a sense of loneliness and a lack of roots. They knew that eventually they would pack what few belongings they had and move on. Where they moved to usually wasn't important. There was nothing for them where they were, but there was some dim hope that somehow things would be better where they were going. That dream would seldom be realized, but they didn't know it.

One day, Phil Taft hopped a freight train and headed for Philadelphia. It was the start of an eight-year odyssey that would take him to all parts of this country (except the Deep South) and into Canada, and would bring him into contact with the labor union movement, a movement that would give direction to his life.

Phil Taft's understanding of work came from firsthand, practical experience. Between 1915 and 1923, he labored as an errand boy, a factory worker, a stable boy for trotting horses, coal passer on the ore boats of the Great Lakes, harvest hand in the grain belt of the Midwest, potato picker, a pipe liner in the oil fields of Kansas, Oklahoma, and Texas, mule skinner on construction jobs, longshoreman, swamper in the woods of British Columbia and Washington, and brakeman and switchman on a railroad in Chicago.

The first union affiliation for Taft came when he was

working the harvest fields and joined the radical Agricultural Workers Industrial Union, a branch of the Industrial Workers of the World (IWW). The union's recruiting methods were somewhat unorthodox, according to Taft. Strong-arm men would enter the boxcars where drifters were riding and would offer the men a dubious choice – join the union or get tossed off the fast-moving train. It may not have been democracy in action, but the methods were effective. The IWW took in more members in 1915 and 1916 than it ever had before.

Taft signed up with the IWW and within a year had become a member of the Agricultural Workers' Organizing Committee. During 1922-23, he wrote several articles for the IWW's *Industrial Solidarity*. He was twenty years old and hadn't even finished grammar school.

The IWW did play an important role in Phil Taft's transformation from unskilled laborer to college professor. It was in the labor halls of the IWW that he first gained a nodding acquaintance with books. Taft recalled that period of his life in the Oral History interview: "A union hall meant that you didn't have to go to a skid row bar. A hall also provided a place where you could read. I found out that I enjoyed it. You might find things by Marx in there, or by some of the other radical writers and revolutionaries. But those things are difficult reading, conceptually, and I wonder how much I learned, except words. I had left school in the sixth grade, and I came from a family that wasn't literate. So my vocabulary was not extensive. To get through a book by Marx when you haven't gone to school is tough reading."

There was a common thread of experience with labor organizations and the American socialist movement through Phil Taft's early years. The radical literature found in the IWW halls was, without question, an influence on the young man's thinking. So, too, was the Branstetter family of Chicago. Otto Branstetter served as secretary of the Socialist Party of America (1918-23), and his wife, Winnie, also an active socialist, operated two rooming houses on Chicago's West Side. The family included a daughter, Theresa. While Phil Taft was working on the railroad in Chicago in 1922, he rented a room from the Branstetters.

During that period, the friendship between Phil Taft and Theresa Branstetter was cordial but casual. After a few months at the Branstetter home, Phil was laid off by the railroad and left Chicago. He and Theresa didn't meet again until the early 1930s when Taft returned to

Chicago to visit with Otto Branstetter. In the eight or nine years between their first and second meetings, both Phil and Theresa had married briefly and been divorced. However, their second meeting marked the start of a close friendship, which led to their marriage in Washington, D.C., on July 30, 1936.

After being laid off from the railroad job in Chicago in 1923, Phil Taft returned to New York City, still a drifter, and got a job running an elevator in a high-rise apartment. Then "purely out of boredom," he began attending night classes, earning a certificate a year later for his grammar school work.

"My interest was aroused at this point, and I now had confidence that I could handle academic work," Taft said shortly before his death. "The next step was to register for night classes at DeWitt Clinton High School. It was a difficult struggle, since I worked a ten-hour day and then had classes from 7:15 to 10:15 in the evening. Still, I managed to graduate." The year was 1928, and Phil Taft was twenty-six years old.

Later Taft would look upon his decision to return to school as the turning point in his life. In the Oral History interview, he suggested that if circumstances had been different for him in 1923, he might not have become a schoolboy again. "If I had had a girl friend, I would not have gone to night school," he said. "Between my job and school, I was on the go from 7 a.m. until nearly 11 p.m. You can't keep a girl on those hours. Probably a wife, but not a girl. And without schooling, maybe I would have become a union officer, or something like that, but certainly never a professor."

After getting in touch with several universities concerning admission, Taft was accepted at the University of Wisconsin, then one of the principal centers for the study of labor and trade unions in the United States. Under the direction of John R. Commons, the university had gathered a collection of documents on the beginnings of American labor. In 1910-11, the *Documentary History of American Industrial Society* was published there in eleven volumes. The first two volumes of *History of Labor in the United States* were published in 1918 by Professor Commons, and in 1928, the year Taft entered the college, Professor Selig Perlman published his *A Theory of the Labor Movement*.

In contrast to his earlier life, college was relatively easy for Phil Taft. Several small scholarships helped ease the financial burden, but Taft continued to work. He was up before daybreak to deliver morning newspapers to the campus and then, during the lunch hour,

he worked in the campus cafeteria.

Just before Phil graduated in 1932, fate took a turn in his behalf. Gary M. Fink, professor of history at Georgia State University in Atlanta, who revised and edited Taft's final book, *Organizing Dixie* (Greenwood Press 1981), recalled the situation in his introduction to the book. "Roger Baldwin, one of the founders of the American Civil Liberties Union, was visiting Madison," he wrote. "Taft had met Baldwin several years earlier while serving as secretary of a defense committee to defend IWW members being held for deportation. After meeting Taft once again in Madison, Baldwin asked William Ellery Leonard, a respected poet and scholar on the university's humanities faculty, if he could do anything for Taft. Leonard contacted Selig Perlman, thus inaugurating a relationship beneficial to both men and one that marked a critical turning point in Taft's academic career."

Upon graduation in 1932, Taft received his first academic job, working with Professor Perlman on the *History of Labor in the United States* at $65 a month. Taft did the research and then drafted the chapters. Later, he and Perlman would sit down for rewrite work. Most of this book belonged to Taft, with the graduate student producing more than 2,000 pages of manuscript. This work, which was published listing Taft and Perlman as co-authors, became the fourth volume in John R. Commons's monumental history of American labor and provided Taft with a reputation in the labor field.

Shortly before securing his doctorate in 1935, Phil met a government official from Washington, D.C., who was impressed with Taft's work and offered the young labor historian a job in the Labor Department. Any job at all in those Depression years would have been welcome. Getting a position in the Labor Department seemed too good to be true. It was. "This is a sure thing," the government bureaucrat said. "I've just got to get back to my boss for final approval."

Phil waited for a week, two weeks, three weeks, and then started to make inquiries. As it turned out, the man from Washington had suffered a heart attack on the train and died on his way back to Washington. Taft would tell this story whenever he wanted to emphasize that there is no such thing in this world as a "sure thing."

Phil Taft spent the first two years following his doctorate working with several New Deal agencies. Then, in 1937, he accepted a one-year appointment in the economics department at Brown. He had finally found a permanent home.

The Phil Taft who arrived at Brown in the late summer of 1937 was slight of build, vigorous, and very expressive. He loved to talk. He also loved to argue. But he argued without insulting. He tried to make his points as strongly as possible, but without ever becoming personal. He gave the impression of one who felt that his views would not necessarily be accepted unless he went to a great effort to explain them. This may well have been because, in his mind, the thirty-five-year-old Taft questioned whether or not a man of his background would readily be accepted by the faculty of an Ivy League college. Therefore, he somehow felt compelled to explain in detail to both his colleagues and his students what his positions were. This compulsion remained a part of his character until his dying day.

Taft also came across as a very friendly but nevertheless a very personal and reserved individual. This was not surprising since he became deeply involved in the labor movement in a period prior to the enactment of federal legislation institutionalizing and recognizing labor unions. He had been in the vanguard – a lonely spot at that time – of a very important social movement.

George Borts, a member of the economics department since 1950 and its chairman from 1964 to 1967, points out that the Brown faculty of 1937 differed greatly from the faculty of today. "It was poorer," Borts says, "far smaller (perhaps one-fourth the current size), primarily white, male, and Protestant. The emphasis on research had not become the obsession it is today. I recall Phil saying that a good way to halt a lunchtime conversation at early-Wriston Brown was to inquire, 'What kind of research are you doing?'"

It bears mentioning here that Phil Taft came to Brown at a point when the philosophy of how economics should be taught was changing rapidly. Prior to the middle 1930s, the training of an economist included

Taft during his first year at Brown.

some rudimentary calculus, some mathematics, some statistics, and not much more. The analysis that was done was accomplished in simple graphical terms. The economist considered it his main job to describe the functions of the economic institutions about him, including labor unions and labor-management problems. This was useful work and served a clear-cut purpose.

"When Phil took his degree, he took it in economics because labor history wasn't in existence then," Theresa Taft says. "But, he always thought of himself as a historian. In the late 1930s, someone reviewed a book of his and referred to Phil as a 'so-called historian.' Later, this became a big joke with us, and he would sometimes refer to himself as 'that so-called historian.'"

In the mid-1930s, a change took place in this teaching philosophy, as more and more technically trained people began to find the problems of economics interesting and amenable to mathematical analysis. There are some who feel that gradually economists began to live with such highly active mathematical models that they lost sight of the world with which they were supposed to be dealing. Phil Taft was not a mathematical genius, and he came out of graduate school almost precisely at the time when most non-technically trained people were being pushed to one side and considered old hat. Mark Schupack, a long-time member of the Brown economics department, its chairman from 1970 to 1974, and currently associate provost of the University, comments on this situation:

"In some sense, people always wondered about Phil's work because he was not technically trained. He came into economics just at the time when the style of training was shifting from a literary style to one that emphasized mathematics. So, you'd have to say that Phil was not a mainstream economist by the standards of the past forty-five years. During this stretch, most of the men who became well-known nationally – Paul Samuelson at MIT and Milton Friedman at Chicago, for example – used mathematical methods to make sense out of what they were doing. The amazing thing here is that Phil Taft, even though in this sense he was out of step with the times, was so good at what he did that he also achieved a national reputation in his field. Very few other economists who used the old literary style made any sort of name for themselves throughout this period.

"Phil never pretended to learn math, or felt that he *had* to learn mathematical analysis. But he didn't denigrate people who did know math, which was practically the rest of the department at Brown. The key is that Phil Taft always brought *some* analytical insights as to what was happening, as compared to straight description. And that's the difference economists always try to draw. It doesn't take much intelligence to just describe something, but the real question is 'Why? What's the implication?' The people in Phil's field of labor history felt that he had given them new insights and new appreciation of historical events. And on this, his reputation stands."

Phil Taft did not win any honors with the students during his first few years at Brown. At that time of his life, Phil was a no-holds-barred person. Perhaps it was a combination of his upbringing, plus his years at Wisconsin. The students there – the only college students Phil had ever known – were not prep-school graduates as many of them were at Brown. Phil probably came across at first as just a little bit rough for the Brown students.

Some students of the period regarded Professor Taft as a radical. This was because his ideas were different from those of the majority of the students. However, Phil Taft was certainly not a radical in the sense of someone who would seek drastic or dramatic changes in the institutions around him.

At any rate, when the student evaluation of the faculty appeared in the spring of 1938, Phil received a very poor rating. He didn't score much higher the following spring, either. But when the Pembroke class of 1947 voted him its "favorite professor," Taft went around the campus beaming for weeks. In a humorous acceptance speech at the Pembroke campus, Taft made reference to his rocky start in the classroom nine years earlier, and concluded:

Instead of the unreasonable, uncompromising, stony-hearted martinet, I have become the gentlest, most reasonable, and, if I have to say it, one of the sweetest members of the faculty. This character change, this transformation from an exacting autocrat to a tolerant guide, fitted to run a column giving advice to the lovelorn has been a source of wonder and inspiration to me, and I hope to you.

Taft and President Wriston arrived at Brown in the same year. Phil respected Wriston, called him an "out-

There was time for laughter in Taft's I.C. course.

standing president," but felt that he could never get close to him. "He wasn't the sort of person a faculty member could sidle up to and relate the story he had just heard at the corner pub," Taft once said. Phil's respect for the new Brown president didn't prevent him from standing up to Wriston when the occasion called for it, as Professor Borts recalls:

"Phil and Jim Hedges in history were two of the faculty members who had the intellectual and moral strength to take a stand if Wriston did something that irritated them. Phil's vehicle for expressing his displeasure with Wriston was the personal letter. He was always upfront with Wriston. He never ran to the *Brown Daily Herald* and let them say things for him. I think Wriston also respected Phil."

Mrs. Taft recalls how Wriston handled a misunderstanding he had with Taft during World War II. This was at a time when the president held a monthly meeting at the Hope Club for university professors. Traditionally, the meetings ended with a brandy.

"On one of these occasions," Mrs. Taft says, "Phil tried to say something and Wriston, who conducted the meetings in his usual high-handed manner, cut him off. Phil didn't stay for the brandy. He just got up and left. The next day he received a hand-written note from Henry saying, 'I'm afraid that something I said or did last night offended you, and I'm sorry. I didn't intend it to be that way.' I still have that note. It has to be a collector's item now, because I don't imagine Henry said 'I'm sorry' too often. It wasn't his nature."

Taft and Wriston had a considerable correspondence between 1937 and 1955, when Wriston retired. Some of the letters leaving Taft's office in Robinson Hall were real scorchers ("hand delivered in asbestos envelopes" was the way one colleague put it). The matter of Taft's status at Brown was one topic of dispute.

When Phil came to Brown, he replaced Professor George Bigge, who had taken a leave to work in Washington, D.C. A problem arose when Bigge couldn't make up his mind whether or not he wanted to return to Brown. The years went by – four or five – and Bigge was still straddling the fence. Taft felt that enough was enough, especially since the handling of the matter had left him without any raises through those years or a promise of tenure. One of Taft's "blistering" letters went to Wriston, suggesting in language that left little to the imagination that it was time Professor Bigge made a move – one way or the other. In short order Taft got a handsome raise and tenure.

President Wriston appointed Taft chairman of the economics department in 1949 for what turned out to be a four-year term. During his chairmanship, Taft shook up the personnel in the department, as we pointed out earlier, and this was good for the department and for Brown. But Phil Taft was not a detail man, and the daily duties associated with running a department were not to his liking.

"Every time a piece of mail came in – ledger sheets, budgets, you name it – you could hear loud noises coming from Phil's office," Professor Schupack says. "Mert, Mert,' he'd yell. 'Come in here. Hurry up.' And Mert Stoltz [professor of economics and later provost of the University] would go in and huddle with Phil. In fact, Mert did most of the paper work for the department while Phil was chairman."

Phil Taft never claimed to be a clean-desk man. His office was completely cluttered. Papers he was working on were strewn about in wild and happy disarray, along with assorted journals. Books lined the walls, surrounded with enough dust to lend authenticity. Yet Phil claimed that he knew precisely where everything was at every hour of the day. The only time he had any trouble, he said, came a few years earlier when a Manpower secretary, hired to work in Robinson Hall

for a few days, decided that she should tidy up the Taft office and put everything in its proper place. "She was a disaster," Phil said. "I couldn't find a damn thing for weeks."

While Phil was chairman, and for some time after that, he and Theresa enjoyed entertaining members of the department. In his own home Phil Taft could be the life of the party. He'd get started on some subject that was close to him – and he'd be hard to stop. One night, though, he stopped himself.

To appreciate this story, you have to understand that Phil Taft felt that certain groups were out to get him. To Phil, publishers were "difficult as a class," lawyers were "experts at the small print," and doctors were – well, several steps lower than lawyers.

Members of the department were dining one evening at the home of Professor Martin Beckmann, who was new to the faculty. Right after dinner Phil started in on the medical profession. "Those damn doctors," he said, "they cheat you blind. They have all this market power and high income, and none of them is any good." As was usually the case when Phil finished one of his soliloquies, there was a moment of silence. Then Mrs. Beckmann piped up. "Mr. Taft," she said, "I guess you don't know my daddy. He's a doctor in Minneapolis." Phil just smiled, pushed his hair back from his forehead, and was quiet the rest of the evening.

One of the men Taft hired during his chairmanship was George Borts, who, in 1950, was a graduate student at the University of Chicago. Late that spring, Taft met Borts at the Tropical Hut, an unpretentious restaurant in Chicago. Borts admits today that at first blush he didn't know what to make of Taft. He expected to see somebody very formal and institutionalized, someone who could describe what Brown was like and what the standards of employment were. Nothing of that sort came across.

"Sitting in a booth in the Tropical Hut, we just had a wild discussion of his views on life in general," Borts says. "He offered some very frank opinions of some of my professors in graduate school who even now, thirty-two years later, are quite controversial. I didn't know what the devil to make of it. I said to myself – well, if he thinks Milton Friedman is a jerk, then my chances aren't very great.

"But I was impressed. My final opinion was that Professor Taft was an interesting guy. Here was a man who was old enough to be my father but was perfectly willing to discuss all his professional and personal opinions with someone who was a total stranger, and to bring that person into his confidence and give him the benefit of his thoughts."

Although Phil Taft had a pleasant disposition, little irritations could throw him into a momentary rage. Then, thirty minutes later, he'd be his old self again. Phil claimed that his moments of anger were deceptive. "When I'm *not* very mad, I'll shout about things," he once said. "But when I'm quiet and don't say anything, then I'm very, very angry." It was to his credit that he never let these irritations affect his relations with his colleagues on a day-to-day basis. Most of them revered Taft. All had their lives enriched by him to some extent.

This was partly because Taft was extremely fair. He was able to accommodate people with different backgrounds or with different types of training. One of the reasons the economics department functioned so well when he was a part of it was that Taft could bring together people who were doing all kinds of work and give them the feeling that they were wanted and useful. But his ethic was *work*. As long as these people were working, he felt that they were contributing. And by working, he meant scholarly work.

When it came to this thoughts about the University, Phil Taft was one of the old school. "People who teach here have damned good jobs," he once said. "Just think about the guy who works in a foundry when it's 103 degrees outside."

Mark Schupack comments further on this matter: "In Phil's mind, the University was a good place to work, and you came in just as a laborer came in. There were certain work conditions to follow, and you followed them. He was very upset with at least a couple of members of our department, who, he thought, simply were not giving the University good value for its money. He used to rail about their lack of work ethic. 'For what we're paying them, they're cheating us,' he'd say. It was the same thing when anyone began talking about academic freedom. 'Academic freedom has to do with conditions of your employment,' he'd storm. 'It's no God-given constitutional right.' To Phil, academic freedom was not a civil rights issue. It was just like any other labor contract clause."

When Professor Taft was in his office, he usually wore jacket, slacks, shirt, and tie. This attire would have appeared casual by the standards of the 1930s, especially if the jacket and slacks didn't match. Near the close of his career, when most of his colleagues had gone the sport shirt route, Taft continued to dress as he had throughout his Brown years. "I think he enjoyed dressing neatly," George Borts says. "I know he well remembered the days when he was a graduate student and had only one pair of pants. I recall his saying bitterly, 'I didn't even have enough money to buy a second pair of trousers.'"

The writing career of Phil Taft entered its productive period in 1953, shortly after he gave up the departmental chairmanship. From that point until his death twenty-three years later, he worked every day and many nights, either browsing through the archives of some library or sitting behind his typewriter. Of his fifteen books, eleven were written after 1953, and four of those eleven were produced in the nine-year period between his retirement and his death.

"His method of research was historical, but his thinking processes were analytical," says Professor Borts. "He approached archival material as data for the testing of hypotheses about union, trade association, and government activities. As an institutional economist, he derived such hypotheses from the political, historical, and social forces operating on the institutions.

"Phil played an important role in defining the characteristics of the American labor movement and in preserving its identity against attempts by Socialist and Communist writers to interpret its activities to suit their purposes. In this regard, his role as a scholar paralleled the political and organizational activity of those leaders who were the focus of his books: Samuel Gompers, William Green, and George Meany."

In 1956, Taft was asked to write the history of the A. F. of L. The man who asked him was Arthur Elder, then an advisor to George Meany on taxation. After arranging for a sabbatical from Brown and being awarded a Faculty Fellowship from the Ford Foundation, Phil agreed to take on the job. Working at the A. F. of L. headquarters in Washington, he was given space for his research, a modest budget, and something

much more important – the keys to the building. This marked the first time in the history of this union that its keys had been given to anyone except the executive staff.

"I'd be in there earlier than anybody and would stay long after everyone else had gone," Taft recalled in the Columbia Oral History interview. "I would take the executive council minutes out of the shelves, bring them downstairs, and read them. I never violated their trust."

In the same interview, Taft pointed out that the A. F. of L. executive council never published minority opinions. The feeling was that their views would have meaning only if they were put out as the unanimous opinion of the council. No man was ever quoted, and

there is no breakdown of who voted for or against specific issues. Taft did note that Gompers was admonished once by a member of the council after the head of the union had gone on the floor and made a motion to overturn a council decision. "This fellow wrote to Gompers," Taft said, "and he told him, 'You are not the entire council, and you should not have done that.'"

Ironically, while the two-volume history of the A. F. of L. made Taft an international reputation, it didn't earn him much money. "I may have made a couple of thousand dollars from the sale of the book," Taft told Margot Honig in the Oral History interview, "but if I needed money badly, I think I could have found other sources that would have been more remunerative. I have never gotten anything from the labor movement except work. I'm not complaining about this, but one of their favorite arbitrators will probably earn more in one week than I've earned in forty years from the labor movement."

The man who had no interest in the day-to-day detail involved with the running of the economics department was the very master of detail in his research for the writing of a book or an article. Larry Spitz '51 ('76 Hon. LL.D.), a former student of Taft's who became assistant to the president of the United Steelworkers of America, comments: "When I was in Pittsburgh, he came to the International Union office of the Steelworkers to see me concerning an article he was writing on the Land-rum-Griffin Act and its impact on the labor movement. Well, Phil wasn't content to talk to officials of the union or its attorney. He had to contact local union offices and rank-and-file members to hear first hand their experiences under the law. Later, when I arranged to open the archives of the Steelworkers in Pittsburgh for Phil, he would disappear for hours and miss meals unless we'd go down to his office to haul him out. He spent countless hours talking to our members, and they sensed in him a person who understood their problems."

Because his handwriting was very bad, and tiring, Taft would knock out the first draft of a book on his old black Royal typewriter. He was a fast typist, made few mistakes, but never produced final copy. And, despite the frequency with which he turned out manu-scripts, he found it difficult to relax while writing a book. "I get very bad habits when I write," he said. "I drink too much black coffee, I work long hours, and I get very nervous. My Mrs. would never say anything to me when I was nearing the completion of a book. There was pressure on her, too. I always wished that I could have saved her that pressure."

Theresa Taft, who was totally supportive of her hus-band, frequently accompanied him when he was doing research at various points around the country. She was secretary, notetaker, and typist for Phil, as well as a motivating factor in his life for forty years. Phil always referred to Theresa as, simply, "My Mrs."

Not too long before his death, Phil and I chatted about what was involved in writing a book. At that time, he stressed that if someone had a book in his future, he should stick to a few firm guidelines. Rule one was to stay with a subject with which the author was comfortable. "I know only one subject," he said, "and I don't purport to know that in its entirety, either. The subject I feel comfortable in is labor, and I've never written anything of importance outside of labor."

He also cautioned about being too structured when you start the project. Remain flexible, he suggested. "I've always operated on the theory that a man never writes a book. You know, you start in, then maybe you get interested in something unexpected, and you sort of nibble at the edges. Then, the book follows.

"When it comes to writing a book, I'm a pessimist in the sense that I believe in the imminence of failure. Be prepared for failure. It's always around the corner. For one thing, people are more happy when you fail. You'll never get any sympathy about failure."

From Phil Taft's point of view, an author is better off working alone. "One time, I tried working with a fellow on a book," he said. "It was a great mistake. You know, I am not orderly. But I am systematic in my work. If I work on a project, I work every day – Saturdays, Sun-days, holidays. I get up and I go to work, because there's nothing else to do at 5 o'clock in the morning. I'm not driven, or anything, but in a sense the only thing I have is pride. I am like any workman who has a skill and enjoys using it. If you hook up on a book with someone else, and if he's not as dedicated, well – you have problems."

The people who were heroes in the eyes of Phil Taft were mainly from the field of labor. There were excep-tions, such as sports columnist Red Smith and former President Harry Truman. Taft termed Smith "the best darned sports writer who ever lived, a writer who could really burn the hair off your head." Phil was an early admirer of Truman, supporting him enthusiasti-cally before it was popular to do so. He may have seen something of himself in Truman. Certainly, there were similarities between the two men. Both were feisty and both were self-made. There was probably one other reason. Truman was considered effective in han-dling American foreign policy, in which Taft took a strong interest because of what happened to the Euro-pean labor movement after World War II when it was threatened with infiltration by the Communists. Taft felt that Truman's influence in the immediate post-war years helped halt what otherwise might have been a major takeover of the unions.

Although he spoke out against John L. Lewis on several occasions, Taft did admire the strength and leadership ability of this man. "Lewis certainly dominated the miners," he told me one afternoon. "But you know the fable of Achilles' heel. Every man has his weak spot. For Lewis, his great defect was his ego. But he was a man of tremendous ability, and he could dominate any movement he was in, or any conversation, or anything else. I'm told there was one exception. It was in 1944, and President Roosevelt had a campaign train going into the anthracite belt in Pennsylvania. Well, Lewis got on the train and was shown into Roosevelt's private car. But he didn't dominate there! There were some drinks, some stories being told, but F.D.R. dominated the scene, as he always did."

The person Taft admired above all others was George Meany. A letter from Meany was received as a message from heaven. It made no difference whether it was a complimentary letter or one that was critical. Taft discussed Meany in a 1973 taped interview with Art Hatton, then acting director of the Brown News Bureau and now assistant to the president at the State University of New York College at Geneseo.

"Don't ever underestimate George Meany," Taft said. "He has a mind like a steel trap. He is a very nice man, but the best way to deal with him is to be straightforward. Always have your facts straight, and do not assume that George Meany is incapable of logical analysis. He may not have studied Euclidean logic, but he sure knows how to use it. He has a very, very good mind. It's just that he's not the sort of man to sparkle."

Taft would bristle when people complained about what they perceived as the growing power of the labor unions. Phil would patiently point out that the United States was fortunate in having the type of unions that exist here, that there are no political strikes in this country, that unions are not interested in nationalizing any industries, and that unions are completely reliable whenever the government is engaged in any sort of foreign adventure.

Labor, however, was not Phil Taft's *entire* life; it just seemed that way sometimes. Among other things, he had a reputation, justly earned, of being one of the most perceptive sports fans on the faculty. He could pull names and statistics out of baseball's past just as easily as he could recite the batting averages of the current stars. The moves of the managers intrigued him. So did the trades and the gossip of the off-season. "An afternoon at the ball park with Phil was a singular treatment," says Selig Silverman, a New York attorney who was a college classmate and long-time friend. "You would get sports history, a running social commentary on racial segregation in the major leagues, and his views on the economic life of ball players – all this for the price of one admission."

Professor Taft was also a Brown football fan – a fanatical fan. He liked to go to the games with George and Dolly Borts. Mrs. Borts sat in between the two men, until she realized that this was a mistake. As Brown moved the ball up and down the field, George would be pushing Dolly from one side and Phil would be hitting her with elbows, a shoulder, and an occasional knee from the other. After a season or so of this treatment, Dolly sat elsewhere.

Taft was sometimes tough to "live" with *away* from the ballpark or stadium. When Eleanor Roosevelt spoke at Sayles Hall in the fall of 1948, Taft, an enthusiastic supporter of the former First Lady, was seated in the audience directly behind Edward A. Bloom, professor of English. Mrs. Roosevelt had no sooner started her talk when Taft began to tap Professor Bloom on the back, gently at first and then harder and harder as Mrs. Roosevelt warmed up to her task. "Did you hear that?" Taft fairly shouted at one point, from a strategic location just east of Bloom's right ear. "Isn't she great? Isn't she great?" he bellowed, emphasizing his point with a straight arm to Professor Bloom's upper back. "It got so bad I was hoping Mrs. Roosevelt would say something Phil *didn't* like, just so he would ease up on me," Ed Bloom recalls with a chuckle.

Walking on the sidewalk with Phil Taft was also quite an experience. When a particular subject had been bothering him for a while, Taft loved to buttonhole a colleague and verbalize his thoughts. Larry Spitz sometimes found himself the catcher, not the pitcher, in one of these conversations. He writes: "His white hair would be flying in the wind, his arms waving, and periodically he would wheel around in front of you, blocking your path and compelling you to stop while he finished his dissertation."

There was a story on campus, perhaps apocryphal, about the time Phil and a colleague were locked in heated debate in Robinson Hall, the home of the economics department at the corner of Waterman and Prospect Streets. At 12 noon, the two professors, still jawing, put on their coats and headed for lunch at the Ivy Room in Sharpe Refectory, not more than 300 yards away. Phil stopped his colleague at several points along the way to hammer home a particular point or two, and it was 12:30 before they reached the front steps of the "Ratty," where their discussion went on and on. Finally, Taft looked at his watch. "My God," he said, "it's 1:15." With that, the two men slowly headed back to Robinson Hall, still shoulder to shoulder, still debating the issue of the day and oblivious to the fact that they had not remembered to eat.

Although Phil Taft was a very intense man, he always had a safety valve. He knew how to relax. For him, relaxing might mean a few moments alone at the piano, reading in bed or on a train, listening to classical music or musical comedies, or taking a long walk. Professor Schupack talks about Taft's walking habits:

"I think Phil was most relaxed when he took one of his walks, whether it was at the beach near his summer home in Middletown or in Providence. But even when walking, when trying to relax, he couldn't completely resist talking business. Those were the occasions when he could get some of the probems of the day off his chest.

"There was only one thing about walking with Phil. If he wasn't in deep debate with someone, he really liked to step out. He would sometimes complain to me that Professor Beckmann walked too slowly. Well, Martin *does* walk slowly. I tried to play squash with Martin once. It was fine as long as I hit the ball *directly* at him. Phil and I would walk home together once in a while, and he'd complain to me, 'I like walking with Mart, but he walks so damn slowly.'"

There were few things Phil Taft enjoyed more than sitting at the piano and hammering out a tune. All of his "concerts" were confined to the Taft's Irving Avenue home – and all were private. Theresa looked upon him as something less than Bach. "Phil was in his fifties when he started to play," Theresa says, "and he would joke about not being a child prodigy anymore. He had no eye trouble, but he said that if he ever did, the piano

would become his form of relaxation. Then he wouldn't have to be reading and using his eyes twenty-four hours a day."

According to some reports, Phil enjoyed his lessons more than he enjoyed hearing himself play. He and the instructor, Ivan Waldbauer, professor of music at Brown, had a grand old time. Right in the middle of a cadenza, something might pop into Phil's head, and he would spin around on the piano stool and launch into a lively discussion of the subject at hand. Suddenly, the roles were changed as pupil became teacher. Ivan could feel control slipping away from him, but he didn't mind. He was completely fascinated with Taft's fertile mind. "I don't know whether he should pay me or I should pay him," he once joked.

Jogging was another form of relaxation that Phil Taft took up late in life. It started as an alternative to reading, on those days when he awoke at the crack of dawn. When he found out that jogging seemed to improve his health, Phil continued it on a daily basis, along the quiet streets of East Side Providence or in Mobile, Birmingham, Austin, Chicago, New York, Atlanta, or wherever his research took him. Occasionally he encountered some interesting companions.

"Early one morning," Phil said, "as I was running along 56th Street in New York City, three young men hailed me. 'Sir,' one of them yelled, 'do you know where we can find three nice girls?' Without breaking stride, I yelled back, 'I should think you'd ask this of someone much younger than I.' And the kids stood there grinning from ear to ear. Another morning, I was hailed by a prostitute. 'I see you all the time running. Why do you do that?' she asked. Well, I stopped and the two of us chatted for three or four minutes. I didn't try to convert her. Nor she me."

Although most people do not remember Phil Taft as a witty person, he did have a good sense of humor. He was not expert at telling jokes or coming out with quick one-liners. And he gave wide berth to puns. But Taft was not a deadly serious person. He was lively, friendly, animated, and very good company. Perhaps his forte as a humorist was in illustrating events that happened to him, either on campus or when he was off on one of his trips.

One of his favorite stories concerned the time he and Theresa were living in Williamstown, N.Y., on the outskirts of Buffalo, where he was doing some research at the university. Each morning when Phil would go jogging at 5:30 or 6, he would pass a particular horse in a field on the outskirts of town. After a day or two, when it appeared to Phil that a certain compatability existed between the two early risers, he would bring an apple or a lump of sugar with him and would stop and feed the animal. Phil enjoyed this respite, and so, presumably, did the horse. One day as Phil was completing his morning exercise and was about to enter his apartment in the center of town, he heard a familiar sound behind him. He turned, and there trotting up the middle of the street, braying as he came, was the horse. "That," Phil would always tell his listeners, "was carrying friendship *too* far."

After living with Phil Taft for more than forty years, Theresa feels that it is safe to describe her husband's humor as "dry." Much of his humor was unexpected. She illustrates:

"Shortly after Phil retired, he was made a consultant at the Department of Employment Security in Providence. He had no set duties down there except to attend a committee meeting once a month. But he would drop in twice a week, just to see if there wasn't something he could do to help. And sometimes Mary Hackett, the director, would say, 'Phil, will you write a press release or type me a statement on this subject?' So, Phil would take off his coat, roll up his sleeves, and sit down in front of a typewriter. One day, a woman who had known him at Brown walked by, saw him typing, did a double-take, and then said, 'Why, Professor Taft! What are *you* doing here?' Taft looked up. 'Oh, well,' he said, 'you probably read in the paper where I retired, and they have given me a job down here as a typist.' The woman gave him a funny look and went on about her business."

One of the constant enjoyments in Professor Taft's life was attending the theatre, both in Providence and in the cities he would visit. If Phil had a free evening and there was a good play in town, he would be there. James O. Barnhill, former chairman of the theatre arts department at Brown, would frequently receive first-

hand reports from Phil on how he viewed the productions. "He had strong convictions on everything, including plays," Professor Barnhill says. "He was seldom neutral. 'That was a thoroughly *lousy* production I saw last night,' he might tell me. 'I saw absolutely nothing to recommend it to anyone.' But he really was a very fine critic. He loved the theatre, knew what to look for in a production, and could smell a turkey a mile away."

The Taft who loved to talk and relished a heated one-on-one debate became the Taft who rarely spoke when he attended faculty meetings, which he did religiously. "In small groups, Phil was fine," Professor Borts says, "but he was not comfortable in debate or speaking before a large audience. There was another reason why he, and others, were quiet at those meetings. A faculty meeting chaired by President Wriston was like a day at the Roman Colosseum with Wriston as the lion. Anyone who didn't toe the line was made a fool of by the chair, or by somebody on the floor who got up to please the chair. I mean it was guided democracy of the worst type, and I think Phil lost any taste he might have had for faculty debate as a result."

The reading habits formed in the IWW halls when he was a young man stayed with Taft all of his life. His personal library consisted of more than 2,500 books in all fields of learning except science and math. He could discuss philosophy with philosphers, literature – modern and ancient – with literary scholars, and history and political science with historians and political scientists. And, although he was a non-believer, he was well read in the various aspects of Protestantism and Catholicism. In fact, two of his many articles dealt with Catholicism: *The Association of Catholic Trade Unions* and *The Pope Points the Way to Social Justice*. He read the Bible as great literature, and it was always on the coffee table or at his bedside. Scarcely a day went by that he didn't open the Bible and read from it for a while. He also had an enormous collection of books on the "isms," as he called them: anarchism, bolshevism, fascism (Italian, Spanish, and German), and socialism. He read Russian without a dictionary and had several hundred books on Russia, some in English and others in Russian.

"The wide amount of reading he did impressed me," Professor Schupack says. "After earning her bachelor's at Brown in 1966, my wife, Helene, took her master's in English literature here in 1970, and she enjoyed talking to Phil because he knew the field so well, in a semi-professional way. I remember taking a trip with him once, and he was reading Joseph Conrad's *Lord Jim*. Actually, he was rereading it. Phil would read some books two and three times, which is not something one would expect from a person whose main interest is labor economics and who came into intellectual work late. I think his voracious reading was an effort to make up for lost time."

Much of Phil Taft's reading was done in the middle of the night. He retired early, but he frequently had trouble sleeping. So, he would get up, take a book down from the shelf, and start reading at 2 or 3 a.m. Then, by 5 or 5:30, he was pulling on a pair of old trousers and (in the cold weather) his fur cap in preparation for his morning jog.

"I had a bit of trouble with Phil when we were first married," Theresa says, "because I was the sort of person who would like to get up and have a cup of coffee and not talk to anybody. Phil would bound out of bed and into the shower and then bounce into his chair at the breakfast table. He was going from the moment he opened his eyes. This energy remained at a high level right up until a few months before he died."

Phil took delight in getting to Faunce House each morning before the newspapers arrived at Fiore's counter in the Trophy Room. And when the Blue Room opened at 7 a.m., he was the first person through the door for a cup of coffee. It followed that Phil Taft was the first man to turn the key in the lock at Robinson Hall each morning. Rumor has it that when, on occasion, the janitor forgot his keys, Phil let *him* in. Although he scheduled his office hours at 8 a.m. (for his own convenience), the students came anyway. The Brown undergraduates found him an interesting man.

"Phil was informed and up to date," George Borts says. "Even if his ideas didn't agree with what the younger people were thinking, he was willing to confront them, challenge them, and argue on specific issues with them. The students did not treat him as someone who was out of touch with things."

Professor Schupack feels that Taft would have done well in any student poll during the 1960s. "However, one should keep in mind," Schupack says, "that Phil was never really close to the undergraduates. It wasn't his style to be a buddy to his pupils. Despite his outgoing nature, in many ways Phil Taft was a very private individual."

Extremely popular as a lecturer, Taft usually had one or two large classes each semester. His style tended to be a combination of well-researched notes and personal reminiscences or illustrative stories. He brought his particular sense of humor to the classroom, frequently making himself the butt of his own jokes.

No one would accuse Phil Taft of being absent-minded. Still, several stories from the middle 1960s do come to mind suggesting that occasionally he was so deep in thought or so engrossed in conversation that strange things did happen. Paul F. Mackesey '32 recalls:

"After a party at Alumni House one night, Ed Sulzberger [a 1929 graduate and a prominent realtor in New York City] told me that he couldn't find his coat. The case of the missing coat remained a mystery for several months, until one day when I received a call from Theresa. 'Do you know anyone named Sulzberger?' she asked. 'Phil put on a coat this morning, found a pair of unfamiliar gloves in the pocket, and panicked.'

"On another occasion, a colleague noticed that his hat was missing as he was about to depart from the Faculty Club. Acting on an inside tip, he called Phil the very next day. 'Oh, was that your hat?' Phil countered. 'I attended a meeting in New Haven last night, and as I was leaving, the hat check girl handed me this hat. It didn't fit right, so I said to her, 'That's not my hat,' and I left it there.'"

As Taft's career drew to a close, he could look back on a life that was productive, interesting, and rewarding. He did research and lecturing at nine major universities. He was one of the founders of *Labor History* and served on its editorial board until his death. He was elected a Fellow of the American Academy of Arts and Sciences in 1949; eleven years later, he was elected president of the Industrial Relations Research Association. He was a public panel member of the National War Labor Board during World War II, presided over the New England Trucking Commission, which supervised wage changes in the industry, and for more than twenty-five years was a consultant to the Rhode Island Department of Employment Security.

After World War II, he also did some arbitration, although he never really enjoyed it. "While I'm not anti-social, I am not the sort of person who is a great lover of meeting people," he said in the Columbia Oral History interview. "This is not snobbery on my part. I mean, I would just as soon meet somebody who drives a truck as a college professor. Many times rather. They're frequently more interesting."

It's hard to imagine Phil Taft not enjoying anything he undertook, including arbitration. And in the Oral History interview, he did recall one case that brought him more than a modicum of satisfaction. Phil was involved in arbitration at the Washburn Wire Company in East Providence, which had just experienced a long strike with the Steelworkers. Arbitration was going slowly, mainly because of the stubborn stance of the company attorney, whose name rang a bell with Phil. Then, one day while walking off lunch, Phil suddenly remembered. The attorney who was giving him so much trouble had been a leader in some of the Communist demonstrations of the 1930s. When negotiations resumed after lunch, the situation was the same – no progress. During a coffee break, Phil took the attorney aside for a brief chat. "After that, by God, we settled in a half hour," Phil said. "He thought I would go and tell his company about his Communist affiliation. I wouldn't have, but ...."

Phil Taft had power in the labor field and sometimes used it to achieve an objective. But he didn't enjoy the process. At heart he was shy and embarrassed easily. I've been in his company when someone would praise him for a recent achievement. "Aw, no," he would say as he turned away, his face coloring slightly. "It was nothing."

Late in his career Phil delighted in being compared in appearance to Carl Sandburg. In the mid-1960s Phil was returning by train from a meeting in New York City, accompanied by Provost Stoltz and Professor Schupack. During the time they sat and chatted in the club car three or four people came by, did a double take, and said, 'Aren't you Carl Sandburg?' Phil would smile, lower his head, and politely explain that he was not Sandburg. But he was pleased.

There were a number of things that were disturbing to Taft during his final years at Brown. He never lost his enthusiasm for what he was doing or for life itself. But he was troubled. One of the things that bothered him most was the drastic change in moral standards among the students with respect to sex and drugs. This was something Phil just couldn't understand. He had been brought up in hard times, and the idea that

young people could come from affluent backgrounds, have the whole world in front of them, and destroy themselves physically and emotionally was something that he could not comprehend. This was especially true in terms of drugs.

If the drug situation made Phil sad, the disruptions on the college campuses in this country in the late 1960s and early 1970s caused him to boil over with anger. He felt that college administrators were much too soft with the student protesters, and too reluctant to take the steps that might at least have minimized the problem.

"College officials may never again experience this sort of thing from students, where they curse them and shout obscenities," Taft said in the early 1970s. "Just picture a student sitting on the other side of the desk from the president of Yale or Cornell and cursing him in language that would bring a blush to the cheeks of a $2 tart. When you allow this, you've lost the battle. When things get this far out of control, it would have

Taft and his granddaughter, Nancy Ellen Blake, on a Commencement morning.

been better to close the place down."

Phil Taft also could not understand the reaction on campus to the Vietnam War. In his support of the war, he was out of step with almost all of his colleagues. Professor Borts recalls sitting with Phil and discussing the situation:

"Phil and I were very close friends, even though there were many things we didn't see eye-to-eye on. And yet, we could tolerate the differences. I could sit for hours with him discussing George Meany's views on the war in Vietnam, trying to figure out why the American labor movement was not being critical of the war. I remember having a very bitter discussion with Phil about this. His position was that you have to support the government. The President with all his informational sources knows what's right. It was obvious that he was very uncomfortable defending the labor position, and it was also obvious that I made him very uncomfortable attacking labor's position. But it didn't have any effect on our personal relationship."

If Phil had respect for a person, as he did for George Borts, he could accept criticism graciously. He was especially close to Jerome Stein, professor of economics at Brown, who read the manuscript for one of Taft's last books, *Defending Freedom* (Nash Publishing, 1973), and was brutally frank in his comments to the author. In the preface, Taft publicly thanked Professor Stein for his "sharp eye and unmerciful criticism."

For a number of years, Phil had experienced a slow heart beat. Finally, his physician suggested that a pacemaker might be helpful, and Phil was admitted to the hospital for a series of preliminary and presumably routine tests. Unfortunately, the results were *not* routine. Every day, the doctors came up with a different malignancy.

"Phil had never smoked in his life," Theresa says, "and he had never been near chemicals. Yet, these growths showed up in his lungs. He knew that he was seriously ill. His reaction was what we might have expected – stoical. I was extremely uptight. It was a very difficult time for me."

During his hospitalization, Phil said that he hoped death would come quickly, "not for my sake but for my Mrs." Because he had never really retired in the formal sense of the word, his death on November 17, 1976, created a void on the campus.

Phil would not have liked that. He would have much preferred that some of his old companions from the economics department – Borts, Schupack, Stein, Stoltz, Beckmann – got together at the round table in the Faculty Club for a heated discussion on a topic of current interest.

Even better, Phil would have enjoyed joining in on that debate – loudly.

Chapter 3 ❧
Only he drew smiles from the provost at budget time

On a frosty morning in the winter of 1947, President Henry M. Wriston summoned Otto Neugebauer, the distinguished professor of the history of mathematics, to his office. "Otto," Wriston said crisply, "find me an Egyptologist."

Professor Neugebauer found Richard A. Parker, then a highly competent assistant professor of Egyptology at the University of Chicago. The two men had been collaborating at long range for five years on Egyptian astronomical texts, collecting and interpreting them and then arranging for publication.

By the fall of 1949 Neugebauer and Parker were collaborating at extremely short range: from adjacent offices in the basement of Sayles Hall. A congenial Dartmouth graduate who numbered among his close friends James T. Farrell, author of *Studs Lonigan*, and Nelson Rockefeller, Dick Parker proved to be an excellent choice to head Brown's new department. He also proved to be a very interesting man – equally at home studying papyri in the British Museum, telling a joke at his favorite club, or slouched on his couch – a pile of jazz records scattered about him – listening to Duke Ellington and the Cotton Club Orchestra play "Shout 'em Aunt Tillie."

During his days on College Hill, Professor Parker was the only department chairman the provost greeted with a smile at budget time: That was because the De-

partment of Egyptology is completely endowed and has never cost Brown one single penny. The money to set up the department and keep it in business came, indirectly, from the financial rape of New York City between 1869 and 1871 by William Marcy "Boss" Tweed, in one of the great political scandals of the nineteenth century.

That brings us to the second man who plays a leading role in this story, Charles Edwin Wilbour. A member of the Brown class of 1854, Wilbour was a struggling journalist when he became involved with the Tweed Ring. Several years later, when he sought self-exile in Europe, Wilbour was a wealthy man who never worked again. Out of his association with the unsavory Tweed came lush Paris apartments, house boats on the Nile, friendships with some of the great men of his era – and Brown's Department of Egyptology.

Wilbour, whose ancestors settled in Little Compton, Rhode Island, about 1690, early developed a fascination for languages. Reportedly he drove a wagon load of hay into a ditch one day because he was more interested in the Latin grammar in his hands than he was in the direction his horse was taking him. He entered Brown in 1850, majored in languages, took a prize for proficiency in Greek, but didn't graduate.

Wilbour headed for New York City in 1853, where his first job was at the *New York Tribune* of Horace

Greeley and Charles A. Dana. Starting out as a reporter, he quickly gained some knowledge of shorthand and soon was promoted to the post of court reporter. Stenography was new at that time, but Wilbour became an expert at the trade and patented a system of rapid courtroom stenography. He also earned a law degree and practiced briefly while continuing with his journalistic career.

Greeley, who took a liking to this young newspaperman who was both bright and ambitious, befriended him in a number of ways. Wilbour became the owner of a small block of *Tribune* stock, which he expanded considerably in later years. Greeley also helped his protégé to rise in the social set, paving the way for his entry into the drawing rooms of the established literary circle. As Wilbour rapidly moved up in the world, he made friends in all walks of life. One of his new acquaintances was William Marcy Tweed, a coarse and ill-bred ward politician who has been referred to as "a drinking licentious Falstaff, with a facility for making friends."

Shortly after the Civil War, Tweed established the political machine that eventually was to plunder New York City. High on his priority list as he put this machine in motion was a desire to create a complacent press, and one of Tweed's first moves in that direction was an attempt to buy the support, or at least the silence, of the Fourth Estate.

Tweed had the *Times* in his hip pocket, a good start toward his objective. Some of the giants of the profession fought back, among them Nordhoff of the *Evening Post*. Then, one day it was suddenly announced that Nordhoff was taking a long vacation in Europe – with pay.

As part of its plan to control the press, the Tweed Ring took control of the *New York Transcript* and brought Charles Wilbour over from the *Tribune* as manager. In a related move, Tweed assumed control of the New York Printing Company. Again Wilbour was on the scene, this time as president of the publishing house.

A. Oakey Hall, the new mayor of New York City, was among the political puppets who danced when Boss Tweed pulled the strings. "Call me O.K. Hall," he liked to say. Thomas Nast, the political cartoonist and the biggest thorn in Tweed's side, frequently referred to the mayor as "O.K. Haul," in obvious reference to the money that was being hauled out of the taxpayer's pockets. He was also known as "Elegant Oakey," in reference to his style of dress and his pen-

Charles Edwin Wilbour was known as Abu-Dign, "father of the beard."

chant for high living.

O.K. Hall was a central figure in the inner workings of the Tweed Ring. Through his office, key city positions were filled with a series of characters that would have been completely at home in a Damon Runyon story. Among them was Richard B. "Slippery Dick" Connolly, an undistinguished bank clerk who awoke one morning to find himself Controller of Public Expenditures for the city; and Peter "Brains" Sweeney, the Park Commissioner, a somber and seclusive man.

In a period of thirty months between 1869 and 1871, Boss Tweed and his cronies bilked the city of almost $45,000,000 and added more than $50,000,000 to the public debt. It's not clear how deeply Wilbour was involved with this group, but Denis Tilden Lynch, in his book *Boss Tweed*, wrote:

"The Boss was also a newspaper publisher. His paper was the *Transcript*, a struggling morning newspaper when he took it over. The Boss engaged one of his Republican editorial friends, Charles Edwin Wilbour, to manage it. Editor Wilbour held at least three jobs simultaneously. He was stenographer in the Bureau of Elections at $3,000 a year, stenographer in the Superior Court at $2,500 annually, and the Examiner of Accounts at $3,500. The *Transcript* became the official newspaper of the City of New York, and no journal fared so well in the matter of municipal advertising."

In another book about the Tweed era, *Thomas Nast: His Period and His Pictures*, by Albert Bigelow Paine, the New York Printing Company, run by Wilbour, got good play.

"The entire amount distributed by the Ring during a period of about thirty months for public advertising alone was $7,168,212," Paine wrote. "The greater part of that amount was paid to the New York Printing Company, owned by the Ring."

Paine also mentions that in 1871 Tweed gave orders to the Board of Education to reject all bids submitted for school books by Harper, publisher for the cartoons of Nast. In addition, all Harper books then used in the New York school system were destroyed at a net loss to the taxpayers of approximately $50,000. The books were replaced with new ones printed at Wilbour's New York Printing Company.

Thanks largely to the constant crusading of the *Times*, under new editors, and by Nast, the people of New York were finally shocked into an awareness of what was happening to them. During this journalistic crusade, the caricatures of the Tammany Tiger drawn by Nast became the symbol of the fight against Tweed. As the *Times* pounded home the truth with its pitiless exposures, the gang began to break up under an ever-mounting wave of public indignation. Jailed in 1871, Tweed escaped to Spain, but was returned by the Spanish government in 1876 and died in prison two years later at age fifty-five.

At some point in the fall of 1871, while the steamer lines were being called upon to arrange an unusual number of hurried departures from New York to Europe, Charles Edwin Wilbour and his family quietly sailed for France. Wilbour was thirty-eight years old when he left the country. One life was behind him and a very different life was about to begin. In the twenty-five years that were left to him, Wilbour made contributions in the field of Egyptology that earned him both the admiration and the respect of the world's experts in this field.

David Patten, former feature writer for the *Providence Journal*, described the Wilbour of that period in one of his "In Perspective" columns: "Charles Edwin Wilbour was only one jump from the soil. He was the product of a thousand years of yeomanry, but it took only a few decades to polish him into something little resembling his father. He was tall, broad-shouldered, with a fine head, and his blue eyes snapped under busy white brows. His fingers were strangely slim for a son of the soil, and they frequently stroked the white mustachio and the full white beard that fell in a stroke almost to the middle of his body. None dressed for any occasion better than he, and his whole presence was that of a man at home in any waters."

In 1858, Wilbour had married Charlotte Beebe of Norwich, Connecticut, a lady of breeding. She was described by some as "stylish and noticeable" and as a figure among the intelligentsia. One of her family lawyers, a Mr. Cook, saw her differently. In a letter to John Cooney, then director of the Cleveland Museum of Art, he described her as "that old buzzard." Charlotte was a founder and first president of the Sorosis Club of New York, the pioneer women's club in the United States, perhaps the world. She was an active leader in the movement for women's suffrage more than 100 years before women's liberation entered the picture.

She was also a true Victorian, always addressing her husband as "Mr. Wilbour."

In Paris, the Wilbours continued to find the literary set stimulating and satisfying. In turn, Paris was impressed by the Wilbours. Dave Patten writes: "Except for Zoe, the youngest child, they were six feet or more tall, with sturdy physiques and, in exile, they consorted with writers and artists, even with the mighty Victor Hugo. When they entered the ateliers and salons of the Right Bank or the Left Bank, the whispers spread: 'Those Americans! Those Wilbours!'"

Wilbour respected the burly strength and passion of Victor Hugo, and the two men enjoyed the good life of Paris. He also met Gaston Maspero, at that time one of the three leading Egyptologists in the world. Wilbour had begun to study the ancient civilization of the Nile Valley in his earlier New York days, and these years abroad gave him the opportunity to advance this study in the libraries and museums of Paris and Heidelberg. It was Maspero from whom Wilbour acquired an exceptional knowledge of hieroglyphics.

Urged on by Maspero, Wilbour made the first of his annual visits to Egypt in 1880, traveling the Nile on a government gunboat. Then, in the fall of 1886, he bought his own sailing *dahabiyeh*, naming her *The Seven Hathors* after the ancient Egyptian goddess of fortune. He and the members of his family spent every winter on this vessel, usually returning to Paris for the summer months.

In Egypt, *The Seven Hathors* became known as a resort for traveling members of the social set, friends of Wilbour who had also come under the spell of Egypt's past. The boat was loaded at the start of each winter for its leisurely cruising of the Nile, carrying an extensive professional library, souvenirs of the past, and an equally impressive group of his peers. This was the life Wilbour wanted – and enjoyed.

During the last sixteen years of his life, Charles Edwin Wilbour sailed the Nile deep into the recesses of a fabulous civilization, probing the mysteries of the temples and monuments, studying hieroglyphic texts and Greek inscriptions. Above all, Wilbour's passion was to copy inscriptions, and he was happiest when he had a chance to read a text that no other modern had seen. "It is a great pleasure," he once said, "to be the first after 2,500 years to read what has been a sealed

The *dahabiyeh* on which Wilbour sailed the Nile was *The Seven Hathors*.

book so long."

Although Wilbour acquired some very fine antiquities, which are now in the Brooklyn Museum, collecting was of minor interest to him. He approached this phase of his work cautiously, purchased carefully, and would not pay high prices. As his New England neighbors of the time might have said, he was "near with money." The highest price he ever paid, and this was only once, was $25 for a gold chain. Even then he insisted that the chain be weighed to make sure its gold content matched the price. Unfortunately, Wilbour rejected as too expensive many masterpieces that now are the glories of major museums around the world.

To the Arabs, who delight in descriptive names, Wilbour became known as Abu-Dign, "father of the beard." Abu-Dign he may have been to the Egyptians, many of whom were adopting him as their own, but at heart Wilbour remained the New England provincial, as when he wrote about a young woman on a visiting *dahabiyeh.* "She is a sweet lady," he said, "even if she does come from Chicago."

Wilbour was an unusual scholar in that he was unwilling to publish. Apparently, his interest in Egyptology was purely scientific and without thought of self-aggrandizement. Yet he made extraordinary discoveries, including the Famine Stela on the island of Sehel in the First Cataract in 1889, and his name and reputation in the field are secure.

Although brusque and sometimes salty, the Brown alumnus always had the respect of his peers. Britain's A. H. Sayce termed him "the best Egyptologist living." When someone countered with the name of Maspero, Sayce replied, "Maspero is less inclusive."

Heinrich Brugsch, head of the Khedive's School of Egyptology in Cairo, had this to say: "Wilbour is more than merely conversant with results of research in the field of Egyptology. He is a scholar in the truest meaning of the word, a clear thinker, a conscientious critic, and what puts the crown to all of the rest is that he is the most enthusiastic of our young Egyptological recruits in discovering and studying unknown monuments, especially inscriptions."

Apparently the constantly pursued objective in Wilbour's life after he sought his self-imposed exile in 1871 was to study today so that he might study more tomorrow. But having researched knowledge, he seemed content to let others share, and even exploit, this knowledge freely.

The late John Wilson, former Andrew MacLeish Distinguished Service Professor of Egyptology at the University of Chicago, discussed this aspect of Wilbour's personality in his book, *Signs and Wonders Upon Pharaoh.*

"This gifted man," he wrote, "despite his friendliness to others, despite his generosity in distributing copies of his discoveries, was withdrawn into himself, a collector, not a scholar whose chief desire was to organize knowledge. He was happiest when he was copying a newly discovered text or checking someone else's copy against the original…The former protégé of Boss Tweed was a man who could no longer find a full and assured life. His inner fires were banked low; they did not inflame him to generate a heat of scholarship."

The winter of 1896 was Wilbour's last on the Nile. He died the following fall in Paris at age sixty-three. Mrs. Wilbour returned to New York and established the family in a large apartment in Central Park South. There had been four children, but Zoe, the youngest, had died at an early age in Little Compton. Remaining were Victor, named after his father's boon companion of the Paris years, and two daughters, Linnie and Theodora.

Victor was a gymnast of some ability in his youth, littering the lawn at Little Comptom with his trapezes and bars. He boxed with professionals through the north of France and apparently gave a good account of himself. He also joined the French Foreign Legion and sired at least one illegitimate son. In his old age, Victor lived in apparent poverty on West 57th Street in New York City where the neighbors, mostly poor Irish, took pity on him and brought food and clothing. When the obituaries reported that Victor was a millionaire and that he had left his large fortune for the maintenance and development of his father's collection at the Brooklyn Museum, two of the neighbors who had helped keep Wilbour warm and well fed, filed claims with the estate. Each collected $5,000.

Linnie, the oldest surviving child, while in France met and married a young American painter, Edwin Howland Blashfield, who became one of this country's foremost muralists. The bulk of his work was on the sentimental side, with most of the paintings looking like enormously enlarged Christmas cards. Blashfield is immortalized in many public buildings, including the Library of Congress. Linnie died four days after the 1918 Armistice.

Theodora, who outlived the rest of the family, spent the remainder of her days worshipping her father's memory. Her main occupation seems to have been keeping a wary eye on the administrators of the Brooklyn Museum, which had inherited the bulk of the Wilbour collection in 1916, two years after Mrs. Wilbour's death.

Visits to the museum by Theodora were impressive affairs, according to John D. Cooney, former curator of ancient art at the Brooklyn Museum and most recently holder of the same title at the Cleveland Museum of Art. He speaks of Theodora from first-hand observation.

"The visits were made with an air of solemnity surrounding royalty," Cooney writes. "A tall, heavily built woman, she insisted on being taken through the galleries in a wheel chair, her chief lawyer on her left, a curator on her right, and, of course, a museum guard pushing the chair. She was not hesitant to express *ex cathedra* opinions in her very low voice. She kept an eye on papa's mementoes, partly through sentimentality and partly to make certain that they were exhibited."

The strange trips of Theodora to the Museum continued until 1928, at which time a disaster occurred that set the stage for the creation of Brown's chair in Egyptology. Some years earlier, Theodora had placed on loan at the Museum a fine collection of English silver, which she had assembled over the years. Included was an eighteenth-century cucumber slicer of which she was particularly proud.

On the tour in question, a curator not known for his discretion made some disparaging remarks concerning the cucumber slicer. A brief but heated argument ensued, with several other administrators flying to the defense of their colleague. Theodora left in a huff and never set foot in the Brooklyn Museum again.

The silver collection was immediately withdrawn and presented to the Museum of Fine Arts in Boston, where Theodora maintained excellent relations with the curator and other officials. She had little further to do with the Brooklyn Museum, which up until the cucumber affair had expected to inherit her very considerable fortune.

Three years after her break with the Brooklyn Museum, Theodora wrote to the registrar at Brown asking for information about scholarships and fellowships. A check of the records indicated that on September 4, 1931, Vice President James P. Adams replied in a detailed two-page letter. Theodora took up the pen again a few days later, this time asking about special courses in Greek, Latin, German, the Romance languages, history, and literature. Again Vice President Adams sent a courteous reply, this time enclosing a catalogue of the University.

There is no evidence that Charles Edwin Wilbour ever maintained his association with Brown after he left the campus, or that Theodora had any connection

The Parker family paid a 1946 visit to the Temple of Karnak.

with the University prior to her correspondence with Jim Adams in the fall of 1931. However, three years later, on June 18, 1934, when Theodora made out her will, she included five fellowships to Brown University – each for $10,000 – in oratory, Classical English, Latin, Greek, and Classical French from the sixteenth century. She also willed to Brown one half of her residual estate as a permanent fund, the income to be applied towards the establishment and maintenance of its Department of Egyptology in memory of her father. The sum from the residual estate came to $750,000.

Theodora died on February 26, 1947, at age eighty-six, and President Wriston wasted little time in putting the terms of her will into effect. That was when he summoned Otto Neugebauer to his office and issued his "find me an Egyptologist" order.

Once Henry Wriston put anything into motion, he liked to see it come to a rapid conclusion. Neugebauer knew this and he pushed hard to find the right man for the job. He had done graduate work in Egyptology in Germany and had written a doctoral dissertation on Egyptian mathematics. He knew the field and he knew the people in it. None impressed him more than young Dick Parker at the University of Chicago. The years the two men had worked together on Egyptian astronomical texts had been very productive.

Professor Parker was interested in the Brown position – but there was a hitch. He had just been appointed field director of the Epigraphic Survey, a permanent expedition of the Oriental Institute, with headquarters in Luxor, Egypt. The expedition, which was out each winter for six months, was halfway through recording the great mortuary temple of Ramses III at Medinet Habu, a project that had been started in 1924. Parker felt a commitment to the project and, frankly, was looking forward to the honor of serving as its director. His answer to Dr. Neugebauer was a tentative "no," with the option of first refusal when the will was settled.

But Henry Wriston also had an obligation – to fill the chair in Egyptology at Brown – and there was an able Egyptologist circulating around Luxor who could solve the problem. In the spring of 1948, Wriston sent a letter to Luxor inviting Dr. Parker to become the first Wilbour

Professor of Egyptology at Brown. That May, Dick Parker arrived in Providence on his return from Egypt and immediately made an appointment to see President Wriston.

"I was impressed immediately by Wriston's informality," Dr. Parker says. "As soon as I had entered his office and the introductions were dispensed with, Brown University's president stretched out on his couch and stayed that way through most of the conversation. All the while, I was sitting somewhat stiffly in a straight-backed chair. Right away, Wriston had put me on the defensive.

"Wriston told me that he rarely used a 'marriage broker' when recruiting staff, but that in this case he had great confidence in Neugebauer to come up with the right person for the position. He was persuasive, offering me a research professorship which included funds for trips to Egypt and for publishing. Wriston also agreed to allow me to return to Luxor the following fall to break in my successor as field director. Really, he couldn't have offered much more. I told him that I accepted the position and we shook hands on it.

"As I was leaving, Wriston walked to the door with me. 'Dr. Parker,' he said, moving those large eyebrows up and down, 'I hope you understand that while you are in Luxor, you will be on the payroll of the University of Chicago.'"

Having finally nailed down his man after a two-year hunt, Henry Wriston wasted no time in getting a notice on the appointment out to the media. A person who left nothing to chance, the Brown president may have felt that if the story appeared in print immediately, then his once elusive Egyptologist could not very easily change his mind. At any rate, the next morning the *Providence Journal* reported the appointment on page one, and noted that Brown had hired "one of the few American experts on the history, culture, and language of ancient Egypt." The reaction within the Parker family, however, was mixed.

"My wife, Gladys, was pleased with the news," Dick Parker says, "and I was extremely relieved that a major decision affecting the future course of my life was finally behind me. But the children, Michael, five, and Beatrice, three, had more important things on their minds than my meeting with President Wriston on the previous afternoon.

"Remember, they had known only two homes up to then – Chicago, and Luxor, Egypt, and on their return trips they always felt that they were not back in the

United States until they had reached Chicago. Seeing their father's picture on page one of the Providence newspaper was no big deal to them. Michael and Beatrice were more interested in getting on the train that would take them back to the good old U.S.A."

In the minds of most people, an Egyptologist is a person who roams through Egypt excavating tombs and making priceless discoveries. In reality, there are two types of Egyptologists: archaeologists, those who deal with artifacts; and philologists, whose main concern is language. Dick Parker is a philologist, a man who spent the better part of a lifetime deciphering and interpreting papyri and inscriptions uncovered by the archaeologists of the world. In his field, his reputation is secure for all time, based both on his discoveries and on his writings, which have shed new light on the language of ancient Egypt.

A man precise in his use of the English language, Professor Parker becomes upset at the bastardization of this language and of the misuse of certain words, such as "unique." Still, he agrees that it was a unique opportunity, indeed, that came to him in the fall of 1949 when he set up shop on the Brown campus as the Wilbour Professor of Egyptology. In addition to being chairman of the only department of Egyptology at any university in the United States, Parker found himself with ample private funds for expansion of the department, travel, and bringing in visiting scholars.

From the time the Department of Egyptology first opened its doors in the basement of Sayles Hall, Parker's objective was to spend money on people and research rather than on collecting objects that would eventually require a museum. The one-man staff was doubled in 1952 with the addition of Ricardó Caminos, an Argentinean who had studied under Dr. Parker at the University of Chicago and who became chairman of the department in 1972 upon Parker's retirement. Caroline Nestman Peck, who had also studied under Parker at the University of Chicago, later became the third member of the department.

In 1951, Professor Parker took a giant step toward bringing world-wide recognition to the department. He instituted a visiting scholar program that each year brought to the campus a professor from abroad. In the ten years that this program was in existence, scholars were brought in from England, Egypt, Israel, France, and Belgium. One of the visiting scholars was Dr. Edwards, then the Keeper of Egyptian Antiquities in the British Museum and the man directly responsible for bringing King Tut's Exhibit to England in 1972.

"I thought it would be a once-in-a-lifetime experience for foreign scholars to come to Brown as visiting professors for a year," Dr. Parker says. "They would not only give the students the benefit of their special knowledge, but they would also – with a Wilbour travel grant – be able to move around the United States and become acquainted with other universities and museums for their own enrichment as scholars. During that decade, we attracted some of the very best men in the field."

From its inception, Brown's Department of Egyptology was research-oriented and aimed primarily at graduate study. However, there were courses for undergraduates in the language (one or two students a year), history (twelve students), and the art and architecture (fifteen students per year) of Egypt. Only two students took graduate degrees during the Parker years – Caroline Peck in 1958 and Richard H. Pierce '57 in 1963. Pierce is now a professor of Egyptology at the University of Bergen in Norway.

"Frankly, there is not a great call for Egyptologists these days," Dick Parker admits. "There are very few areas where a pure Egyptologist can earn a living. Because of this exclusiveness, Brown encouraged only the extremely gifted to participate in its programs."

Presently, there are only fourteen teaching and research posts available in this country, according to Parker. Five are at the University of Chicago, two each at Brown, Penn, and UCLA, and one each at Yale, Johns Hopkins, and Berkeley. Add to this some positions at museums and you have about covered the field. Some graduate students in Egyptology have been forced to accept positions teaching ancient history and classics, either at colleges or secondary schools.

When he has the proper audience, Professor Parker likes to spin a wry yarn that illustrates the scarcity of openings in the field. It seems that on one of his trips to England, Dr. Parker was driving a small English car along the highway between Oxford and Liverpool. In the car were two other prominent Egyptologists – Jaroslav Černy of Oxford and Ronald Williams of the University of Toronto. As the car, a Morris Oxford, rounded this particular corner, a very large truck was coming directly at them at a good clip and taking up a liberal amount of the road. Only a quick twist of the wheel by Parker prevented a collision. For a moment, no one in the car spoke. Then, Professor Černy broke the silence. "Gentlemen," he said, "for a quick moment, I thought that there might be three openings in Egyptology."

Professor Parker served as chairman of Brown's Department of Egyptology for twenty-three years before reaching retirement age in 1972. But, retirement to him was merely a word, not a change in his way of life. He was in London in 1972 for the opening of King Tutankhamen's Exhibit at the British Museum. Later the same year he returned to London to speak at a two-day symposium on ancient astronomy, sponsored by the Royal Society and the British Academy, of which he is a Corresponding Fellow. Since then there have been other trips to Europe to attend the International Congresses of Orientalists.

Professor Parker has published widely. Before coming to Brown he wrote *Babylonian Chronology* and the *Calendars of Ancient Egypt*. His publications continued through the Brown years and the retirement years as well. The list is impressive, including seven volumes in the eight-volume Brown Egyptological Studies series. One of these works, *The Edifice of Taharqa*, was started while he was still on the expedition in Luxor and was completed in 1979 with the collaboration of two French colleagues.

His most famous publication, however, is *Egyptian Astronomical Texts*, based on his long association with Otto Neugebauer and published jointly with him in 1960, 1964, and 1969 as part of the Brown Egyptological Studies. Considered the definitive work in its field, *Egyptian Astronomical Texts* is a collection, analysis, and interpretation of all the known texts from ancient Egypt that pertain to astronomy in any way.

"If Professor Parker had published nothing else, his fame would be secure from this work alone," Professor Neugebauer says. "The thing that is quite important about Professor Parker's work is that he has contributed greatly in making texts available that were not available before. The true test of a scholar, you know, is whether or not he opens up new materials for others to use. Professor Parker spent his career doing that. It is as if he were born to be an Egyptologist."

Perhaps Dick Parker wasn't born to be an Egyptologist. But he did start leaning in that direction as a small boy in Chicago, where he was born in 1905. His first knowledge of Egypt came from the pages of *National Geographic*, which carried frequent articles on the Land of the Pharoahs. But his imagination was also stirred by Burton Holmes, who came to Orchestra Hall in Chicago on several occasions just prior to World War I to give slide lectures on Egypt.

The Parker family, which also includes a sister two years Dick's junior, lived on the southwest side of Chicago, near Ogden Park. When he was sixteen, the young Parker achieved a modicum of respectability with his peers by winning the junior tennis championship held on the well-manicured grass courts in Ogden Park. His debut as a budding star several years earlier, however, had been a disaster.

"When I first showed an interest in tennis," Professor Parker recalls, "my parents bought me a brand new racket and a pair of tennis shoes. So far, so good. They also purchased a pair of white ducks, which I thought were fine until I put them on one day and started to walk toward Ogden Park. It took only a few steps for me to get the message that these white ducks were not appreciated by my confréres on Laflin Street. My pals, the boys I played stickball with in the streets, thought I was going 'uptown' on them. They started to toss cat calls my way as my cheeks got red and I lengthened my stride to get out of earshot as quickly as possible."

By the time Dick Parker had reached high school age, the family had moved to the southeast side of Chicago and the young athlete added basketball to his interests. A lean six-footer by the time he enrolled at St. Cyril Academy (now known as Mount Carmel), Dick Parker was the tallest man on the basketball team and, naturally, was placed at center. When Parker talks about his basketball days, he reminds his audience that he played in the age of the center jump after *every* basket, thus putting extreme pressure on the man handling the pivot position

A glance through the St. Cyril Academy yearbook reveals that the term "scrappy" was used frequently to describe the basketball team, which usually means that losses outnumbered victories. ("We didn't win much," Parker confirms, "but we sure had a lot of fun"). According to Parker, the scrappiest man on this very scrappy team was a 5'5" bundle of fighting energy named James T. Farrell. This is the same Farrell who, by the mid-1930s, had written his trilogy, *Studs Lonigan*, and achieved almost overnight fame.

"We had very good instruction in writing in high school," Professor Parker continues. "Father Dolan, our English teacher, had a theory that the more you wrote, the better you wrote. Every week we had to produce a theme. There was also a literary magazine, the *St. Cyril Oriflamme*, which provided an outlet for creative writing. I was managing editor for three years and Jim Farrell was athletic editor for the same period.

"Looking back, I think that Jim and I really became fast friends after we had graduated from high school. We both worked for a while, trying to save some money so that we could go to college. I worked at LaSalle Extension University, at 41st and Michigan Avenue, from 1923 to 1926, and Jim worked at a filling station at 42nd and Michigan. From time to time, I would drop in at the filling station on my way home and we would get into long discussions on our hopes for the future.

"Jim was very bright, inquisitive, and sensitive to people around him. We corresponded regularly until his death in 1980. When Jim wrote his *Danny O'Neill* series in the late 1930s, he put some of his classmates into one brief episode in Jackson Park, and I found myself in the book as Bart Daly. I remember showing the section to a colleague with some pride. 'You'd better enjoy it,' he said, cutting me down to size. 'It's probably the only book you'll ever be in.' Little did he know!"

Jim Farrell left for the University of Chicago in the fall of 1926, and Dick Parker headed for Dartmouth College. Dick was sold on spending four years in scenic Hanover, New Hampshire, after talking with Norman S. "Cy" Gordon, a former football player for the Big Green and one of the college's most enthusiastic recruiters. When Gordon told Parker that all he had to do to earn a scholarship to Dartmouth was prove financial need, his case was won. Although the Parker family lived comfortably, Dick's father did not earn a great salary and money was tight.

Tuition at Dartmouth in September of 1926 was $400 a year. Dick's scholarship covered this amount, and something toward room and board. With this help, plus the savings from his four years working at LaSalle

Extension University and some loans from relatives, he managed to get through his four years without experiencing any hardships or enjoying any luxuries.

There was another freshman at Dartmouth in 1926 who had to live close to the vest. He was Nelson Rockefeller, son of the richest man in the world, John D. Rockefeller, Jr., an 1897 Brown graduate.

The year before Dick Parker arrived in Hanover, the Dartmouth Indians had won the national football championship with a team that compiled an 8-0 record and averaged 42.5 points per game. Football fever was still very much a part of the Dartmouth scene in 1926. The big game that year was the mid-season meeting with arch rival Harvard at Cambridge. Some Dartmouth undergraduates started making their plans for the Harvard weekend immediately after registering in September. On the Friday before the long-awaited weekend, the trains leaving White River Junction for Boston were jammed. Friday evening the campus was deserted, except for a few students who couldn't afford the trip. Two of the students who remained in Hanover were named Parker and Rockefeller.

"I fully understood why I had no funds for such things as trips to football games," Parker says. "However, I found it difficult to understand why Nelson Rockefeller was in the same boat.

"The day of the game, we walked down to the athletic gymnasium, which had a grid graph set up against one wall. The grid graph was very popular in its day. It consisted of a large facsimile of a football field mounted on a frame which had a light behind it. The light was the 'ball,' and as the plays came in by telegraph directly from the stadium, an operator would move the 'ball' up and down the pseudo field according to the reports.

"Nelson had a bag of apples with him, and we sat on a very hard bench and ate apples while 'watching' the Dartmouth-Harvard game. Frankly, I don't remember who won that day [it was Harvard, 16-12], but fifty-five years later I can still remember Nelson sitting there with a bag of apples in his lap and the two of us munching on them all through the game."

Dick Parker majored in English literature at Dartmouth, not exactly a direct route to Egyptology. However, he did come under the direction of two professors who had a strong influence on his life. One was Sidney Cox, who worked Parker hard on his writing and awakened his sense of creativity by leading him into poetry as a means of expressing his deep

feelings. The other professor was Royal Nemiah, who
drilled him in the study of Greek as a language, which
proved to be a big help many years down the road
when he was studying the late stages of the Egyptian
language.

It's safe to say that going through college in the Roaring '20s was a different experience for Dick Parker
from that of the romanticized characters in a Scott
Fitzgerald story.

"All I know is that I didn't do much roaring in the
'20s," Parker says. "It was an ideal period to start collecting jazz records, artists such as King Oliver, Bix
Beiderbecke, and Louis Armstrong. But as I look back
now at that colorful era in American history I have to
chuckle, because the closest I came to experiencing the
flavor of the period was when Al Capone's mother
moved into my parents' neighborhood. I only saw
Mrs. Capone once and didn't ever catch a glimpse of
Scarface. This didn't bother me a bit, nor presumably
did it bother him."

The class of 1930 at Dartmouth was the last one for
many years to which large organizations sent representatives to drum up prospects for employment. The
Great Depression forced most American firms to stop
hiring and start firing. It wasn't a buyer's market again
for college undergraduates until more than fifteen
years had passed and a world war had been fought.
But in the spring of 1930, Illinois Bell Telephone Company sent a representative to Hanover who offered

Parker a job in Chicago that June. After four years with
Bell Telephone, and at age twenty-nine, Dick Parker
had sufficient money to enroll at the University of
Chicago graduate school to pursue his childhood ambition of becoming an Egyptologist.

For a budding Egyptologist, the University of
Chicago was the logical place to seek out a doctorate in
the field. On its campus was housed the Oriental Institute, which was financed by John D. Rockefeller, Jr.
The campus was also home-base for James Henry
Breasted, who wrote the first history of Egypt in English, a work that for years remained a classic in the
field.

For all that this University offered to a man interested
in becoming an Egyptologist, Dick Parker might never
have gone beyond his first day on the campus if he
had been the type of person to be easily discouraged.

"The first professor I talked with was Professor Billy
Edgerton," Parker recalls. "He promptly endeavored
to dampen my enthusiasm for graduate study. First,
he pointed out how few Egyptologists there were in
the United States at that time by telling me that he
could count them on the fingers of his two hands. He
went on to assure me that they were all young and

healthy men who were going to live for years and years. He also reminded me that I had a good job – a rarity for those Depression years. I can see him now, throwing both hands in the air and saying, 'For God's sake, man, don't be a fool. Stay at your job.' But I was a fool. I immediately went out and completed my enrolling process, *despite* my talk with Billy Edgerton!"

Earlier in 1934, Dick Parker had taken another important step in his life. On February 10, he had married Gladys Anne Burns, a young women he had met while working at LaSalle Extension University a decade earlier.

Most of the country was still struggling with the Great Depression in August of 1938 when Parker received his doctorate from the University of Chicago. He received more than a degree that summer. He was also given an appointment with the Epigraphic Survey in Luxor, Egypt. The Expedition, begun in 1922, was originally intended to combine both epigraphy and excavation. By the time Parker arrived for the October-15-to-April-15 "season" of 1938, all excavation had ceased, which meant that the long-range aim of the Expedition was now the recording of the temples of ancient Thebes. The immediate target in 1938 was the great mortuary temple of Ramses III and a smaller temple of the God, Khonsu.

The Epigraphic Survey that year was made up of a field director, two epigraphers (one of whom was Parker), and three artists. The method devised earlier by James Breasted for getting the most accurate record of what still remained on the temple and tomb walls was complicated, time consuming – but very thorough.

First, the photographer would take a picture and blow it up to a large scale. This print was then taken by the artist to the temple wall where, after studying the remains of the hieroglyphs and the scenes, he would ink in the photograph to the best of his ability. The artists were not Egyptologists, but over the years many of them did acquire an extensive knowledge of hieroglyphs and were able to make a lot out of mere traces.

When the artist had finished inking in the photograph, it was then bleached, leaving only a black and white drawing. From this, blue prints were made and distributed to the epigrapher, who was skilled in the language (inscriptions). He would cut up the blue print into small pieces, paste them to the center of a large sheet of paper, and then take this to the wall to compare what the artist had produced with what he, as an expert in the language and the art of Egypt, was able to see. Frequently, the epigrapher made additions or corrections to the artist's drawings.

After one epigrapher had gone over it, the second epigrapher checked the first man, to be sure he had missed nothing or had not come to an erroneous conclusion about the traces. In the end, when the two epigraphers agreed, the corrected blueprint was handed back to the artist. He entered them in the drawing, which was then ready for a page in a publication of the future. The purpose of this slow process was to make sure that the Egyptological team had the most accurate record that could be obtained from any one scene or inscription.

Parker had only one more season in Luxor before World War II forced the closing of Chicago House for the duration. He spent the war years teaching at the Oriental Institute on the University of Chicago campus, started his long-range association with Otto Neugebauer, and by 1948 had made the decision to come to Brown. Although Parker wrapped up his duties as director of the Expedition in the 1948-49 season, he returned for a three-month stay in the winter of 1951 to recheck some of his previous copies of astronomical ceilings and to record a few new ones that time had not permitted him to record before.

Parker's report on this trip to Luxor was contained in the June 1951 newsletter of the American Research Center in Egypt. It read in part:

Most of what I had to do was concentrated in the Valley of the Kings. The astronomical ceilings in the tombs of Ramses VI, VII and IX had to be rechecked; and copies had to be made of those in Merneptah and Tausert. This was all fairly straight-forward and not unpleasant work, difficult only in the necessity of getting up as close as possible to the vaulted ceilings by stepladder and of getting sufficient illumination on the subject. A flashlight and a lantern hung from the end of a long pole were usually adequate. Fortunately I had excellent photographs taken by Charles Nims of Chicago House to help me. Some of his experiments in photographing the same subject with different films and different filters have produced really astonishing results. In some cases in our future publications it will certainly be necessary to reproduce the same subject at least twice to do full justice to it.

One tomb, however, which I was *not* looking forward to working in was that of Pedamenope, the largest of the private tombs, having twenty-two chambers. This had been closed for years because it had for so long been the haven of bats, and they had so impregnated the tomb with ammonia that it was exceedingly unpleasant to enter. Though it is now accessible, there is no ventilation other than the door; and years must elapse before it will become a stop on the itinerary of the ordinary tourist – though its size and its unique features make it well worth a visit. To reach the sarcophagus chamber, which has a vaulted astronomical ceiling, it is necessary twice to descend pits about twenty feet deep. This can be done only by bringing in ladders. From this lowest level another shorter ladder is needed to mount to the sarcophagus chamber. As one goes down in the tomb from level to level the heat and the smell increase until the greatest concentration of both is reached in the sarcophagus chamber. And then of course I had to mount a stepladder and get as close as I could to the ceiling! I have never perspired as I did in that situation.

Perhaps because there are so few Egyptologists roaming the land, it's hard to determine what a member of this specialized profession should be like. But there is nothing stuffy or absent-minded about Brown's Egyptologist, Richard A. Parker. A warm and friendly man with a keen sense of humor, Dr. Parker brought good fellowship to a wide variety of committees on College Hill during the past thirty-three years. Former Alumni Executive Officer at Brown Paul F. Mackesey '32 once commented that Dick Parker was "one of the few men around who is invited to serve on committees as much for his good companionship as for his knowledge of the subject at hand."

On at least one occasion, Professor Parker delighted the entire Rhode Island Community. In the spring of 1965, Joe Mullaney, then basketball coach at Providence College, was quoted in a *Providence Journal* feature story as complaining about all the free advice a coach has to take "from bank presidents to hot dog venders; from professors of Egyptology to sixth grade students."

As you might well imagine, Dick Parker rose majestically to the defense of the Egyptologists in their moment of plight. His tongue-in-cheek reply to Mullaney was in the form of a letter to the editor of the *Providence Journal* and was considered by many as a classic in its field:

The Gentleman Doth Protest

In a touching little article in the March 7 Sunday *Rhode Islander* Joseph Mullaney, prominent Rhode Islander and basketball coach of Providence College, speaks of the overwhelming amount of unsolicited advice the coach of a sport, by implication himself, receives from "bank presidents to hot dog vendors; from professors of Egyptology to sixth grade students." It is flattering to have Mr. Mullaney choose "professors of Egyptology" as the pendant to "bank presidents" in his dichotomies. Does he rank them over college presidents, or has he no evidence on the latter's behavior?

Perhaps as a layman he is misled, as I was as a boy, when my peers told me that the Bible spoke of basketball when it related how Moses dribbled and Joseph played in the court of Pharaoh. Higher criticism, however, has eliminated that game as an invention of ancient Egypt, and Egyptologists can claim no special knowledge of it. But I am afraid I digress. Bank presidents, hot dog vendors and sixth grade students must protect themselves against Mr. Mullaney's accusations as they see fit. I am here to deny in toto his charge that Egyptologists have given him advice, either in private or as loud-mouthed spectators.

To begin with there are precious few of us Egyptologists, and we tend to stand out by reason of rarity. In all New England there are but four, three at Brown and one at Yale. I am quite sure that my colleague at Yale does not advise coaches and those farther afield, at Johns Hopkins, Chicago and California, are hardly likely to be directly known to Mr. Mullaney, so that anything he might charge to them would be from sheerest hearsay and not admissible.

There remain we three at Brown. I have this morning questioned my two colleagues. I fear that I may wound Mr. Mullaney's *amour propre* when I say that they not only couldn't identify him but that neither one had ever seen a basketball game. That seems to leave only me, and lest my standing in the Brown community drop by reason of the suspicion that I have been giving aid and comfort to the enemy, let me here reaffirm specifically my already given general denial. I don't know Mr. Mullaney personally (though I do know who he is, at least) and I have never advised him either in private or public. If I considered myself expert enough to give such advice it would be my friend, Stan Ward, who would get it, but since I consider him one of the top coaches in the country, I know enough to keep my mouth shut as far as advice is concerned.

If Mr. Mullaney can name the guilty, let him now do so. Otherwise let this libel on professors of Egyptology be stricken from the record.

Richard A. Parker
Wilbour Professor of Egyptology
Providence

At various times during his Brown years, Parker served on the Library Committee, Curriculum Com-

Wilbour Hall was "saved" by a rumor.

mittee, and as a member of the Faculty Club's Board of Governors. He served as faculty advisor for the varsity basketball team and for a decade was Brown's faculty advisor to the National Collegiate Athletic Association. His two terms on the Athletic Advisory Council totalled eight years. And some of the best sub-committee meetings of these groups were held at the Parker home between choice selections from his jazz record library.

If Professor Parker has a vice, it is his addiction to the crossword puzzle, especially to the more difficult English version, which he gets regularly from the *London Times*. "Once that paper arrives, Dad just disappears," says his daughter, Beatrice, a teacher in the Providence school system.

"To handle these English puzzles intelligently, you really have to be an Englishman," Parker admits. "You have to know their sports, their slang, the history of their country, everything about England. And you have to know it well. Most people who work the puz-

zles can take the *New York Times* puzzle, for example, sit down with it for a short while, and be finished. I'll work on some of the English puzzles for several days. Some I never finish at all. The longest run of completed puzzles from the *London Times* that I finished, without error, was twelve. I don't want to sound like a football coach taking a new job, but it is the *challenge* that appeals to me."

There is one other thing about Brown's Egyptologist, something that may earn him the scorn of many women who idolize a tidy home and the support of most men who feel that a home should look lived in: Dick Parker is an avid collector. To make matters worse, where some people collect specific items, such as baseball cards or old beer cans, Parker doesn't even have the courtesy to specialize.

He has a fine collection of jazz records of the 1920s, detective stories in great quantity, innumerable other books, including some rare editions, memorabilia from his extensive travels, and a vast collection of odds and ends. He has even saved his 1913 wind-up train set. "If there is room, we keep it" is the Parker motto.

When the occasion calls for it, Dick Parker can also be something of a Machiavellian character. In the early 1960s, when the Rockefeller Library was being planned, there was talk of tearing down Wilbour Hall, the old Delta Phi fraternity house, which became the home of Egyptology in 1951 and which stood in the library's way at the corner of George and Prospect Streets.

Otto Neugebauer had been bounced from office to office before finding what he thought was a permanent home in Wilbour Hall. Another move didn't meet his fancy. But the construction plans were drawn, the bulldozers were poised, and there seemed little that could be done to halt the course of events.

Then one day a rumor started to make its way across the campus to the effect that if Wilbour Hall were demolished, Professor Neugebauer, the world's leading authority in the history of mathematics, would pack his bags and depart. There was even a quotation attributed to Neugebauer, which went something like this: "If I have to move my books once more, I move them to Princeton." It didn't take long for this rumor to reach the ears of President Barnaby C. Keeney. The danger of losing a man of Neugebauer's stature was unthinkable. This danger was the one thing that could, and did, save Wilbour Hall. And that is why that red brick Victorian building with peaked gables facing toward various points of the campus still stands on the corner of George and Prospect Streets in sharp contrast to the modern Rockefeller Library just a few feet away.

Considerably later it was learned that the only person on campus at the time who hadn't heard the rumor about Neugebauer's departure was Professor Neugebauer himself. The entire thing was a plot, a successful one at that, and the man who put life to the rumor was none other than Richard A. Parker, Egyptologist.

Chapter 4 ✍
His students followed him in an eternal search for greatness

Someone once said that Alex Robinson was an archaeologist who combined a tireless interest in the past with a bent for adventure. On his first visit to the American School of Classical Studies at Athens in 1923, a companion sitting beside him in an automobile was shot and killed by bandits. In subsequent trips, Professor Robinson was once separated from his family by a Greek revolution and another time stranded in the Syrian desert.

When Robinson prepared to leave on sabbatical for the American School in 1947, the Greek civil war was in full flower. "Won't you be in danger?" a concerned College Hill colleague asked. "Well, my friend," Alex replied, "if the bombs start to fall I'm going to run. Wouldn't you?"

Returning to Brown from a summer session of the American School in the late 1950s, Alex was approached by a well-meaning member of the administration, who asked, "How did your tour make out this summer?" Alex Robinson, who did not suffer fools gladly, exploded. "Let me tell you, young fellow, I was not conducting a tour. The students were not tourists. And I don't run a travel agency. In the future if you insist on making conversation, first find out what you are talking about."

Professor Robinson had a right to be indignant. The American School of Classical Studies at Athens, of which Brown was a founding member, is perhaps the most important foreign academy in Europe. And Alex Robinson was one of the most brilliant, colorful, and effective classicists of his era. He was a world authority on Alexander the Great (he wrote five highly acclaimed books on the subject); a leader in the most important excavation ever conducted in Greece, that of the Athenian Agora (or market place) from 1931 to 1954; and an exciting classroom teacher on the Brown faculty from 1928 until his death in 1965.

To some, Alex Robinson was also a larger than life figure, a person to be treated with extreme deference. In certain ways he symbolized the authoritarian strength of the Brown faculty in the community. He certainly had an introduction to most of the drawing rooms on the East Side. Many people worshipped him, some idolized him, and a few hated him with a passion.

When I first knew him, Alex Robinson was a large man carrying about 250 pounds on his 6'1" frame. His round, ruddy face was topped by closely cropped white hair and included sparkling blue eyes. He spoke in a deep, imposing voice that could turn a casual comment into a declarative statement.

Alex Robinson was a generalist, capable of teaching all areas in the fields of classical antiquity, whether it was Latin or Greek, ancient history, or archaeology.

His whole purpose in scholarship and teaching was to encourage the attainment of greatness. He was not interested in small names. Alex liked the big leagues.

For him, a Solon, a Pericles, and an Alexander the Great meant Greek history. But if you mentioned someone such as Peisistratus – well, he was just a person between Solon and Pericles. When students raised questions about Thebes in the period after the fall of Athens, Robinson would snort that Thebans came and Thebans went, but they never amounted to anything. Besides, Alexander the Great leveled their city, and, after all, what can you say of a people whose city was leveled.

On numerous occasions Alex referred to himself as "simply an historian." Others regarded the tweedy professor as a human telescope to antiquity. In his encouragement of students Robinson stressed that it was fine to read all the great books about the great events, but above all it was essential to see the vision of what it all stands for and, more particularly, what it means in your own personal life. "If you want to understand the present, know the past," he would tell his students.

When Professor Robinson looked to the past, he looked to Greece. In a 1959 interview with Jesse R. Victor '62 of the *Brown Daily Herald Supplement*, Alex Robinson discussed the value of the classics. "Take art," he said. "Study the Parthenon. Is it the most beautiful thing in the world? I don't know. It certainly is a beautiful thing. You must study the background of it – what it came out of, what it is made of, and who paid for it. Take Sophocles or Plato. You are coming up against first-rate minds. Thucydides, one of the greatest minds. Solon, the extraordinary political reformer. That is the thing about ancient Greece – everything was first-rate."

Robinson admitted that defining the concept of beauty and the theory of great art was purely subjective. To illustrate his point, he liked to quote A. E. Housman. "Someone once asked Housman how it is possible to know whether a piece of art is great," Robinson would tell his class. "Housman replied, 'When it gives me a pain in the belly.' I would say when it gives me a chemical change in my bloodstream. University Hall does this, but the other buildings on campus don't."

Most people didn't expect Robinson to have a kind word for modern art. But he did. "A person is very foolish to love just Graeco-Roman art or modern art," he said. "The sensible, urbane individual loves the great art of *any* period. The more you love Greek art, the more you love Picasso."

While Alex could show pride toward his students, those young people who joined him in his everlasting search for greatness, he could be a holy terror with members of the administration. This was particularly true if he thought his academic freedom was being challenged. F. Morris Cochran, the business manager of the University, ran into the Robinson buzz-saw in the early 1950s.

From time to time, Cochran (who reportedly never said yes to any proposal that cost money) would hire efficiency experts to keep tabs on unnecessary expenses run up by the whims of the professors. Along about 1952 the American School of Classical Studies in Athens put on the market an elaborate set of slides of all sites, archaeological and otherwise, in Greece. Alex had the department chairman, Herbert Couch, order this set at a cost of $100, claiming that he could not teach either history or archaeology properly without those props. "I must have the very best for my students," he said.

The Robinsons spent part of 1936 in Athens.

"The efficiency expert was quickly dispatched to our department," says Professor John Rowe Workman, a long-time Robinson friend and colleague, "and Couch sent him up to see Alex. Never have I heard such a commotion on the second floor of Waterman House. Apparently the expert had told Alex that the slides would have to be sent back to Athens and further warned that there would be no more new slides. Well, no one went around *warning* Alex Robinson about anything!

"As was usually the case after such an encounter, Alex rushed down to my office. 'Did you hear that uproar, my friend?' he asked. He then proceeded into the most eloquent defense of academic freedom and the unfettered nature of the professor to determine what was to be done in his own classroom that I have ever heard. Alex at that moment taught me an important lesson – that when the professor closes his door and commences class, it is nobody's business what goes on in that classroom. In his own classroom and in preparation for that class the professor is master of his destiny, and no efficiency expert has any business prowling around counting the cost.

"Alex lost no time getting on the phone to Morris Cochran, telling him to get rid of his so-called expert. Alex then scribbled a hasty note to President Wriston explaining his grievance. The efficiency expert seemed shortly after that to disappear into thin air and was heard of no more."

At some point in the mid-1950s, University Secretary Howard S. Curtis and his staff made plans to put Brown professors on television in a weekly series on Channel 10. Although Alex did not completely believe in TV, he nevertheless consented to do a program on his specialty, Alexander the Great. Once he learned, however, that his carefully written script was to pass through the hands of several editors and censors, and that it was planned to have background music, and that slides were to be shown while he was speaking, Alex exploded and the program was cancelled.

"That one was a dilly," Professor Workman told me recently in his book-cluttered office on College Hill. "He objected strenuously to non-professionals reading and editing his script. Also, the slides were to come from *National Geographic*, which Alex did not consider to be a learned publication. The cancellation caused something of a flap, but at least the office of the Secretary of the University, the News Bureau, and others became aware of what professorial privilege meant and that full professors were not to be monkeyed with or pushed into a salad mold of developing TV personalities."

Through most of his Brown years Alex had a friendly rivalry with Professor Robert George, a popular lecturer in history who could make Wellington at Waterloo or Nelson at Trafalgar come alive for his students. Alex had the classics distribution courses, D_1 and D_2 and Bob George had the equivalent courses in history. These were large lecture classes and each man was afraid the other would have the larger enrollment.

"Alex would approach me at the start of each semester," Professor Workman says. "'John, you didn't happen to hear how many students Bob George has, did you?' Then I'd meet Bob either at the Faculty Club or in the Ivy Room and he'd put a hand on my arm. 'Say, John, do you have any idea how Alex is doing for numbers this semester?' It was a great rivalry, considering that each highly respected the other as a person."

These large classes were held in Alumnae Hall, which Alex called his "megaron" – his great room. This terminology, incidentally, didn't sit well with several members of the classics department who didn't think that Alumnae Hall was *his* room. But that sort of reaction never bothered Alex. Alumnae Hall was and would always be his megaron. It's interesting to note that even in these large classes of between 200 and 300 pupils, Alex made a specific effort to learn the name and something personal about each student. Those who took other courses with him found that Alex never forgot.

Even the Alex Robinson exams in those big classes were calculated to capture or instill greatness. The questions were always broad, never specific. After turning the portable blackboard around and exposing the question, Alex would seat himself on his desk – he called it his Olympian Heights – and say, "Gentlemen, on this exam I want to find out what you *know*, not what you don't know." One year he asked an extremely broad question. "What do you think of Plato? And why?" One of my friends, who, I must admit, came to the exam in a complete state of unpreparedness, filled the entire exam book by repeating, "I love Plato, I love Plato, I love Plato." Alex, of course, was outraged that anyone would make sport of Plato.

According to reports that circulated on the campus, Profesor Robinson handed the exam book to the late Dr. Charles A. McDonald '03, then the resident psychiatrist, and asked him to study the contents and then report back on what exactly was wrong with the student. Dr. McDonald, who had a sharp needle for things other than medicine, thought he'd have some fun with Alex. So in due time, he wrote Alex a letter saying that it wasn't the student who was at fault, it was Alex who must shoulder the blame for writing such a broad question. "Well, what does he know about it," Alex is reported to have replied. "He's only a psychiatrist."

Charles Alexander Robinson, Jr., was born on March 30, 1900, in Princeton, N.J., the son of Charles and Sarah Westcott Robinson. Alex's father was raised on a farm in the village of West Hebron, N.Y., a tiny and somewhat remote farming community even today. Charles Robinson and his two brothers (both of whom became ministers) prayed with their parents at the hay-mow in the barn. They were devout Presbyterians and apparently exceptionally able, as all three brothers attended and excelled at Princeton.

Charles Robinson majored in classics at Princeton, studied at the American School of Classical Studies at Athens (as his son, Alex, would later do), taught at Princeton, and eventually made his life's work in secondary school teaching and as principal of Peekskill Military Academy. Alex Robinson was among his father's star pupils in classes in both Greek and Latin. Mr. Robinson also owned a boys' summer camp in the Adirondacks, which specialized in mountain climbing. While undoubtedly approving of "a sound mind in a sound body," Charles Robinson never participated in the hiking feats which he oversaw, but Alex pioneered those hikes both as a boy and later as a counselor.

After graduating from Peekskill Military Academy, Alex attended Phillips Andover and then enrolled at Princeton. There, his predilection for Periclean culture and for Alexander the Great was sparked by Professor William Kelly Prentice. When Alex returned to Princeton for graduate work, he and Professor Prentice came together again under somewhat unusual circumstances. Alex was the only student in the class.

Alex once told of one of his first sessions with Prentice. "Read all of the *Iliad* and count the number of days' actions," Prentice said. Alex thought to himself that this would be a semester's project. Then the pro-

fessor added, "Come back with the answer tomorrow, Alex." He did, having worked all night.

Another time Alex quoted Professor Seymour of Yale in the presence of Prentice, who said, "Who is Seymour?" When the student replied that he thought Seymour was an authority, the professor pounced on him. "Alex, if the archangel Gabriel came down and said he was an authority, he wouldn't be. There is no authority. *You* decide." This work in close harmony with Prentice was great preparation for Alex's own scholarship and teaching – and for his independent thinking.

While studying at Princeton, Alex won a two-year fellowship to the American School of Classical Studies in Athens. However, he gave up the second year to accept the broader challenge of the Prix de Rome Fellowship at the American Academy. It was a decision that had a dramatic effect on his life, for it was there that he met his wife-to-be, Celia Sachs.

As Celia remembers it, "I was sixteen at the time and was in Rome with my father, Paul Sachs, who was on sabbatical from Harvard, and my mother. We were settled in a beautiful apartment overlooking the gardens of the Pincio, and one morning I walked from there to the American Academy, where my father's friend, Professor Charles Rufus Morey, of Princeton fame, was head of the Classical School. He arranged for me to take some courses, and on my first archaeological trip to Lake Nemi (near Castel Gandolpho, the Pope's summer residence) I met Alex and shared my delicious chicken sandwich. Shortly after that, Alex took me to lunch at the famous Alfredo's restaurant on the Via della Scrofa, and half-way through the meal he said, 'How would you like to eat breakfast across the table from me the rest of your life?' I laughed and hardly knew what he meant, but in the taxi going back to our hotel I found out, of course. And we did eat breakfast together all of his life."

Alex Robinson returned to Princeton as a John Harding Page Fellow in Classics before coming to Brown in 1928 as instructor in Greek and Latin. His strong academic background and his immediate success as a classroom teacher prompted the University to make him an assistant professor the next year. He became associate professor in 1935 (at that time, one of the youngest men ever to hold such an appointment at Brown), full professor in 1945, and David Benedict Professor of Classics in 1959. Among the many honors that came his way was the invitation to deliver the

Martin Classical Lectures at Oberlin, a distinction highly prized by classical scholars.

His books, all of which had the advantage of being both readable and informative, included: *The Ephemerides of Alexander's Expedition*, *Hellenic History* (with G. W. Botsford), *Alexander the Great*, *Ancient History*, *The Spring of Civilization*, *The History of Alexander the Great*, *Athens in the Age of Pericles*, and *Alexander: Conqueror and Creator of a New World*.

As an authority in his field, Robinson was frequently called upon to review its important books. His appraisals appeared in such publications as *The New York Times Book Review*, *Saturday Review*, and the *Chicago Tribune*. In addition to scores of articles for magazines and newspapers, Alex wrote for several encyclopedias and was author of a number of books on Greek history and on Alexander the Great for young readers.

Despite his early and extensive success as an archaeologist and a writer, Alex Robinson considered himself a teacher above all. While filling out a Univer-

sity biography form in 1963, he wrote: "The thing that matters most in my life is the fact that every Monday afternoon since 1928, Mrs. Robinson and I have been at home for my students." These "at home" sessions, whether at 12 Keene Street in Providence or at the American School of Classical Studies at Athens, featured tea and cookies, good humor, and lively debate.

The Robinsons had been married in 1927. Celia's father, Paul J. Sachs, was professor of fine arts at Harvard and associate director and genius of its Fogg Museum. Together, Alex and Celia constituted perhaps the most entertaining couple at Brown. The spacious Robinson residence on Keene Street was a museum, and the artifacts displayed there were all originals, not reproductions. The nerve center of that residence – the most impressive room in the large three-story frame house – was Alex's study, and he was always on guard to maintain its status. Many professional people on the East Side had rooms set apart for professional purposes, and these rooms were referred to as "dens."

Monday afternoon tea was a ritual at 12 Keene Street.

Nothing brought Alex to indignation so completely as when some light-hearted man or woman referred to his study as a "den." Again and again he would correct these people in tones most severe.

During our Monday afternoon teas with Alex and Celia Robinson, we were frequently drawn to Alex Robinson's study. There were shelves to the ceiling filled with books in the field of ancient history and classical antiquity. All available wall space and tables contained exquisite artifacts. On his large desk would be a collection of things: books to be reviewed, papers relating to the book he might then be working on, and proofs waiting to be read. Stacks of correspondence from publishers would be in another pile, and sheaves of writing paper were in still another. Alex would not accept the fact that his desk was cluttered. "My friends, let's just say that the desk is full," he would explain. Suffice it to say that there was room left for Alex to write, but just barely.

"The Robinson home was full of treasures," according to C. Gail Wright '64, library assistant at the American Bible Society in New York City. "You could sit on the floor and look at them – a fifth-century Greek vase here, a Picasso there. John Crawford of the class of 1937, one of the most prominent art collectors in the United States, first became aware of art sitting on the floor at 12 Keene Street," Gail said.

"These afternoon teas featured more than art. Celia was a wonderful cook and there were always yummy things to eat – date nut bread and cream cheese sandwiches were her specialty – that contrasted with the mystery meat we ate on campus. Those afternoons with the Robinsons were so civilized, so much fun."

Gail Wright recalled that Professor Robinson enjoyed provoking discussions at these teas. "One day I made a statement with which he obviously didn't agree. 'What was your source?' he asked. '*Time* magazine,' I answered. Well, he was horrified that I could believe *anything* I'd read in *Time*. After that he always called me 'Little Miss *Time* Magazine.' Sometimes he would make a statement to one of us that was almost insulting and Celia would say, 'Now, darling, did you really mean that?' To me, and to many others away from home for the first time, those Monday sessions at 12 Keene Street meant everything."

The rule of thumb was that the afternoon teas were strictly informal, with students wandering casually about the house, chatting with Alex or Celia, or just relaxing. On a particular Monday in the late 1940s,

Alex asked us all to gather in one room while he expounded on the virtues of a recently acquired piece of Greek antiquity. This sudden change in format caused a problem for two students, Dick Gempp '51 and Don Alsop '51. "We were seated on a priceless Oriental rug, jammed in by fellow students, smoking cigarettes, and there wasn't an ash tray in sight," Gempp says. "Experience taught us that you did not interrupt Professor Robinson when he was enthusiastically discussing some element of Greek art, especially a Greek vase. You especially didn't interrupt to ask for something as mundane and modern as an ash tray. We solved the problem the only way gentlemen could – putting the ashes in the pockets of our sports coats and butting the cigarettes, painfully, in the palms of our hands."

According to Professor Workman, Alex used his Monday teas as a vehicle for talking to students. He enjoyed challenging them, finding out what they were thinking. And almost every week he would stop in and tell Workman what he had heard from the undergraduates.

"Whether it was in the Museum of the Rhode Island School of Design, in Alumnae Hall, or in Faunce House Theater, Alex had the ability to arouse a student's historical and aesthetic faculties," Professor Workman said. "Students liked to talk in class and answer his broad questions. It was almost a preceptorial with a large group or a Socratic dialectic, and students were quick to respond. On two occasions I happened to be in the RISD Museum and witnessed Alex pulling out students about a work of art. If we had nothing else to go on to judge this man, that dialectic twixt student and professor over a vase or some other work of classical art was the mark of the greatest teaching ability in the world. If I had tried that same approach, the student would have frozen in his tracks, but Alex had the special ability to elicit responses from even the most modest and shy types."

To appreciate fully Alex Robinson as a teacher, you had to take one of his courses in Greek history and art or Roman history and art. Only about thirty-five to forty students sat in on these sessions, which were held in Rogers 12. The courses included classics majors, non-classics majors who made it a point to take every course Alex gave, and a smattering of athletes. Alex had the reputation of being an easy grader. That was not completely true. Actually, he could be lenient when he wanted to, and he could be stern when that seemed the better course. However, he was sympathetic and understanding toward his students who showed even a modicum of interest in the subject he loved, especially those who, as he put it, "made a contribution to the campus," by getting involved in such things as Sock and Buskin, the *Brown Daily Herald*, and athletics. If one of his students had a good game, there would be some quick, offhand reference to it from Alex the next time we came together in Rogers 12.

I first met Alex Robinson in 1947, shortly after returning to Brown following service in World War II. My first paper in his Classics D2 course received a grade that I felt was too harsh. An appointment was made, and we sat down together in his small Waterman House office. The grade wasn't changed, but in a friendly fifteen-minute discussion we did strike the spark of a friendship that was to last until his death eighteen years later. Alex, who had a casual way of drawing students out about their activities, seemed interested that I was writing sports for the BDH and said that he would watch for my by-line. A few weeks later as class was breaking up he walked by. "Read you in the *Brown Daily Herald* this morning, my friend. Your grade on that story is a triple A plus."

These small classes in Rogers 12 were nearly as informal as his Monday afternoon teas. He'd be talking as he entered the room, sauntering down the center aisle toward his Olympian Heights. "What shall we talk about today, my friends? Why don't we talk about Solon? What do you know about Solon, Mr. Scott?" (John Scott '50, co-captain of the 1949 football team and a Phi Beta Kappa). And with that we'd be off on a lively discussion about one of the great men in the history of the world.

Some days Solon, Pericles, and Aristotle never got off their sedilia because Alex thought it more important to spend the hour discussing what the 1948 election between Truman and Dewey would mean to the future of the country or whether or not America was wise to have used the atomic bomb against Hiroshima and Nagasaki.

Gail Wright was impressed with Robinson's accessibilty: "He had that open, sunny face and those big blue eyes. Obviously he was someone you could go right up to. He certainly was a commanding figure when he stood on that stage. Incredible spirit. Overwhelming personality. Vitality. There was no way you could ignore him.

"I always felt Alex was a fine actor. He certainly knew how to handle himself in front of a crowd. And he was a hell of a speaker. He didn't give a damn what he said to anyone. Occasionally he'd say something outrageous – just to see if you had the guts to come back at him. But most of all, perhaps, he provided an example of how to do things in a fine way. As a person dealing with human beings and forming them, this great drive of his for excellence was contagious."

There were certain things you came to expect from Alex Robinson. One was the long pause and then the almost sarcastic "marvelous" when someone gave the wrong answer in class. In his small sections, Alex frequently threw questions at his group. Some claimed that he marked more on the basis of those impromptu questions than he did on his exams. Each semester we could expect to hear Providence referred to as "the Athens of America," although his tongue was well back in his cheek when he said it. And he never could hide his "horror" at the construction of the World War I monument that stands in Market Square, or the pseudo-Greek insurance building blocking the view of the Meeting House from downtown.

George S. Kirkpatrick '56, now vice president of Bache Halsey Stuart Shields, Inc. of Providence, took every course that Alex offered and still carries fond memories of him. "He had an underlying interest in the young, and it was this interest that commanded the huge following that he had," George told me recently. "Frankly, I worshipped the man. I took attendance in every course he gave at Brown. Alex liked to use me as his foil and I seldom disappointed him. During a discussion of Roman history one day, he said, 'Mr. Kirkpatrick, how many bathtubs would you say were in Rome at that time?' Without hesitating, I said, 'Oh, somewhere between 600 and 700.' 'Gad, Mr. Kirkpatrick, your knowledge of the classics never ceases to amaze me. There were four.' The class roared and, of course, so did he."

With those of us who took all of Alex Robinson's

courses, the professor could do no wrong. He took great pride in us and we, in turn, felt a great camaraderie with him. If any of his "regulars" got into a jam on campus, Alex would stick by us against other faculty members or even the dean, if that was necessary.

A long editorial in the BDH at the time of his death expressed quite well how the long line of students felt about Alex Robinson: "Enthusiasm is the first word that comes to everybody's mind. Professor Robinson was a man whose interests were as wide as his friendships were deep. He approached people and his duties with a kind of ebullience, and this exuberance was contagious.

"The enthusiasm was matched by his youthfulness, a quality that was with him to the very end, a quality manifested in the way he dressed, the way he talked, and the way he wore the Old School tie. He talked big. His language was embellished by superlatives; his respect for his colleagues, his students, his environment was enormous."

At the same time, the *Providence Journal* had this to say: "Professor Robinson was a large man, and he moved ponderously on the lecture platform, but during the hour of a lecture the days of an ancient civilization – perhaps the life of the Minoan City of Knossos in 1400 B.C., of the Athens of Pericles, or the concourse of ships desperately assembled at Salamis, or the mighty empire of Persia – these became alive, almost contemporaneous."

Not surprisingly, a healthy number of Alex's students went into ancient history and became classical archaeologists. One who has achieved extraordinary success is Joseph W. Shaw '57, associate chairman of the department of fine arts at the University of Toronto. Professor Shaw has his own excavation on the Minoan site on the island of Crete, where his discovery is said to rival that of Sir Arthur Evans at Knossos. Shaw doesn't have behind him the funds that Evans had, so he may not ultimately erect a museum and publish six volumes on the subject. But he does have the Canadian Research Fund behind him, and he has the University of Toronto behind him, and the results of his research may put the history of Crete in an entirely different light.

Another student who is still remembered on campus is Richard H. Pierce '57, not only because he is now professor of Egyptology at the University of Bergen in Norway but also because he stood up to Alex in a classic classroom confrontation. Alex had a funny looking, 3-inch-by-4-inch archaic horse made of bronze. Few things in his vast collection were closer to his heart than that horse, and once each semester he would carry it carefully with him down Brown Street, through the Faunce House Arch, and into Rogers 12 to show proudly to his students.

One morning he placed the horse beside him on his Olympian Heights, extolled its virtues for ten or fifteen minutes, and then looked out at his class. "Mr. Pierce, what do you think of my horse?" And Pierce is reported to have said, "Well, if you really want to know, I think it's a stupid looking horse." "Well, Mr. Pierce, it's *my* horse!" But Pierce stuck to his ground, claiming that it was a stupid looking horse. And it really was.

You didn't have to go into the field of classical antiquity to carry with you the effects of studying under Alex Robinson. Gail Wright comments: "I find myself still going to museums – the British Museum, the Vatican Museum, the Louvre – to look at things he loved, and taught me to love. I remember he once said that if you want to see the Parthenon, to *really* see the Parthenon, you should be up there at 7:30 in the morning when there are no people, no buses, no fumes. On a recent trip to Greece, I did climb up to the Acropolis and looked at the Parthenon in the early light of day. It was an incredible experience. And as I stood there all by myself, I thought of Alex Robinson."

One of the areas most important to Alex through his adult life was the American School of Classical Studies at Athens, whose chief task has been to train American graduate students in the history, literature, and archaeology of Classical and Byzantine Greece and to widen the knowledge and understanding of antiquity by excavation and publication. In addition to being a student there from 1923 to 1925, Alex served as professor of Greek literature and archaeology in 1934-35 and again in 1948. He excavated with the school at Corinth, Nemea, Phlius, and Prosymna, and was one of the authors of the first volume published by the school on its excavations at Corinth. From 1935 to 1954 he was a member of the Commission for the Excavation of the Athenian Agora, the market place and civic center of the Athens of the golden fifth and fourth centuries B.C. He was chairman of the school's alumni association from 1940 to 1946.

Alex also served for a long period as secretary of the managing and directing committee of the school. In this capacity he had a great deal to do with the appointment of Brown students to the school – undergraduates for the summer sessions and graduate students to go there as fellows in the winter time. For a period of thirty years, no college – not even Princeton, Harvard, and Bryn Mawr, which traditionally take the greatest number of fellowships – had greater representation at the American School than Brown.

This seemed appropriate because of Brown's long and close connection with the school. On June 22, 1881, Professor Albert Harkness met in Cambridge with two Harvard professors and two laymen to establish an American institution on Greek soil. Shortly, Yale, Johns Hopkins, and Cornell joined Brown and Harvard in an intercollegiate project which, as Alex liked to tell us, is the oldest in America except for the Harvard-Yale boat race and the Princeton-Rutgers football game.

The school that Professor Harkness helped to found continued to have Brown support. The late John Nicholas Brown was a member of its board of trustees, and the late John D. Rockefeller, Jr. '97, through the Rockefeller Foundation, provided the funds both for the purchase of sixteen acres in the middle of Athens in 1931 as the site of the Agora excavation and for the reconstruction of the ancient Stoa of Attalus as a museum some years later.

Originally the museum (the design was by the late William T. Aldrich '00) was to have been located on the southwest side of the Agora. However, when Alex Robinson's crew began digging trenches to make sure the new building was not covering anything of historical significance, the archaeologists found the masonry walls and foundation of an ancient building. The find turned out to be the Athenian law courts, where, in 399 B.C., Socrates stood facing his accusers and where the jury of 501 citizens convicted him and sentenced him to drink the fatal draught of hemlock. Among the ruins were found some of the jurors' bronze discs, the little metal markers used by the jurors to vote their belief in the guilt or innocence of a defendant.

Alex believed that students will not achieve greatness unless they have greatness thrust upon them. This theory led to another of his special activities – the Lectureship Committee at Brown, which he headed and

which also included the president of the University, John Nicholas Brown, and perhaps another member or two of the Board of Fellows. Alex was always proud of the number of prominent archaeologists whom he invited to lecture at Brown, and on each occasion the lecture was crammed with students who had been worked up to a fever pitch of enthusiasm over the contribution the scheduled lecturer had made to the field.

Alex and Celia Robinson were hosts to many groups, but none was more remarkable than the gathering of the Faculty Shop Club at 12 Keene Street six or seven times a year. Membership consisted of a very large circle of Alex's faculty friends, one of whom would give a paper, which was followed by comments, criticism, and conversation. Generally the subject under discussion would be one of some controversy, such as curricular revision, addition of a medical school or law school, the make-up of the Brown Corporation, or faculty salaries. Barney Keeney was a regular participant, even after he became president.

W. Chesley Worthington '23, editor emeritus of the *Brown Alumni Monthly*, once described this loosely knit group: "It had no officers, just a man who found someone to lead a discussion about some University matter, just a man who saw that colleagues got one-line notices on bits of flimsy paper, just a man who started the cheese and beer on its way around the room after giving a speaker the central chair. Perhaps nothing was decided officially in such gatherings, but many a proposal which later became University policy had its first serious hearing in the give-and-take of the ready dialogue."

Alex was the cornerstone of another group known simply as the Shop Club, an organization of eight or ten professional persons closely associated with Brown and the community who met for lunch monthly. The late Bill Edwards '19, former senior partner of the Providence law firm of Edwards and Angell, was a prominent member. Alex was particularly fond of this group, for wits were sharp, humor was abounding, and professional expertise was abundant as each member illustrated problems in his own profession.

Some years back Alex talked about his motivation in

forming the Faculty Shop Club and the Shop Club. "I believe in the value of good conversation," he said, "in getting people together to meet and talk, whatever their concentration or background. Getting intelligent people together to talk about worthwhile things is one of the greatest forms of civilization."

By choice Alex Robinson was never chairman of the Department of Classics. He didn't want the details that went with the job. "I would never think of becoming chairman," he would say. "It's all right for Herbert Couch to roll up his sleeves and move papers around if he wants to, but I don't do that kind of thing. My job is to educate the young and get on with it."

In a sense, Alex had the best of two worlds. He wasn't saddled with the administrative details that go with the chairmanship, yet he ruled the department. He was so strong, so famous that the various chairmen found themselves coming to him *for* advice, not to give advice.

Alex and Professor Arthur Lynch, two very different people, had a few skirmishes within the department. Arthur was a detail man, very particular about dates, times, and places when he taught a course. Alex? Well, he was just seeking greatness in the classroom. Alex would get indignant when Arthur would suggest that Imperial Rome in the second century A.D. represented one of the great moments in history. "The people were vegetables hanging onto the status quo," he would say. "That period produced no great books, no new

The Classics staff: Robinson, left, Chairman Herb Couch, and a young John Rowe Workman.

ideas in science or art. Collapse lay just ahead. There was a terrible fear of Parthia and the Christians. It was a period of gross materialism and pessimism featured by a general loss of initiative." Obviously, Professor Lynch would do some bristling of his own when Alex took off on this subject.

One afternoon at a staff meeting in Waterman House Arthur said that he wanted to start his Classics D2 course the following semester with Romulus and Remus. "You can't do that," Alex replied, "because they haven't had Alexander the Great yet." Then, with a wave of the hand and in a breezy fashion he added, "Besides nothing famous ever came out of Rome except Cicero and Julius Caesar." Well, that got Arthur hopping mad because Rome was his historical specialty. Eventually, Arthur refused to teach the course. Alex took it over, and then Alexander the Great was prolonged until spring vacation. After the students came back, Alex talked about only two people, Cicero and Julius Caesar, using them as examples of Roman history.

Alex got along well with most members of the faculty, although there were vexations there also. One of the most prestigious honors that a classicist can earn is the Prix de Rome of the American Academy in Rome. Alex Robinson had won the Prix de Rome, and with the honor went a special baldric and *bulla* worn as part of academic costume. Shortly after Alex had donned his new regalia, his good friend, Bob George, remarked: "Well, Alex, is Celia giving you things out of her linen closet to wear?" Alex was furious about this slur, especially coming from Professor George, who should have known better.

"But Bob George was not the only person to comment on the ratty appearance of the baldric and the brown *bulla*," Professor Workman says. "Even today the baldric of the Prix de Rome looks ratty. Of course, Alex asked me what I thought about its appearance, and he was consoled when I told him that it was the honor which counted and that Bob George could never even compete for the Prix de Rome. 'John, you're a nice guy,' he said, walking out of my office with his head held high."

It was generally accepted that Alex Robinson was extremely loyal to his friends and colleagues, even if he had to go out of his way to express that loyalty. The late Alonzo W. Quinn, professor of geology, benefitted from Robinson's support one afternoon during a battle over curriculum reform.

Now, if there was one thing Alex was *not* fond of it was the curriculum experimentation that seemed to go on endlessly at Brown. "If people want to play around with the curriculum, that's fine," he'd say. "I have too many important things to do." Alex always claimed that great teaching and the intellectual world would transcend any curriculum. And any attempt to abridge his own courses would be unthinkable.

Professor Quinn was visibly upset because his Geology D1 had failed at one point to be listed among the distribution courses. He confided in Alex, who decided that he would come to the support of his old friend. So, at a faculty meeting, and in tones most dramatic, Alex cited the absolute necessity of having geology available for all. He spoke of the archaeologists' need for geology and how geology was essential for all science and all life. When he finally sat down, one prominent economist was heard to ask no one in particular, "What the hell does *he* know about geology?" Whatever the case, Alex started a movement that day that put geology back in the distribution line-up.

T here were a few strong-willed members of the college community who would never be listed among Alex Robinson's close friends. One was Margaret Shove Morriss, dean of Pembroke, with whom Alex had a running battle over the shades in the Pembroke dormitory located right across from his home. Alex's concern was that many of the young women were careless about pulling down their shades while approaching the state of undress. A constant flow of memos on the subject went to Dean Morriss's office, each stating that he was in the habit of entertaining visitors of international scholarship, prominent people from the community, and distinguished students and that the shade situation was an embarrassment. Rumor has it that the memos went quickly from Dean Morriss's desk into the nearby waste basket.

When Nancy Duke Lewis became dean in 1950, Alex thought he'd see where she stood on the shade issue. So, off went a memo. It so happened that Professor Couch and Dean Morriss were in Dean Lewis's office when the Robinson memo arrived. "Professor Robinson seems very disturbed," Nancy said. "What should we do about it?" Dean Morriss rose from her chair and

picked up the piece of paper. "Just this," she replied, dropping the memo into the waste basket.

On at least one occasion, Alex had a problem with the *wife* of a member of the faculty. It involved a concern that Alex shared with several other faculty members (notably those of the French and English departments), and shared with horror – the bi-annual French play that Dorothy Brown, wife of Professor Harcourt Brown, insisted on presenting. Dorothy had fought bitter battles with Ben Brown about the use of Faunce House Theater, which she wanted for her play but which Professor Brown said was off limits because of Sock and Buskin and Brownbrokers' commitments. Ben even had the locks changed so that Dorothy and her cast could not enter.

"Smarting and humiliated, Dorothy then turned her attention to using Alumnae Hall," Professor Workman said. "Now, Alex was not opposed to drama, but he soon learned that Dorothy Brown's idea of a French play tied up everything completely. Alex sensed the closing pincers as more and more equipment was fetched into Alumnae Hall, where Alex held his large lecture class. When orders were given to take down the screen from the stage and move the podium to floor level, Alex rebelled.

"Rebellion, in this case, consisted of getting the departmental chairman, Herbert Couch, to sound a warning to Dorothy that neither the screen nor the podium could be moved. Herbert Couch, of course, was aware of the nettles involved with Dorothy, because she and her husband and Couch were all former Canadians and University of Torontonians, and Dorothy was bi-annually becoming more difficult about the French play. Still, Couch sought to work through Harcourt, and much was done to tone down the complete renovation or rebuilding of Alumnae Hall. Well, the play was performed, Ben Brown's establishment was left unmolested, Alex kept his screen and podium in place, and Dorothy left a trail of vituperation in her wake about Alex and Couch and Ben Brown. As usual, Alex had the last word. He once told me that during the two weeks in which plans for the French play were underway, he lectured on Sophocles so that his students in Alumnae Hall would know what 'great' drama really was!"

Alex also had a certain horror of the interruption or intrusion by parents into the academic programs of their children. Nothing could aggrieve him more than a letter from a complaining parent or a snide comment from a worried mother. Alex believed that the students were entrusted to the professors, their tuition paid, and that the parents must not interrupt the course of instruction. He was jovial to any stray father who might sit in on his lectures on occasion, but the gentleman soon learned that Alex was the educator and the father was the bill-payer.

Small people who kept nipping at his heels also bothered Professor Robinson. High on that list in the 1950s were the young women who worked in the Registrar's Office. "Back in those days we were supposed to write in a professor's comment on all failing grades," Professor Workman said. "Alex would never fill out the little cards. He would give them to his secretary and say, 'Just tell them he doesn't know anything.'

"Well, these slips of paper would be sent over, and before long some girl from the Registrar's Office would be on the phone. I could hear all this from my office, for Alex had a booming voice that could be picked up at any point in the building. 'Hello, now who are you, my friend?' and 'Well, but I don't know you. Why are you calling me up?' And the conversation would go on like that. 'Well, I don't know a thing about it. I did submit a grade. It's your job to find the students. I just teach them.'

"Later, Alex would come down to me. 'Now, my boy, do you fail students?' And I would tell him that indeed I did. 'Well, now, what do you do when you fail someone?' I'd patiently tell him that a comment had to be put on the card. 'Who has these cards? Can you share those cards?' I'd tell him, no, that they were distributed by the Registrar's Office. 'Well, I didn't get any.' And so I'd assure him that we would get some for him. No, that kind of detail was not Alex's forte. He was all for getting on with the job ahead, the big job. But just when it seemed we were in for open warfare between Waterman House and University Hall, Alex would saunter over to the Registrar's Office and charm those girls right off the wall."

Alex Robinson was completely at the mercy of all things mechanical. He was especially terrified of slide machines. "You've got to get me a projectionist," he would tell Professor Workman prior to one of his lectures. "I want a good projectionist, a *great* projectionist." He also never completely mastered the operation of an electric typewriter. "After all, my friends, some people earn their living running a typewriter!" He had particularly strong sentiments about the Hammond typewriter that Arthur Lynch was always trying

to get to work, with its interchangeable type fonts. Arthur never gave up with sealing wax, paper clips, and rubber bands trying to produce efficiency from the Hammond, which Alex always referred to as "Arthur's electric train." Alex became mildly interested in the department's duplicating machine until he found the ink and rolling process a real nuisance. He drove a car occasionally but admitted that he had no idea what made it run.

Knowing that Alex had strong likes and dislikes, President Keeney used to enjoy playing a practical joke on him occasionally. John Workman recalls one such incident. "Barney and I were walking up Brown Street to one of Alex's post-lecture parties when we spied a little black alley cat. Aware that Alex abhorred cats, Barney picked up the animal and put it in his coat pocket.

"Alex came to the door. 'Ah, my friends, come right in. The eminent Professor Workman, the great president of Brown University, and – oh, oh, there's a cat. Who does that dreadful cat belong to?' 'That's my cat,' Barney said. 'Oh, that's a nice cat, a marvelous cat,' Alex replied. 'Do bring him in.' Barney, who liked to pull tricks like that on any member of the faculty, was in stitches."

Through Alex Robinson's long career, when almost every day seemed to be a new adventure, he had a marvelous woman at his side in Celia, always a person of real joy. She soothed his passions and his anger. She also had an income that enabled him to put on the great performance – the lavish entertaining at 12 Keene Street and the frequent trips to Europe. She was motherly to her family and also happened to be a woman of great good sense. Some years after Alex died, she married Richard Stillwell, one of Alex's classmates at Princeton, later professor of classical archaeology there, and the man responsible for the great Morgantina Excavation in Sicily. At this writing, the couple lives in Princeton.

Alex and Celia were very proud of their three sons and anxious that each enter a profession, which they did. Alex III '51 became a teacher, coach, and an official in the National Basketball Association, Sam is an attorney in Boston, and Frank is director of the Museum of Art at the Rhode Island School of Design.

"Alex was a wonderfully warm and loving husband and father," Celia said. "He insisted on working in his study at home with all of us around him and his books, although at times he seemed oblivious to everything

Celia and Alex with their son, Frank, and Celia's father, Paul Sachs.

but his work. One evening the big drapes from the window by his desk crashed to the floor and he did not know it! Alex usually worked until midnight, at which point I'd bring him a plate of Welsh rarebit and we'd chat before going to bed.

"We returned to Athens and the American School throughout our married life, and almost always with the children. Alex and I were rarely separated, although one time he did take off for Syria with a young architect from the school. They were headed for Dura Europas (where Yale was excavating) but unfortunately became lost in the desert and had to return to Beirut and then to Athens. On another visit we took at trip to the Peloponnesus during a minor Greek revolution. While returning to Athens we were confronted by soldiers with rifles and fixed bayonets pointed toward us. Alex said 'Bah' loudly and directed our Greek dragoman to drive on."

It has never been claimed that Alex was a big help around the house. He always boasted that he had never gone into the cellar or attic. That probably was true. On the day the family moved from Angell Street to the beautiful home on Keene Street, Alex left early for the campus and came home only after everything was moved and settled. "Darling," he said on seeing Celia, "I'm exhausted just thinking of you having to move us." He often said to the boys after dinner, "I hate to see your mother in the kitchen. Go in and help

her." Once when one of the sons gave him a dish towel, Alex beat a hasty retreat to the relative safety of his study.

Alex was a prolific writer. In this area of his life he was completely disciplined. "There's only one way to write a book," he told me in my *Alumni Monthly* office one day. "Just apply the seat of your pants to the seat of your chair." Alex followed his own advice. When he was in the writing process, he would sit at his desk in Providence every evening until well after midnight. He also wrote at his gas-lit summer home at Willsboro in the Adirondacks, which was sufficiently primitive to discourage guests. *Alexander the Great* was revised three times in the privacy of that cabin in the summer of 1946.

His hobbies were his work, his family, classical music (the Robinsons seldom missed the Boston Symphony in Providence), and life in the Adirondacks at the family log cabin. He enjoyed cutting trees, planting ferns, and taking short hikes. Alex and Celia had breakfast at 7:30 on the front porch while watching the birds. Then he would go to his log cabin next door and work until 12:30, when Celia rang the ship's bell signifying lunch.

"One day," Celia said, "when I was forty years old and we were in the village of Willsboro, marketing, Alex said out of the blue, 'How would you like to buy a cemetery lot in Lake View?' So we jumped in the front seat of Bert Peterson's old truck and bought two lots that very day for $100. Later, Alex had some advice for his sons on this subject. 'The three most important decisions you have to make in life,' he told them, 'are where to go to college, whom to marry, and your cemetery lot.'"

Alex enjoyed umpiring at some of the local baseball games, especially if one of his sons was playing. His oldest son, Alex III, brought a few ringers from college to join him on the summer baseball team, men such as John Chernak '51, Jack Gilbert '51, and George Kirkpatrick '56. "Dad always supported us whenever we played sports," young Alex says. "He was a real tiger when he went to ball games in which any of us were playing. No one cheered louder and no one got into more arguments with other fans. Dad had a way of calling people 'my friend' when giving them hell, and I guess he gave plenty of people hell in his day."

George Kirkpatrick, who spent one summer with the Robinsons at the log cabin in Willsboro, recently recalled the strong practical side to Alex Robinson: "He never missed a ball game the summer I was up there, and he almost never missed getting into an argument whenever he came to the park. One of the best occurred during a very tight game when he was standing, as was his practice, to holler encouragement to us on the field. One of the more muscular natives seated behind him finally shouted, 'Sit down, you big hulk, so the rest of us can see.' Professor Robinson turned and stood, rising to his full, impressive height. 'Sir, I object to you referring to my avoirdupois in that manner, as I don't believe we have been introduced.' The good professor continued his enthusiastic cheering with no further comments from the man to his rear."

Frank Robinson, talking from his office at the Rhode Island School of Design, remembered his father as a man who always had a soft spot in his heart for his friends. "There was this old professor of his from Princeton, a productive scholar and a fine teacher, but a man who, in his dotage, had written a not very good book. Well, my father was given this man's book to review. He debated how he could write the review. He knew he couldn't praise the book, but at the same time he didn't want to hurt his old friend. Finally he just wrote an essay on how great this teacher had been and that got printed as the review. Shortly after the review appeared, the professor wrote my father. 'Thank you,' he said. 'I know it wasn't a very good book.'"

Alex Robinson was a moral man who believed in morality and spoke often of it. "A side of him was also quite formal and reserved, although his hearty greetings sometimes may have confused the picture," his son, Sam, told me. "I feel certain that never once in his life did he utter a vulgarity. He believed, and often said, that divorce was not an option open to people. His capacity for labor, which he actually enjoyed, was part of a general idea of duty, laboring deliberately and happily and purposefully in job, family, and life in general. Dad always worked for something better. He always 'looked forward,' as he so often said, because man has the capacity to make tomorrow better, in effect, thereby eradicating yesterday's unhappiness and shortcomings."

Of Alex's numerous virtues and principles of character none was so strong as his intense loyalty to the institutions and organizations that were part of his genius – the Brown University faculty, the classics department, his own students in class, Princeton University, the American School of Classical Studies at Athens, and the American Academy in Rome. He had several opportunities to leave Brown but didn't follow through on any of them. Duke University offered him an open contract in the 1930s, and in the late 1940s, after his *Alexander the Great* had become a national success, he was offered a post at Harvard.

Alex Robinson enjoyed *good* food. He especially enjoyed steak. "Whenever a departmental luncheon was planned, Alex would check with me on the menu," John Workman said. 'Now, what are we having?' he'd ask. 'Well, I thought we might have chicken Kiev.' 'Now, what's that?' 'It's a kind of chicken, and then they take the bone out and put stuffing in it.' 'Oh, and do they put gravy on that?' 'Yes.' 'Oh, so you're going to have this, what do you call it?' 'Chicken Kiev.' 'Yes, well, that's most interesting.' That was his message to me that he didn't want chicken Kiev as the main course. Alex was a choice-cut man."

The Latin Carol Service in Alumnae Hall is a Brown tradition, one that brings Christmas cheer and satisfaction to both campus and community. There is no word spoken other than in classical Latin or Greek from the moment the master of ceremonies gives his welcome. Alex was a frequent participant, but he insisted on doing his part in Greek, not Latin. And, as one might imagine, for Alex the preparation of the reading was a major production.

"Alex really threw himself into the Carol Service," Professor Workman says. "I think he was staggered at first to realize that we could get such a mob out for something like that. He liked big crowds. He liked to see students sitting on radiators and swinging on chandeliers.

"Each year he'd come down to my office. 'Now, there are numerous ways in which Greek can be pronounced,' he'd say. 'How do you want it pronounced?' I'd suggest that he give it the Germanic pronunciation because that's what the students would know best. Later he would appear in my office with a Greek New Testament and say, 'Now, I want you to read this to me.' I would and he'd say, 'So that's the way it's supposed to be.' I'd say yes. 'Would you read it again?' he'd ask. And as I did he'd mark things. Alex would always do the Last Gospel near the end, and the students who had Greek would bring their Greek testaments and follow it. He especially liked that."

Christmas was celebrated with gusto at the Robinson house, especially on the night of the annual Christmas party for faculty, administration, neighbors, and friends from the community. Between 200 and 300 people would come to 12 Keene Street, each one greeted at the door by Alex with his big booming voice. During the early part of the evening, while the children sat on the floor in the front parlor or under the piano, Lois Bigelow, wife of Vice President Bruce Bigelow '24, would play the piano and another woman would play the violin. The adults remained in the back of the room singing the Christmas carols. Everyone drank punch and ate cookies. Outside on the street the huge brass mosque candles (the Robinsons purchased them in Constantinople) burned brightly.

From time to time Alex would ring a little bell that a shepherd boy had given him in Greece many years before, and it would announce a reading of a Christmas classic by Bob George, Ivory Littlefield, or some other old friend. Dr. Bill Buffum and Vice President Jim Adams took turns reading the Bible story. Later in the evening the youngsters went home and the adults took over the party, only to be replaced when they ran out of steam by the teenagers who put on records and danced until the early hours of the morning. All generations were served at an Alex Robinson Christmas party. It was Town and Gown, and much more. He liked it that way.

One day in 1964 Alex walked into the office of his old friend John Workman. "I have been to the doctor and he tells me I have a fistula," he said. The fistula turned out to be cancer of the colon. His spirits remained high, even after the operation that followed. But the prognosis was not good.

"I well remember the day he returned to the office after his surgery," Professor Workman recalled. "'Gentlemen,' he said, 'I've had the greatest operation anybody's ever had.' And he started naming some of the prominent surgeons who had been involved, most of them long-standing members of Alex's Shop Club or the Art Club."

Samuel Robinson said that his father never became depressed during his final months. "He was above all else an optimist, a man who made everyone else feel better because he seemed to feel so damned good himself. For us, his death was all the more tragic to observe because even it could not completely dispatch his faith in good things and the power of man to achieve them."

His only regret, according to his son, Alex, was the timing of his death. "It's too bad this thing had to happen while I'm at the peak of my mental power," he told Alex one night.

The Latin Carol Service at Brown was taking its normal course in the Christmas season of 1964. The audience and musical groups sang with that special exuberance of long-standing, with familiar carols in Latin translation for both the willing amateurs and trained choruses. As usual every seat in Alumnae Hall was occupied. Some students stood out on the terrace and looked inside through frost-covered windows.

Chet Worthington commented on that service in the *Brown Alumni Monthly*: "The Latin Carol Service of 1964 will be remembered for one particular moment, when Professor Charles Alexander Robinson, Jr., rose to read from the Greek. Though he had lately left his hospital room, his voice had its old booming vibrance, his joy in taking part was as infectious as ever. When Professor Robinson finished, the hall resounded with applause for the reading, yes, but mostly for the man [applause usually did not occur until the end of the service]. It must have been an ovation hard to take, for so many thus poured out their affection at that moment in that way for so long. We are glad that three generations of his family were there to hear the remarkable tribute.

"In all but spirit, Professor Robinson was an ailing, strangely enfeebled man that night, and there were overtones of a leave-taking no one cared to admit. Students, alumni, neighbors, and townsmen were all telling him of their love and appreciation."

Alex returned to teach after each stay in the hospital, and always with his tremendous enthusiasm. At the end of his final lecture, he was loudly applauded by the 200 students in Alumnae Hall. Alex twirled his cane impatiently, as if to signal the applause to stop. Instead it continued, even more loudly. Then Alex lifted a glass of water from a table beside the lecturn, raised the glass, and gave a toast to the class.

Celia was waiting outside the lecture hall to take him home. And as the students passed, many of them spoke to her. The message was the same: "The greatest lecture yet!" Two weeks later on February 23, 1965, Charles Alexander Robinson, Jr., died at Jane Brown Hospital.

Chapter 5 ❧
A tremendous breadth of understanding typified his work

According to President Henry M. Wriston, it was "one of the great games of hide and seek with the government that makes influence peddling understandable – and thriving." Wriston was referring to the 1941 effort to bring to Brown Dr. William Prager, internationally recognized German engineer and mathematician, and the man who later became known as the father of applied mathematics in this country.

Although the effort did represent intrigue at its best, the sequence of events might never have taken place if it hadn't been for the chain reaction of world events put into motion by Adolf Hitler. By the early 1930s, while still a very young man, Professor Prager had established himself as one of the world's foremost experts in vibrations and in the theory of structures. He was also one of the creators of the mathematical theory of plasticity, which revolutionized design procedures in mechanical engineering. Despite Prager's reputation, however, Hitler had the scientist dismissed from the Institute of Technology at Karlsruhe in 1933 because of Prager's strong anti-Nazi views.

Responding angrily to his dismissal, Prager filed a lawsuit against the government, claiming that his tenure had been violated. Eventually, he became one of the few individuals to win a court case against the German government under Hitler. The professor received a year's back pay and an offer to return to work

if he so desired. At that point, Prager was holding the chair in mechanics at Istanbul University in Turkey, was content in his new position, felt it less than discreet to return to Germany, and so officially resigned from the institute – his point having been won.

By 1941, Prager had been at the University of Istanbul for eight years and because of the war conditions in Europe was receptive to Henry Wriston's offer to head up the Program of Advanced Instruction and Research in Applied Mechanics at Brown. The Russo-German War complicated his efforts to leave Europe, as did troubles in Iran and Iraq. The biggest stumbling block, however, was the matter of obtaining a visa. The U.S. State Department got involved, as did Rhode Island's U.S. Senator Theodore Francis Green '87 and Lord Halifax, the British Ambassador. All of this support represented a great deal of clout, but for a long while it appeared that clout was out in 1941, at least as far as Professor Prager was concerned.

Brown made its first approach to the State Department in Prager's behalf on April 18, 1941, in the form of a letter from James Case, secretary of the University, to Eliot B. Coulter, acting chief of the visa department. Case pointed out that Brown had obtained funds from the Engineering Defense Program of the Office of Education as well as from the Carnegie Corporation to set up during the summer of 1941, and continue through the 1941-42 academic year, advanced courses in applied mechanics. Case also noted that Prager would be a valuable addition to the defense program, whether at the University or in industry, or both, and added that Prager would rank favorably with von Mises of Harvard and von Kármán of the California Institute of Technology as an expert on the theoretical side of aeronautics.

Some days later, Case sent a memo to President Wriston and Dr. Roland G. D. Richardson, dean of the Graduate School, reporting on his trip to the Carnegie Institution in Washington, D.C., where he sought the support of its president, Vannevar Bush, in arranging the transit of Prager from Istanbul to Brown. In his memo, Case reported that Bush not only knew very little about Prager but also seriously questioned Brown's high evaluation of him.

"The conclusive fact," Case added, "is that established policies of the defense agencies with regard to defense work prevent them from urging our State Department to give special consideration to a person such as Professor Prager. President Bush said that no confidential work was given out to any person other than an American citizen, and that the approval of the Army and Navy Intelligence Bureau and the FBI was required in every case. He pointed out that no one in Prager's position could be eligible for confidential work for a considerable period of time. That being the case, the defense group would not feel justified in urging the State Department to take special steps to ensure his prompt arrival."

At the meeting with Case, Bush expressed dissatisfaction with the presentation of Brown's program in applied mechanics, noting that a number of his men felt that their efforts were being slighted and that Brown had "overemphasized" the unique character of its program. Bush added that many members of the National Research Council were "rather bitterly opposed" to Brown's undertaking.

That same afternoon, Case met with Howland Shaw, assistant secretary of state, whom von Mises had mentioned as a friend, and possibly a friend of Prager's. It turned out that Shaw did *not* know Prager and was unable to indicate any way in which the State Department would be able to assist in getting the German

scientist to Brown. Concluding his memo on a less than optimistic note, Case said, "As it happens, Mr. Shaw is in charge of the division of the State Department which deals with matters of this nature. I feel, therefore, that we have a pretty definitive decision from the Department."

On May 23, President Wriston personally got involved in the case, sending a three-page letter to Senator Green. He explained that Prager's German passport was due to expire in the middle of July and that no extension would be given since Prager was a German citizen of military age. Wriston also pointed out that there were few options left to the Pragers in their effort to get out of Europe.

"We infer that he will not be able to travel through or touch at any areas under German control," Wriston wrote. "From the events of the last few days, it appears that Syria and other areas under French control will also be dominated by Germany and would prove as dangerous to him as the German areas themselves. As a German citizen, there would be obvious difficulties in bringing him through British territory. Only a direct intervention on the part of the British Embassy here could make that possible."

Wriston informed Senator Green that Brown had consulted with the Rockefeller Foundation, the New School for Social Research, and Thomas Cook & Son, among others, and that there was agreement that the Russo-Japanese route was the most practical, although there was "some difficulty" in obtaining a Japanese visa. In closing, Wriston asked the senator's help in obtaining from the State Department an affidavit in lieu of a passport and in securing a safe-conduct pass from British authorities. "We are attempting to get full information about passage through the Red Sea, as well as passage through Cairo, Capetown, and various points in India," Wriston concluded. "At present, the India route appears to be closed. The availability of the Red Sea route is highly problematical, and the Cairo to Capetown route has the initial difficulty of arranging a method of transportation from Istanbul to Cairo."

If Wriston, Richardson, Case, and other officials at Brown were frustrated by their inability to secure a visa, the Pragers were also feeling extreme pressure. Some years back, Professor Prager discussed with me those anxious days and nights. "Originally, we planned to go to the United States via Odessa, then Japan, and finally a boat to San Francisco. The United States ambassador in Ankara took a special interest in me because he had gone to college with Wriston at Wesleyan. 'You'll never make it through to Japan,' he told me, while implying that he'd like to say more but couldn't. Then, in June of 1941, about the time we had hoped to start our journey, Germany attacked Russia."

A late-spring telegram to Brown voiced Prager's concern: "Japanese Travel Definitely Closed / Odessa Boat Now Impossible Touching Varna / Expected Developments Indicate Utmost Speed." Prager may have cried out for "utmost speed," but what he got was more bureaucratic delay. In response to Senator Green's urgent appeal for action, the State Department replied, tersely, that "neither the Department nor its representatives abroad may be of any assistance to Professor Prager and his family in affecting their entry into the countries through which they must proceed en route to the United States." Clearly, the State Department was going to be of little help to Brown in this venture.

Lord Halifax was more positive, expressing cautious optimism that some help might be forthcoming. After suggesting that the Pragers should make every effort to travel by some route that would enable them to "avoid touching any British territory," the ambassador added: "If this proves impossible, however, I think the professor should be advised to get in touch with our Ambassador at Ankara, Sir Hugh Knatchbull-Hugessen, who is clearly in a better position than any other British authority to be of assistance and who I might expect may already know of Dr. Prager. When Professor Prager decides on his itinerary, it will be possible for Sir Knatchbull-Hugessen, if he thinks it advisable, to recommend the Professor to the British authorities en route. In the meantime," Lord Halifax added, "I have telegraphed to the Ambassador to warn him that he may shortly be hearing from the Professor."

By early July, nearly three months after negotiations to bring Prager to this country had opened, it seemed that success was finally at hand. These hopes were dashed on July 15 when A. M. Warren, chief of the visa division of the State Department, wrote the following note to Secretary Case at Brown: "The American consulate at Istanbul reports that visas in these cases have been withheld in view of the fact that close relatives of Professor Prager reside in Germany. It is the policy of the Department to withhold visas in the cases of applicants having members of their immediate family living in an area where they might be subject to influences which might affect the applicants after their arrival in the United States. This case has been given careful consideration, and it is regretted that it has not been found possible to make an exception."

This decision by the State Department prompted a poignant telegram from Prager to Otto Neugebauer, professor of the history of mathematics at Brown and a college colleague of Prager's. The wire read: "US Visa Cancelled / Cabled Details Dean / Furniture Sold / Position Resigned / Situation Here Expected Deteriorate Soon / Impossible Stay for Czechoslovakians / Implore Help / Willy."

In short order, two things happened to give the story a happy ending. First, thanks to the intervention of Lord Halifax, Prager was able to meet with the British Ambassador in Ankara. (Prager did not enter into the conversation with an empty hand. Shortly after the war started in September 1939, Prager had become an advisor to the Air Ministry in Britain and, in this role, played a part in the design of the RAF planes that helped save England during the Battle of Britain in the summer and fall of 1940.) There are indications that the British Ambassador in Ankara initiated several moves that indirectly paved the way for Prager's departure from Europe. Dean Richardson mentioned this in a November 21 letter to President Wriston, when he wrote: "I have all along had the feeling that the British had done more to get Prager's exit expedited than the Americans, and in conversations with Prager I am still further convinced of this."

The other important factor in the successful denouement of this story was President Wriston's ability finally to find a somewhat friendly face in the nation's Capital. When the efforts of Senator Green, the State Department, and Lord Halifax failed to produce a visa, Wriston went to see the Secretary of State, Cordell Hull, who startled the Brown president early in the conversation by admitting that he didn't know what applied math was.

"He said that if I could straighten him out on that point, the professor would be admitted," Wriston later wrote. "My last mathematics had been as a college freshman, and there had been nothing applied about it. Nevertheless, I used every term I had heard used by Dean Richardson and made my exposition as long and involved as possible. Whereupon, with a gleam of humanity theretofore hidden by his official pose, the Secretary broke in and said, 'I don't understand all that, and, frankly, I don't think you do, either. But, he can come in.'"

When the elusive visas were finally secured in October 1931, Dr. Prager, his wife, Gertrude Ann Heyer (they were married on September 16, 1925), and their twelve-year-old son, Stephen, set out on a 20,000-mile journey that should have taken eight days but took forty instead. The Mediterranean was closed because Rommel's army was almost to Alexandria. Tobruk had fallen. This meant that the Pragers had to go east. They went to Bagdad by train, proceeded from there by plane to Karachi, India, and then took the next-to-the-last boat, the *President Monroe*, out of Bombay on a thirty-one-day trip through submarine-infested waters to New York via Capetown.

Prager's mind was constantly active, and so his body had to follow. During the first few days out of Bombay, the German scientist was troubled by the confinement of the ship. And then he found an outlet in a highly unlikely spot – the recreation room. For the better part of four weeks, one of the world's most brilliant men

occupied his time by testing his skill against the pinball machine on the *President Monroe*. By the time the ship docked in New York City, Prager had come to a reluctant conclusion – on the basis of a considerable body of evidence – that the best one can hope to do in competition with a pinball machine is break even.

The Pragers arrived in this country in mid-November, only a few weeks before the attack on Pearl Harbor drew America into the war. Awaiting him at Brown University was a difficult task – and a $4,000-per-year salary.

The hard-sell effort by Wriston and Dean Richardson to recruit Prager, a slight, bald, and self-controlled scientist, came about because the threat of war had underscored the insufficient emphasis placed on the sciences in general, and applied mathematics in particular, in the United States. The federal government had decided to do something about the situation, and, Henry Wriston decided, so could Brown.

Late in 1940, Dr. Thornton C. Fry, mathematical research director of Bell Telephone Laboratories, wrote a report on industrial mathematics as part of a project for the Survey of Research in Industry. This report,

Prager, standing, and Dean Richardson, right, brought Professor Tamarkin to Brown.

submitted to the National Resources Planning Board and President Roosevelt, pointed out that the need for mathematicians was increasing and that there was a serious lack of university courses for graduate training of industrial mathematicians.

Dean Richardson, a Yale graduate, had been at Brown since 1907, was a former chairman of the mathematics department, and had served for twenty years as secretary of the American Mathematical Society. A Canadian, he had the British sense of the importance of applied mathematics, a field not yet fully developed in this country. "The last war," he said in 1934, in reference to World War I, "was a chemist's war. If there is a next one, it will be a mathematician's war."

The Fry report both reinforced Richardson's convictions that the United States needed to shore up its training in mathematics and provided welcome backing for it. With the financial support of the U.S. Office of Education and the Carnegie Foundation, and with the moral support of President Wriston, Richardson in 1941 organized a twelve-week summer school called the Program of Advanced Instruction and Research in Mechanics. Although the research institute was to be operated within the framework of the Graduate School, it was felt that its special purpose could best be met by setting it up as a separate entity rather than as a part of the general activity of the Department of Mathematics.

For five successive summers, superior young mathematicians and engineers who had advanced degrees participated in the program. These students received strenuous mathematical training from some of the world's most distinguished applied mathematicians, men brought to Brown as visiting professors. The immediate objective of the program was to prepare the students for work in war-related industries.

As soon as the first summer session had been approved early in 1941, Dean Richardson turned his efforts toward finding a permanent director. What Brown needed was an eminent applied mathematician, an experienced teacher who was young, vigorous, and enterprising. Experience with industrial research was also desirable. After extensive consultation, Dean Richardson located someone who met these qualifications and who also happened to have some personal experience in administration. The search ended in Istanbul – and the man was Prager.

In his book, *Academic Freedom*, Wriston described the circumstances surrounding the Prager appointment.

"Early in my career at Lawrence College," he wrote, "I made some appointments on the basis of papers, records, recommendations – with disastrous results. The appointees were so bad that I determined never again to risk a 'picture bride.' Prager represented the greatest gamble ever: to bring a scholar half round the world to a permanent position with no interview, no knowledge of the man's adaptability to a new environment, or his gifts at developing and managing a new department – for which no funds were in sight. This was academic risk-taking with a vengeance. But Dean Richardson was a good judge of excellence, and so the decision was made."

From the time of his birth on May 23, 1903, in Karlsruhe, Germany, to his death in Savognin, Switzerland on March 17, 1980, William Prager never wasted a minute. In addition to being an engineer and mathematician, he was an inventor, writer, editor, linguist, connoisseur of good food and wines, and a person deeply devoted to teaching as well as research.

Educated at the Institute of Technology in Darmstadt, Germany, Prager received his civil engineering degree there in 1925 and his doctorate the following year. He was a lecturer at the Institute of Darmstadt until 1929, after which he was appointed acting director of the Institute of Applied Mechanics at the University of Göttingen. Prager also held positions as structural inspector of the German Airport League and as scientific advisor to the Fieseler Aircraft Company at Kassel, one of Germany's largest airplane manufacturers. Then, in 1933, he was named professor of mechanics in the Institute of Technology in Karlsruhe, the town of his birth. At twenty-nine years of age, Prager was the youngest full professor in Germany.

Prager reached scientific maturity during a period of remarkable productivity for German applied mathematics. Known as the Golden Age, this era was dominated by Ludwig Prandtl and Richard von Mises. Prager quickly established himself scientifically among that company by publishing a series of papers on structural vibrations and elasticity, six of them in the year of his doctorate, when he was only twenty-three.

During his three years at the University of Göttingen, Prager reported directly to Prandtl. At that point, Göttingen represented what James R. Rice, L. Herbert Ballou Professor of Applied Mechanics at Brown for seventeen years before moving to Harvard in the fall of 1981, referred to as "a firmament of scientific stars the likes of which the world has perhaps not seen since." This period marked the start of Prager's deep interest in plasticity, a field he led to maturity during the next thirty years. He and his first student, K. Hohenemser, published an important paper on plastic behavior under combined stresses. Later, with Hilda Geiringer, he wrote on the theory of slip lines in plane plastic flow.

By 1933, Prager had published more than thirty papers in his specialty and was internationally famous. His work in structure was especially important, since it had a profound influence on the development of lighter yet stronger airplanes and cars. As a colleague at Brown stated a decade or so ago, "When one attempts to think of a single person in the world who established a field and put his stamp on it, you think of Prager and the theory of plasticity."

Prager's knowledge of planes was not obtained exclusively in the abstract. As a young man he developed a keen interest in flying and went up whenever he could. As part of the terms of the peace treaty after World War I, Germany was prohibited from having an Air Force. The Germans, however, were allowed to build gliders, and it was in these fragile crates that Prager first learned how to fly.

Later, while Prager was scientific advisor to Feisler Aircraft Company, he was invited to go up as a passenger in one of the biplanes with open cockpits. Since the purpose of the flight was to check several stress features, the pilot did a number of loop-the-loops before coming back to the field.

"How did you like it?" the pilot asked, as the two men climbed out of the plane. "Were you afraid?" Nodding his head, Prager admitted that he was very much afraid. "You see," he said, "I never found the safety strap. I was just clinging on to the edge of the cockpit all the while."

Although Prager was only thirty when Hitler forced him from Germany, he was already so well known that the Turkish Government immediately offered him the chair in mechanics at the University of Istanbul. He was told that he would have four years to acquire a sufficient knowledge of Turkish to lecture to his students in that language. Prager achieved this objective in two years, eventually going on to write four books

in Turkish on descriptive geometry and mathematics.

Prager was fluent in four languages – English, German, French, and Turkish – and could read Russian, Dutch, and Italian. In late 1968, he told me that he would frequently skip back and forth between them. "A few years ago," he said, "I was scheduled to speak at Brooklyn Polytechnic Institute. Before I went on, I was introduced to several Turkish graduate students and began to talk to them in their native tongue. This went on for about fifteen minutes. Later, when I started to give my speech, I looked out and saw the bewildered faces of my audience. I had still been talking in Turkish."

During most of Prager's stay at the University of Istanbul, Turkey was governed by President Kemal Ataturk, the man who helped defeat the British at Gallipoli during World War I and who then, between 1923 and his death in 1938, personally dragged his country out of the Middle Ages and into the twentieth century. Kemal was especially proud of the many brilliant scientists he had brought to his new university, and the forceful and sometimes dictatorial leader got a vicarious pleasure from holding private discussions with these eminent scholars.

"Being a very busy man, President Ataturk might not find himself free until the early hours of the morning," says Herbert Kolsky, professor of applied mathematics at Brown. "Apparently, it wasn't unusual for Prager's phone to ring at 1 or 2 a.m., with Ataturk requesting an immediate discussion on philosophy, or some other worldly subject. 'I could not very well say no,' Prager would say in relating this story. 'How do you tell the president of the country that you are tired – call me tomorrow!'"

Professor Kolsky believes that Prager might not have accepted Brown's 1941 offer if Hitler's armies had not reached Greece. "All professors were treated with extreme deference in Turkey at that time," Kolsky says. "Also, the Pragers had a beautiful home overlooking the Bosphorus. They were quite content. But, then came the war."

At the time of Prager's arrival in the United States, applied mathematics in this country was still in a relatively undeveloped state. Generally speaking, through the 1930s applied mathematics could be described as that part of mathematics whose active development was in the hands of physicists and engineers rather than professional mathematicians. With several notable exceptions, the few professional mathematicians

Text on blackboard: COMBINED BENDING AND TORSION OF TWO-SPARRED WING

genuinely interested in the field were not held in high professional esteem by their colleagues in pure mathematics because of a widespread belief that you turned to applied mathematics only if you found the going too difficult in pure mathematics. An evaluation committee appointed by President Wriston in 1941 referred to this when it wrote: "In our enthusiasm for pure mathematics, we have foolishly assumed that applied mathematics is something less attractive and less worthy."

It is next to impossible to define applied mathematics. Even Prager admitted this. "It cannot be defined in terms of subject matter," he once said. "The borderline between theory and application is highly subjective and shifts with time. Nor can it be defined in terms of motivation: to study a mathematical problem *for its own sake* is surely not the exclusive privilege of pure mathematics. Perhaps the best I can do is to describe applied mathematics as the bridge connecting pure mathematics with science and technology. I have deliberately described this bridge as *connecting* two areas of activity rather than *leading* from one to the other

because the bridge carries two-way traffic. Its importance to science and technology is obvious, but it is not less important to pure mathematics, which would be poorer without the stimuli coming from the applications."

The environment for applied mathematics greatly improved in the United States during the early 1940s. Brown's Program of Advanced Instruction and Research in Applied Mechanics, forerunner of the Graduate Division of Applied Mathematics, contributed substantially to this improvement. There were similar organizations at a few other universities, such as the Courant Institute of the Mathematical Sciences at New York University.

Through his years at Brown, and into retirement, Prager expressed appreciation for Brown's commitment to the growth of applied mathematics and paid special homage to the foresight of two men – Dean Richardson and President Wriston. Shortly before retiring from Brown in 1973, Prager recalled those days: "Dean Richardson recognized early that, as a result of this country's unavoidable entry into World War II, there would be a sharply increased demand for applied mathematicians, and that an emergency training program in applied mathematics was therefore bound to find financial support. It was thanks to his initiative and drive that the Program of Advanced Instruction and Research in Applied Mechanics could be started in the summer of 1941.

"At the end of the war, the funds that had so far supported the program disappeared almost overnight, and President Wriston had to decide whether to wind up the venture or continue it in some form with little prospect of outside funding. It is thanks to his courage in committing University funds that Brown has a Division of Applied Mathematics today."

Prager and Richardson spent many long days and nights together in early 1942 building a framework for the new department. There was much give and take in these meetings, but there was one point on which the two were in complete agreement: that the first order of business was to build a staff and to do it quickly. They accomplished this by attracting to Brown many of the top mathematicians overseas who were either driven out of Central Europe by Hitler or who, like Prager, chose to leave.

A factor in Brown's ability to attract these world-famous scholars was the promise by Prager and Richardson that the University would not attempt to hold them for more than one or two years. Professor Kolsky, who first came to Brown as a visiting professor in 1955, recently commented on this point.

"It was a good thing for both sides," he said. "I can take a look at you, and you can take a look at me. Yet there was no permanent commitment on either side. The arrangement was good for the professor because he still had his roots at his home university, and it was good for Brown because of the constant influx of new blood."

The availability of these European scholars was known to most college administrators at that time, according to Dr. Daniel C. Drucker, a Prager protégé at Brown who is now dean of the College of Engineering at the University of Illinois. "But the point is that most college administrators hadn't been thinking in terms of bringing these great minds together," Drucker said. "Thanks to the team of Prager, Richardson, and Wriston, Brown University recognized this opportunity – and seized it."

The group that Prager and Richardson drew together at Brown in the early 1940s created a field of applied

Prager and two graduate students examine a German jet engine.

mathematics that had never before existed in this country. Included were such internationally famous names as von Mises, Bergman, Brillouin, Synge, and Sokolnikoff. There is an irony that many of these men normally would have been disbursing their knowledge at European universities. Instead, they were at Brown aiding the American war effort. In 1944, for example, Dr. R. K. Luneberg, formerly of the University of Göttingen, and Dr. Nicholas Chako, professor of the College of Scutari in Albania, conducted a new course in mathematical optics. When published that fall, Luneberg's lectures formed the best treatises on optics in any language and were of immediate use to the major optical companies all over the free world to compute and improve lenses used in bombsights, gunsights, periscopes, range finders, and cameras. Nine mathematical scholars, including two from Canada and one from China, worked with Dr. Luneberg and Dr. Chako nine hours a day that summer in the old Rhode Island Historical Association on Waterman Street, now the site of Graphic Services.

In the middle-to-late 1940s, Brown University was *the place* in the world for applied mathematics. Through the early 1960s, Brown was still the dominant place. Today, many colleges have excellent departments in this field, but it is interesting to note the large number that are still populated either by Brown Ph.D.'s or men who worked at Brown under Prager.

Professor Drucker credits Brown's world-wide reputation to Prager's excellence in his field, his organizational ability, and the facility for recognizing bright young men all over the world and then being able to bring them to Brown. "The ability to form a first-rate group requires certain personality traits," Drucker says, "traits that most great men do not have. Prager had them. He had an understanding of young people and could appreciate their talents *before* they became famous and in danger of being pirated away from Brown."

Professor Drucker also credits Prager with advocating the use of an advanced level of mathematics to solve the general problem, feeling that the smaller problems would then fall into place. "This is where he made his greatest contribution," Dr. Drucker says. "The British

theory, and ours prior to Prager, was to start building up with details to reach a conclusion. In other words, trying to solve 100 small problems before you got to the big one. In essence, what Prager did was to get away from all these details so that he could look at the broad picture and solve problems in the broad sense."

Another former colleague, Paul Symonds, professor of engineering at Brown, maintains that the chief secret of Prager's success in his chosen profession was the ability to see where interesting new problems existed and then to find ways to open them up. "He was great for applying new techniques never used before," Symonds says. "A tremendous breadth of understanding typified his work. He would take ideas from totally different fields and then make them work elsewhere."

Mrs. Prager once cited her husband's tremendous capacity for work as one reason for his success. "An old proverb says that a man works as fast as he eats, and my husband eats very fast."

In William Prager, Brown had secured the services of a man who became a member of both the National Academy of Engineers and the National Academy of Science. At that time, only a handful of scholars belonged to both groups. He earned the highest awards in applied mechanics of United States civil and mechanical engineering societies: the Worcester Reed Warner Medal of the ASME in 1957, the ASCE in 1960, and the Timoshenko Medal of the ASME in 1966.

Prager was the author of twenty books and monographs and more than 200 scientific papers. His six principal books in applied mathematics were written in or translated into half a dozen languages. His book, *The Theory of Perfectly Plastic Solids*, written in collaboration with Philip G. Hodge, Jr. ('49 Ph.D.), was translated into German, Russian, and Japanese. He was the founding editor of the *Quarterly of Applied Mathematics*, which has been published at Brown since 1943, served as co-editor of the *Journal of Applied Mechanics* (1969-72), and as editor of the *Journal of Applied Mathematics* (1966-73). Because of his masterly style, Prager's books and papers were models of lucid exposition.

One thing should be pointed out. Prager was *not* the prototype of the kindly old college professor. Dr. Paul F. Maeder, another Prager protégé and a former vice president of Brown, says: "Through the years, his mind always remained young and quick, and he remained at the forefront, where he always was. As a person, he was not the colorful type. He was logical. At first meeting, he gave the impression of formality, even coldness. When you dug deeper, you'd find that this was traceable to modesty and reserve."

Another colleague put it this way: "Professor Prager was not the sort of man you invited to a cocktail party for laughs. There was very little small talk where he was concerned. He was a quiet, self-controlled man. Rarely did his speech display emotion. He was always the aristocrat of the situation."

According to Professor Kolsky, Prager sometimes was "a bit officious" and could give the impression that he felt he was "pretty good." He adds: "But, he *was* pretty good. The very best. He was a serious scholar, but never solemn. He felt his work was serious, but not something you talked about in hushed tones."

Professors who had occasion to travel with Prager on trips to Boston or New York said that after the first fifteen minutes or so, Dr. Prager would have discussed all the important things that were on his mind. From that point on, the trip would be made in silence. There was never any attempt on Prager's part to engage in light banter just to carry on a conversation.

A member of the department once asked Frances Gajdowski '41, a one-time secretary to Dr. Prager, what the two of them talked about during a typical day. "We don't talk at all," Miss Gajdowski replied. "I just sit there and do what he asks me to do."

Eleanor Addison '38, Prager's long-time secretary, recalls that in his quiet way Prager was a demanding man to work for. "He expected you to do what was assigned," she says. "If you did more, he was grateful. He also expected accuracy. One of his biggest problems with me was that when I did his drawings I was forever forgetting to insert the arrowheads. 'I can't help it, professor,' I'd tell him. 'I just don't remember them.' He'd smile and say, 'Never mind. We'll make you a full professor and then it will be all right for you to forget.'"

When you talk with former friends and colleagues of Professor Prager, one point keeps coming through: his reserve and formality. It is interesting to note that despite his long association with his two secretaries, Prager always addressed them as "Miss Addison" and "Miss Gajdowski." Prager was addressed as "Bill" by his colleagues in the department, but only after he per-sonally gave his permission.

There is an interesting story about the time Prager was trying to bring Eli Sternberg to Brown. Prager wrote an extremely cordial letter, addressed it "Dear Eli" and signed it "Bill." Back from Europe came a letter addressed "Dear Bill" and signed "Eli." In short order, Prager replied. This time it was "Dear Professor Sternberg" and signed "Professor Prager." You see, Prager had not given permission for Sternberg to use the more informal method of address.

Prager was equally proper in his dress. No one on campus ever saw him without a coat and tie, even on the warmest days. His clothes were made by a tailor in London, and he always wore Saville Row suits. "With his formal dress and quiet reserve, Professor Prager always looked like a diplomat who had just walked out of the United Nations," Professor Kolsky says. "I'll never forget the cocktail party the department gave for me when I left Brown in 1958 after my two-year appointment. I probably had a martini too many, and I started to wave my glass about to make some long-forgotten point. Well, some of my martini, which, as I recall, was very good, spilled on Dr. Prager's well-pressed suit. In his gracious fashion, Prager tried to pass it off as nothing. As I look back on that moment, however, I am inclined to believe that the incident was not the highlight of Prager's day."

Prager was particularly close to his graduate students. It was not unusual for a professor to put his name on a graduate student's paper, especially if it was he who had come up with the idea for the paper. Prager always allowed the graduate students to write their papers under their names, thus giving the young people in the department the feeling that they were important, not subsidiary.

Prager's teaching interests were not confined to his graduate students. He took just as great a concern in the undergraduates, including freshmen. "When I was chairman of the engineering division," Paul Maeder says, "I asked Dr. Prager if we could introduce freshmen to the use of computers. He not only agreed, but he met with these students once a week. When the freshmen began to grasp the material and show some enthusiasm for it, Prager started meeting with them on evenings, Saturdays, and Sundays. He was completely at their disposal and showed as much enthusiasm as they did."

It was never necessary for a student to get an appointment with Prager. "I want my students to feel free to come in anytime for help and advice," he once said. "I especially like working with fresh minds," he added, alluding to his work with Brown freshmen, "not with a mentality that already has acquired prejudices. The older students have already formed strong opinions and the challenge there is to open their minds to new viewpoints. But freshmen – ah, they are a pleasure to teach."

Occasionally, Prager ran into opposition from his colleagues at Brown. One such time was his introduction of electronic computers. Carl Runge, with whom Prager worked at the University of Göttingen in the early 1920s, was one of the founders of numerical analysis. As a result of their association in Germany, Prager always maintained an interest – albeit a secondary one – in numerical methods. It was because of this background that he arranged for the first computers at Brown in November 1955.

Prager had the computers installed over the objections of some conservative members of the applied mathematics department who thought that electronic computers would degrade the level of mathematical thinking among applied mathematicians and would tend to replace mathematical arguments with the brute force of computer power. "Exactly the opposite turned out to be true," according to Dr. Walter Freiberger, professor of applied mathematics at Brown. "Without Prager's initiative, the advent of electronic computers in this field would have been delayed by many years. Instead, Brown was among the first universities to use them."

Commenting on this point, Dr. Drucker says that one of Prager's finest qualities was his ability to lead the field. "By the time everyone else had joined in, he was doing something else. Dr. Prager also had an open mind on all things, especially on new directions to take. He never adopted a parochial attitude. If something was good for Brown, he would support it enthusiastically, even if his field wasn't involved. Perhaps this was because his interest was in Brown per se, not just in the engineering and mathematical side of it."

An opportunity to express this broad interest in the University came for Prager early in 1953 when President Wriston asked him to become chairman of the newly formed Physical Sciences Council. This group was composed of the chairmen of the physical sciences departments and the Divisions of Applied Mathematics and Engineering. Its task was to screen all faculty appointments and impose the highest possible uniform standards in these sciences. As one faculty member recently said, "There were a few departments at that time that were not up to snuff. This program raised them up and, by so doing, raised the general level of all sciences at Brown."

In dealing with colleagues in other departments, such as physics and engineering, Prager was all business. He would never walk into a meeting and tell a joke before starting his agenda. Prager did, however, have a sense of humor. It was a humor that usually surfaced on the rare occasions when he talked about his personal experiences. Almost always, the humor was at his own expense.

The story about his first visit to the Biltmore Hotel in Providence is an example. Shortly after he arrived at Brown, Prager was invited to a meeting of all the contributing editors and managing editors of a new publication, *The Quarterly of Applied Mathematics*. Thinking that this would be a very formal occasion, Prager dressed formally – striped trousers, striped tie, and black sack coat. He arrived at the Biltmore Hotel early (as was his custom) and stood in the lobby waiting for his colleagues to show up. In short order, a woman came up to him. "Pardon me, sir," she said, "but where is the ladies' room?" A few minutes later a man approached him. "Can you direct me to the men's room?" he asked. According to Prager, this went on for about twenty minutes. "They thought I worked there," he told a friend. "Never have I worn that suit again."

According to Eleanor Addison, the closest Prager ever came to getting credit for a quick one-liner happened when one of his former pupils, the late Professor Joaquin B. Diaz ('45 Ph.D.), was elected to the Einstein Chair at Rensselear Polytechnic Institute. Also in attendance that day was Professor Herbert J. Greenberg ('46 Ph.D.), one of Prager's graduate students who is now chairman of the mathematics department at the University of Denver. During his graduate school days, Greenberg had wavy hair and kept it very carefully combed. In the intervening years, however, Greenberg had become much more casual in his dress and particularly his hairstyle, to the point where his hair stood on end. Prager was scheduled to speak directly after Greenberg during the RPI ceremonies, and he began this way: "Well, Diaz may have the Einstein Chair but Greenberg has the Einstein hair."

Some have said that Prager got along with everyone at Brown because he never became too close to anyone. In a sense, this is true. He was not a group person. Yet, a factor not generally known was the amount of time he devoted to fellow members of the faculty. "My husband had the kindest heart," Mrs. Prager said recently. "If anyone was in trouble, student or colleague, he'd make every effort to help that person. But it was all low key. There was never any fuss." Comments from former associates bear this out.

"Those of us who were young colleagues of Prager were remarkably fortunate," Professor Rice says. "He was a kind, soft-spoken, and considerate man who would go to extraordinary lengths in the interests of both colleagues and students. Several incidents come to mind. Once, many years ago, I bemoaned in Prager's presence that I did not then subscribe to the Sunday *New York Times*, although I very much enjoyed reading the magazine section. Well, Prager explained that he thought the magazine was perhaps a little too concerned with the trivial, sort of transiently popular issues of the day. Nevertheless, each Monday morning for the next several months he would deposit his own copy of the magazine on my front porch on his way to the University.

"Another time, I went enthusiastically to his office with a solution to a problem on the optimal proportioning of a notch tip. He observed that he thought this was very nice, while noting that he had solved the same mathematical problem, in a somewhat different context, in unpublished works at Göttingen in the late 1920s. He pulled his notes out of a file and commented, in passing, that certain scribbles on the page were made by Prandtl when Prager had reported the work to him. He must have seen my eyes widen because he asked at once if I would like to have the notes. So, now I am the proud owner of a fifty-year-old unpublished document that bears the marks of two of the great pioneers of modern solid mechanics!"

Robert T. Beyer, a former chairman of the physics department, cites another case of Prager's consideration for his colleagues. "Many years ago, I was thinking of leaving Brown," he says. "I had a talk with Dr. Prager and he urged me to stay. Then, without solicitation, he talked to President Wriston and arranged things so that it became possible for me to remain at Brown."

Paul Maeder, who was Brown's first Ph.D. in en-

gineering, admits that Prager extended "a benevolent umbrella" over him on many occasions. "Prager had great influence," he says, "and he didn't hesitate to use it, although usually it was to help someone else."

Another person Prager helped was Professor Kolsky. "If a visiting professor stayed in this country two years or less, he didn't have to pay income tax," Kolsky says. "Well, I was here for two weeks beyond the limit and thought I'd better talk with the Internal Revenue people down town. 'Do I have to pay income tax for those two weeks?' I asked. 'No,' the man replied, with a wicked gleam in his eye. 'You have to pay income tax for *two years* and two weeks. And the sum is $4,000.' I called my wife, but she only laughed uproariously. 'You know we don't have $4,000,' she managed to blurt out. I did know that. So I went to see Dr. Prager. He was very understanding. He was also efficient. He called Wriston, who called a local law firm, and the matter was quickly resolved."

As his secretary, Eleanor Addison spent more time with Prager than almost anyone else. She was especially impressed with his ability to make every person in his department, from the lowest to the highest, feel that he or she was important. "Whether it was myself, the graduate students, or the young staff members – his or her contribution was considered important," Miss Addison said. "No one was ever looked down on. When Professor Prager died, I wrote to his widow and said, 'You're going to get letters telling you what a brilliant scientist your husband was. And I certainly agree with that. But the one thing that stands out in my memory is that he was a very kind man and that he made everyone in our department feel that we were playing a key role in a highly important job.'"

Miss Addison remembers that Dr. Prager was exceptionally considerate of non-academic people and cites an example. "Some years ago we had an old Italian janitor who felt that one of his duties was to save a parking spot for me. Well, one day Prager got to the office ahead of me and took my 'space,' although it was really no one's space. Darned if the janitor didn't ask Dr. Prager to leave. 'That's Ellen's space. That's Ellen's space,' he yelled. As I was driving in, I met Dr. Prager backing out. 'I guess I took your parking spot,' he said somewhat sheepishly. 'We have no spaces,' I tried to explain. 'The janitor told me I had yours,' he added. And he backed right out. Now how many professors would have done that?"

On rare occasions, Prager did get into arguments

with colleagues. When that happened he proved to be a tough adversary. Principally, this was because Prager's style was to present his case with complete Teutonic thoroughness and with no show of emotion.

As a matter of fact, William Prager almost *never* lost his cool. For instance, there was the night the Pragers and several other couples were invited to dinner at the home of Professor Eli Sternberg. Just before dinner, a fire broke out in the kitchen. It was nothing too serious, but the guests did get excited when they saw the flames. Then the firemen came parading through the living room with all their equipment. All the while, Professor and Mrs. Prager sat perfectly still on the living room sofa. They didn't move a muscle. When Professor Sternberg bid his guests good night, he said, "Next time I have a fire, I'll be sure to invite you."

Prager spoke English fluently when he arrived in the United States, although he always retained an accent. In the late 1940s, the department purchased two or three wire recorders, and Prager thought it would be a good idea if he tried them out. "My goodness," he said, after hearing the playback, "listen to the voice of a German spy."

After a twenty-four-year association with a University he loved deeply, Dr. Prager left in 1965 because of

a disagreement with Barnaby Keeney and became professor of applied mechanics at the University of California at San Diego. His departure created quite a stir within the faculty. Many members felt his separation from Brown should never have been allowed to happen. Prager was unhappy, too. He didn't make changes such as this lightly.

In the spring of 1968, University officials agreed that an effort should be made to bring William Prager home. Paul Symonds picked up the phone and made the original contact. Subsequently, he and Paul Maeder met their former colleague in New York City and came to an agreement that brought Prager back to Brown for another five years.

"Dr. Prager was one of the most organized men I have ever known," Professor Symonds says. "His day was organized so completely that he could get much more into it than most people can. In the summer of 1968, when he was planning to return to Brown from the University of California, he came to Providence to check out an apartment. He didn't have much time, but one morning turned out to be more than ample.

"The inspection of the apartment was done in typical Prager style. He had a list of about seventy-five items to check, right down to the details as to the number of switches, and exactly where they were to be located. Because of his organization, decisions were swiftly made and a potentially tedious task was easily completed in a few hours. I recall that at the end of the morning he wanted to check a few decisions with Mrs. Prager, who had remained in California. He did this by telephoning from the manager's office. Occasionally, when privacy was called for, the conversation went on in Turkish. His wife also spoke four or five languages."

Prager also brought this organization into the classroom, according to Professor Freiberger. "Anything he did, he did thoroughly. He'd discuss a problem in the afternoon, take it home with him, and come in the next day with a solution. His lectures were characterized by an exquisite sense of style, perfect timing, and logical construction. His work, in general, was typified by a clarity of conception and a simplicity of execution, in which he managed to bring out the essential features of the problem."

Prager was especially gifted in interpreting the work in his specialty in such a way that people in other fields could easily understand it. When he presented material, it was always clear. The message never got lost.

Miss Gajdowski, who typed many of Professor Prager's reports, says that he worked hard at achieving simplicity. "He would say that although people usually didn't realize it, it took a great deal of work to create a simple equation. 'You are immature if you have pages and pages of equations. Work it all down to the simple.' And he always did just that. As a result, his papers were as brief as he was in his conversation."

The Pragers led a structured life. They would rise each day between 4:30 and 5 a.m., eat a leisurely breakfast, and then relax for an hour or so with the hi-fi before Prager sat down to prepare his day's work. The evening schedule was also rigid. It included a late dinner and more time with his record library (classical chamber music of the eighteenth century through 1830 was his favorite) before he would retire sometime after 10 p.m. Although Ann Prager is an excellent cook, the family usually settled for simple food, but of first-rate quality. A bottle of wine frequently was on the table.

Professor Prager enjoyed a drink now and then, on rare occasions was seen with a Turkish cigarette, but his real weakness was cookies. Mrs. Prager would make them by the hundreds and then have to put the cookies in hiding so that some would be left by day's end. It was a game, really, between the two of them, with Prager constantly looking for an excuse to get into the cookie jar. According to Miss Addison, the professor wasn't above using his house guests as foils in his efforts to satisfy his sweet tooth. "He'd bound up from his chair every once in a while, pass the tray of cookies to each guest, and say, 'But you *must* take one. If you do not, then I cannot take one.' We always obliged. But this would go on all evening until every cookie was gone."

When the Pragers came to the United States, they both drove, although their preference was to avoid traffic by using the car very early in the morning and again before the late afternoon rush hour crowded the highways. Prager took great pride in his car, to the point where he would hastily rush to rub it down if he spotted even a speck of dust. As he grew older, Prager drove less and walked more. Long before his retirement, he had become a familiar figure around the University, walking briskly with his hands behind his back and his trademark, the beige beret, on his head.

Few things gave William and Ann Prager more pleasure than walking. While he was on loan to IBM in Zurich, Switzerland, from 1963 to 1965, Prager and his wife went out for long mountain walks almost daily.

Colleagues at Brown soon learned not to walk up College Hill with Prager, whose long stride left his associates huffing and puffing – and several paces to the rear. "Whenever I had to go somewhere on campus with him," Miss Gajdowski says, "I almost had to run to keep up." Although Prager seldom offered himself the luxury of a vacation, he and Ann did rent a cottage on Nantucket for a week during a particularly hot summer. In exactly three days they were back in Providence. They had already walked the island – and after all, what more was there to do? "Physically, Prager was always in remarkable shape," Professor Maeder says. "Sometimes he would jump around like a small boy."

Occasionally, Prager would find time for pleasure reading. When he did, he often turned to murder mysteries and tales of the sea, which were among the books scattered about his home at the corner of Prospect and Keene Streets. According to a story – probably apocryphal – murder mysteries once got him into a jam. It seems that when Prager first came to this country, he gave a lecture that was heavily sprinkled with profanity, leaving the audience more than surprised. The reason for the questionable vocabulary that day, according to legend, was that he had learned English with a German-English dictionary in one hand and a series of American murder mysteries in the other. Reading the mysteries led him to believe that everyone in this country spoke like Sam Spade.

Other than walking and hiking, Prager had few hobbies. He did love to travel, especially to Paris. He was very meticulous in the hotels he used in Europe and would always make friends with the innkeeper or manager of places he expected to stay in from time to time. In one of his books, Prager wrote: "The quiet hospitable atmosphere of the Hotel Rigihof has again contributed much to the rapid progress of my work."

From the very start, Prager felt that his position at Brown gave him responsibilities in the community. When the Sputnik crisis surfaced in the fall of 1957, it was not surprising that one of the more reasonable statements in the medley of voices speaking out on the subject came from Dr. Prager. In reply to a request from the *Providence Journal* to assess the quality of education in the nation's high schools, Prager said: "In mathematics and science, the average American high school graduate is at least two years behind his European counterpart, and the gap is practically the same at the end of four years of college. This gap can be traced directly to the unwarranted flexibility introduced into our high school curricula. For better or worse, our civilization is now being shaped by technological forces. To understand these forces, future citizens will find mathematics, physics, and chemistry as indispensable as English, foreign languages, and history. The idea that they may be replaced by typing, woodwork, or even by Problems of Democracy and biology is preposterous."

A year later, when Rhode Island was thinking of investing a million dollars in an atomic research reactor, Prager again spoke out. Noting that it was unrealistic to try to decide in advance what would be done with a research reactor, Prager strongly suggested that the reactor be built immediately and uses for it found later. "Even the question of what industries a reactor could be expected to attract here is in large part unanswerable," he said, "because among them will be industries that aren't even in existence now. You can't honestly say what benefits would come from a reactor, but you can be sure that there will be benefits."

As an example of the trigger effect that a first-class research facility has on industrial expansion, he cited the stimulation of the electronics business around Boston by the World War II-spawned Radiation Laboratory at MIT. "I don't agree with the people who say Rhode Island should go after the electronics business," Prager said. "We're too late on that. Let's catch the next bus, and not the one that's already gone to Cambridge."

Prager's son, Stephen, who was thirteen when the family came to this country, was graduated from Brown in 1947 and received his Ph.D. from Cornell in 1951. He's now professor of physical chemistry at the University of Minnesota. His wife, Julianne Heller Prager '46, took her doctorate at Cornell in 1953 and is executive director of technical information at the 3M Company in St. Paul, Minnesota. She currently serves as a member of the Brown Corporation.

During his early undergraduate years, Stephen was torn between majoring in applied math or chemistry, two fields in which he had particularly strong backgrounds. Although Professor Prager was extremely careful not to push his son in either direction, he did

tell several colleagues that he hoped Stephen would *not* major in applied math. "If he becomes better than the father, it will be embarrassing," he said. "If he isn't as good as the father, it will also be embarrassing."

At the time of his retirement in 1973, Brown gave Prager an honorary degree, one of nine he accepted from some of the leading universities all over the world. Equally important to Prager was the retirement banquet in his honor at Agawam Hunt in Rumford. Colleagues from all over the country returned for the occasion, and John Nicholas Brown, Senior Fellow of the University, presided and presented a large painting of Prager, which now hangs in the 1885 Victorian building at 182 George Street, home since 1953 of the applied mathematics department. Professor Prager was always appreciative of things done in his behalf. "Why all this fuss?" he asked that night. "After all, I am only retiring, not dying."

The Pragers retired to Savognin, Switzerland, where there was clear air, open country for hiking, and ample mountains to climb. There were also trips back to the United States, five in all. His final visit to Brown came in the fall of 1979, at the end of a hectic three-week lecture tour in this country. He was noticeably thinner, and he looked tired. "You know, I'm bushed," he told a friend sitting with him at a farewell dinner. "Mrs. Prager said I was taking on too much. She is usually right."

When he returned to Savognin, Prager complained of a pain in his back. A cold had set in. Bronchitis quickly followed, and Prager was hospitalized, first in Chur, and then in Zurich. At times, his condition seemed to be improving. He was in particularly good spirits one afternoon and talked at length with his wife about some papers he was planning to write. When Mrs. Prager arrived back at the hotel a short while later, there was a message that her husband was dead. The date was March 17, 1980. He was seventy-six.

The temptation to pose the question – is the world likely to produce another William Prager? – is difficult to resist. Upon reflection, the answer must be yes. But there will never be another Golden Age, and the great personal contributions of men such as Prandtl, von Mises, and Prager may be replaced by team efforts and computers. Regardless of how the question is answered, there was one William Prager, and he led Brown to unprecedented heights in his field. On that, the record is clear.

ISRAEL J. KAPSTEIN '26
PROFESSOR OF ENGLISH 1928-69

Chapter 6 ✍
He was something of a hero
to students on two campuses

The late S. J. Perelman once recalled the hopes and dreams he shared with his friend Israel Kapstein when they were boys attending Candace Street Grammar School in Providence. "Kappy, who had been reading deeply in the works of Rider Haggard, wanted to be a white hunter in Africa, and I dreamed of one day becoming a world famous shoe salesman. Alas, neither of these goals was to be realized. Our parents were too provincial, too narrow in their outlook, and soon enough our noses were resting against the academic grindstone."

In the years that followed, Perelman was forced to settle for becoming one of the greatest humorists of his era, an era that included Robert Benchley, Ring Lardner, James Thurber, and George Kaufman. Perelman's lifelong friend, Israel James Kapstein, donned the robes of academe and spent a lifetime teaching Brown and Pembroke students about modern novels and romantic poets, with energy left over for some sensitive writing that caught the heartbeat of America in 1941 and propelled him to a place on the best-seller list. His colleagues in the English department called themselves "Kappy's Boys," in deference to the impact he had on them. To his students on two campuses he was something of a hero.

This particular hero was born in Fall River on January 16, 1904. He grew up in Boston, in the atmosphere of

Boston Harbor, and vaguely felt that some day he would automatically enroll at Harvard. Several things happened to change those plans. First, the Kapstein family moved to Providence in 1916. Then, during his high school years, Kappy came under the influence of William T. Peck, an avid Brown alumnus in the class of 1870 who was principal of Classical High. Each spring, Peck took great pleasure in pushing his best students in the direction of his Alma Mater.

According to Kappy, his boyhood was uneventful, even dull. He was an errand boy, soda jerk, newsboy, and mill hand. He also made "honest but uneventful efforts" to make the Classical High football team. This, however, was not the picture Perelman painted on a warm June night in 1969 when some 400 colleagues and friends gathered at Andrews Hall to help ease Professor Kapstein into retirement.

"Man and boy, Kap and I have known each other a matter of fifty-three years, or, in other words, the life span of the Indian elephant – whom, curiously enough, he resembles in repose. We first became acquainted at an institution of learning in the north end of this city, the Candace Street Grammar School. It was there we acquired the fundamentals – the dexterity to clap erasers, a smattering of algebra, and the easy familiarity with the geography of Belgium and Sweden so necessary to humiliate our parents. With that kind of bril-

To Io —
this lyrical little daguerreotype —
Sid

Shortly after he joined the Brown faculty, Kappy
received this portrait from Sid Perelman.

liance, it was unthinkable that we go elsewhere but to
Classical High, where we accomplished a feat unheard
of at that time. You have all seen those gymnasts at the
circus who hang by their teeth from a high trapeze.
Well, Kap and I hung there for four years, threatening
to drop out of the educational spotlight at any
moment.

"There were moments, true, when the temptation to
study was overpowering, when we could have sullied
our ignorance with homework, but we resisted it man-
fully. After all, there were too many cultural distractions
to occupy us – the vaudeville at B. F. Keith Theater,
the movies at the Victory and Fays, and, above all, the
Empire Burlesque on Westminster Street. I know
people whose first recognition of beauty came from
Shelley and Wordsworth. Poor, benighted creatures.
They never saw such visions of loveliness as Rose
Sydell and her Bounteous Belles. Yes, these were the
formative years. But one day childhood toys were put
aside. We had reached man's estate. The mighty Van
Sickle [sic] Gates at Brown University yawned to receive
us – and we yawned right back."

Israel J. Kapstein entered Brown at the start of the
Jazz Age, that dizzy decade that began with the disil-
lusionment that followed the false idealism of World

War I and ended on the same note with the start of the
Great Depression. Woodrow Wilson cried for world
leadership, but his audience was tired of responsibility.
Instead of problems, Americans of the '20s craved
excitement. "How 'ya gonna keep 'em down on the
farm after they've seen Paree?" asked the song hit of
1919. Well, you couldn't. A spirit of frivolity seized the
country, along with a romantic cynicism. This was the
era of the first Youth Rebellion. The gentility of the
pre-war world of Vernon and Irene Castle was replaced
by sensual jazz, rapidly changing morals and manners,
and sheiks with plastered-down hair dancing the
Charleston with flappers born on John Held, Jr.'s drawing board and raised on bathtub gin.

The college campus, usually a mirror of society,
reflected the free-wheeling mood of the decade. Here,
too, old values had gone sour. With their ukuleles and
hip flasks, the self-styled sophisticates of the campus
turned out in droves for football rallies and games.
Some turned out in cars. The captain of the team was
the BMOC, and the "Gentleman's C" became the accepted grade.

When Kappy and 413 other freshmen entered in the
fall of 1922, the social calendar had replaced the
academic calendar in the hearts of many Brunonians.
And the dates marked in red on that calendar were for
the big football weekends with Harvard and Yale, the
Saint Patrick's Day Minstrel, and the Junior Prom.
College songs and cheers were actually *taught* to
freshmen during Chapel, one of the last bastions of
Baptist discipline at Brown. While Sock and Buskin's
first efforts at serious drama played to as few as fifteen
students in the Art Gallery, Brown undergraduates
were shimmying on the dance floors and streaming
downtown to watch Clara Bow, Gloria Swanson, Douglas Fairbanks, and Rudolph Valentino live a life of
fantasy and flamboyance in the silent flicks. And everyone was singing, "In the meantime, in between
time, ain't we got fun?"

Well, almost everyone. There were still some students who went to college for an education, in addition
to a bit of fun now and then. And Kappy was one of
them. "Brown was a great, liberating experience for
Sid and me as well as for a number of fellow students
who were of the same literary bent as we," Kappy told
me on the campus recently. "Our teachers in the
English department were open-minded, knowledgeable, and inspiring men. It was a wonderful teaching
faculty. In addition to the department's advanced writ-

ing course, campus channels of self-expression were open to us: the *Brown Jug* for the humorists among us; *Casements* [a monthly magazine born in January 1923 and written entirely by undergraduates] and the weekly literary supplement of the *Brown Daily Herald* for the more serious."

One of the "inspiring" professors Kapstein talked about was Lindsay Todd Damon, who taught a very popular course in Victorian poetry on the second floor in Manning Hall. Everyone came together in this class – the grinds, football players, and English majors – such was Damon's popularity.

"Damon loved to read from Swinburne," Kapstein said, "and it wouldn't take him long to warm up to his task. His face would get red, his white hair would fly, and he would roll out those lines like an actor on a stage. Sometimes right in the middle of a reading the students would catch the fever of the moment and show their appreciation by stamping their feet in unison until one would think the old floor was going to go crashing down.

"It was something of an experience later to serve under him when he was chairman of the English department. At staff meetings with the young teachers he'd say, 'I want you to rip the guts out of that poem.' This would be said in a Teddy Roosevelt macho style and we'd look at each other and wonder whether or not we could really do what this man expected of us."

Some older alumni will tell you that one of the finest professors who walked the College Green at that time was Ben Clough, a mild man who had no children of his own but who has been accused of being the father of the legendary Josiah S. Carberry. During the mid-1920s, Clough pulled an unusual switch by leaving the English department and joining classics.

Everyone who took a course with Ben Clough loved him. "Ben was widely read, and he gave all of his love of literature to his students," Kapstein said. "Because of the enthusiasm with which he taught the course I'd find myself taking notes on authors I'd never heard of and then literally rushing to the library to get the books by these men."

Another brilliant professor was George W. Benedict, a man who had a great feeling for style, for words, and for the structure of the language. During one of his courses with Professor Benedict, Kappy wrote a novel. This brought the men together for long sessions in Benedict's office on the second floor of University Hall, the professor sitting in his Morris chair with his back to the window and Kappy perched on the window sill looking over Benedict's shoulder as he went over the manuscript.

"I can see him now," Kappy said. "He'd stop, put his pencil on a word, and say, 'I understand what you're trying to say in this sentence, but this word doesn't quite carry the full meaning. Perhaps you might have tried another word.' He would suggest one or two, and then I would say, 'Mr. Benedict, I thought this word conveyed my meaning rather well.' Benedict would walk over to his bookcase. 'Let's look it up in the OED,' he'd say, meaning the Oxford English Dictionary.

"So we'd start by reading the first entry of the word, maybe going back to the twelfth century, and then we'd slowly come up to the present, noting the various changes in the meaning of the word. Frankly, I didn't learn a damn thing about writing a novel from Mr. Benedict, but I became so sensitive about the meanings of words, the overtones, that this has stayed with me all my life. He sensitized me, like rubbing sandpaper over your skin for a long time."

There was a great deal of original writing being done on the Brown campus in the '20s, with many of the writers working professionally in that field after graduation. In Kapstein's class, alone, there was Duncan Norton-Taylor, who went on to become editor of *Fortune* magazine, and Garrett D. Byrnes, who had a long and happy marriage with the *Providence Journal*, ending his career as editor of its much-heralded Sunday supplement, *The Rhode Islander*, where he wrote with nostalgia but without syrup.

And then there was Kappy and his friends – Sid Perelman '25, Nathanael West '25, Quent Reynolds '24, and Jeremiah P. Mahoney '25. It was quite a group, three men of the Jewish faith and a pair of fun-loving Irishmen. Each was an individual, but there was a charisma that brought them together as undergraduates and kept their paths warm through their alumni years. Some of Kappy's fondest memories today revolve around these four men.

Mahoney, the only non-writer of the group, had other virtues. He excelled at Red Dog, a form of poker, and he was a connoisseur of jazz. "I remember one of

Jerry's Red Dog games went until 5:30 in the morning and I had won $92," Kap says. "My only problem was that all but $1.50 was in IOUs. So I did the gentlemanly thing and tore them up. Jerry had a great jazz collection, including some early Louis Armstrong, and every so often we'd head down town to Meiklejohn's on Weybosset Street, take a handful of records into a booth, and hole up for the afternoon."

S. J. Perelman wrote movie scripts for the Marx Brothers, won an Oscar for *Around the World in 80 Days*, and was a regular contributor to the *New Yorker* and other publications. Someone once wrote that his surrealistic, cranky, meticulously polished essays demolished the "warf and woop" of society. He continued his high school interest in drawing by joining the *Brown Jug* as a cartoonist in his freshmen year, but switched to writing when his captions for the college humor magazine drew more attention than his cartoons.

According to Kappy, Perelman had a flair for humor from the time he was a boy. "I heard it as we walked to and from school, and I saw it in his early writing efforts at Classical. I think Ben Clough had quite an influence on Sid's writing while he was at Brown, as did Percy Marks. Sid once told me that of the professionals he was most influenced by Robert Benchley, Ring Lardner, and H. L. Mencken. Of course, Mencken made all the young intellectuals of that period feel good. Sid acquired the knack of using exaggeration to create humor from Benchley, his whacky approach from Lardner, and his cynicism from Mencken."

One of Perelman's first writing efforts in the *Jug* was an ad, with just his initials at the end. It ran this way:

Why Flunk?
Professional tutoring by two Freshmen. We won the Hartshorn Prize and the President's Premium in Algebra and Virgil. Why not have us tutor you in:
    Dante
    Masse
    Billiards
    Psychology
    Money and Banking
    Wrestling
    Biochemistry
We also substitute Chapel and take care of the furnaces. Register now for Phi Beta Kappa – one cowhide bag with every diploma – while they last.
SJP '25

Perelman wrote a variety of material for the *Jug*, including a column, "The Genial Cynic." He occupied the editorial chair in 1924-25, a year in which the magazine's reputation became national. That was when Perelman began to hone the style that brought him fame in the decades ahead. The following piece, typical Perelmania, brought pats on the back from his fellow undergraduates and a summons from the Dean's office:

Students of criminology will find an interesting parallel to the Leopold and Loeb case in the notorious Dugnog Hafiz episode. Dugnog Hafiz, a student of chemistry at Harvard, was suddenly arrested on an inclusive charge of parricide. It was alleged that he had disposed of his parents in some way to his own pecuniary advantage. On investigation it was found that, acting on the suggestion of a famous advertisement, Hafiz had fed his mother and father on raisins and rusty well water until they were chemically about 95 percent iron. He then had them sold to a dealer in scrap iron who, in turn, sold them to a Philadelphia foundry, where they were melted into ten-penny nails and doorknobs. Unfortunately, lack of evidence resulted in the quashing of the indictment against Hafiz, and he was released. He now occupies the Cold-slaw chair of chemistry at Harvard.

Nathanael West came into Kappy's gang late and left early. He was sociable, amiable, and very much interested in being seen on campus in the latest Brooks Brothers suit. He also could be a pampered egotist in the Miss Haversham or Reggie Jackson mold.

Pep West was an excellent writer and was his own biggest fan. His nickname of "Pep" was a misnomer at its grossest. He was slow talking, slow moving, and profoundly lazy. He was tall, stoop-shouldered, took part in almost no campus activity, and studied just enough to get by. West limited his writing efforts to *Casements* and made his debut there with a long, critical, cynical article on Euripides. Indications are that the piece pleased relatives and some friends. Ironically, the four short novels West wrote between 1932 and 1939 – *The Dream Life of Balso Snell*, *The Day of the Locust*, *Miss Lonelyhearts*, and *A Cool Million* – were flops when first published, only later to gain critical acclaim.

"West had a sense of humor, but it wasn't as sharp as Perelman's," Kapstein said. "It was bitter. There was acid in it. But Pep was very much a literary man. His room on campus was lined with books, most of which he had read and committed to memory. He talked about books with enthusiasm and good sense.

But as far as his private interests were concerned, Pep was absolutely unscrupulous. If he borrowed a book from you, you could kiss it goodbye. Or a pair of gloves, or anything else. He never had a sense of guilt or shame for what he did. And yet, I liked him. We became very good friends. Sid later married Pep's sister.

"In his professional writing, Pep really crucified the American middle class. His family had money, but I think Pep looked upon himself as an outsider, like many sons of immigrant parents. The fact that he changed his name from Nathan Weinstein to Nathanael West, the fact that his novels have this negative, bitter, ironical note, indicates to me, at least, that the things he was repudiating were the things that were typical of American life – democracy and the middle class.

"My last memory of Pep dates to the mid-1930s, before his Hollywood years. He and Sid had bought this nice old Dutch-style farmhouse in Bucks County, and Pep was really enjoying the life of a country squire – walking across the wide fields with his gun and his hunting dogs, that sort of thing. We visited him there and thought at the time that maybe Pep had finally found serenity."

Things were never better for Pep West than in 1940. He was married to a charming girl, Eileen McKenney, who achieved vicarious fame as the heroine of Ruth McKenney's best-seller, *My Sister Eileen*, and he was praised by *Time*, which termed him the "most proficient United States surrealist since Poe" and praised his book, *The Day of the Locust*, as "by far the ugliest and best book to date about Hollywood." But on December 12, 1940, the good life ended with dramatic suddenness for Nathan Weinstein when he and his wife were killed in an auto crash near El Centro, California.

The fourth member of Kappy's gang was Quentin Reynolds, a poor Irish boy from Brooklyn who was recruited as a football player by Dave Fultz '98, then a prominent New York attorney and still Brown's all-time scoring leader. The rugged redhead played tackle (he once lumbered 50 yards for a touchdown against Dartmouth), captained the freshman water polo team, and won the college heavyweight boxing championship.

During the Battle of Britain in 1940, America first learned of the true heroism of the British people from two war correspondents, Edward R. Murrow with his radio broadcasts from bomb-torn London, and Quent Reynolds through the stories he sent home to *Collier's*. The first of his more than forty books was a collabora-

tion with Sid Perelman, *Parlor, Bedlam and Bath*. He wrote an original film *Call Northside 777*, and served as associate editor of *Collier's*. His first literary effort at Brown, however, didn't come until his senior year.

One of Brown's most popular diversions in the Roaring '20s was the Saint Patrick's Day Minstrel, normally a series of vaudeville sketches written by the undergraduates. The 1924 production, however, was taken over by Reynolds, Perelman, and West and was a parody of Oscar Wilde's *The Duchess of Padua*. They first named it *The Padded Duchess*, a title that didn't sit well with the administration. So, the trio changed it to *The Plastered Duchess*, a more appropriate title as it turned out because on opening night there were few in the audience who weren't more plastered than padded. Reynolds wrote the script and played the lead (the Padded Duke), West had the minor role of Macaroni but fell asleep during the second act, and Perelman did a surrealistic backdrop which, when torn apart, made excellent souvenirs.

West and Reynolds teamed up on one other occasion, about a month after *The Plastered Duchess* was mercifully put to bed. Early in the spring of 1924 Quent and a college friend started bottling pints of Scotch, gin, bourbon, and rye and then selling them in the men's room of the Green Lantern Tea Room downtown, where Quent had been hired as a bouncer. It was a profitable venture – worth about sixty bucks a week – until a teetotaling alumnus reported the men to Dean Otis Randall. Through a Delta Tau Delta fraternity brother who clerked in the dean's office Quent learned that he and his friend were to be called on the mat the next day. In his book *By Quentin Reynolds*, Red recounted what happened next:

With the thin-lipped face of Dean Randall already seeming to loom before me, I thought of Pep Weinstein. Hurrying to his dorm, I told him what had happened. As one of our good customers who bought at a discount, Pep got the picture at once.

"The dean has ice water in his veins," I said miserably. "We'll never be able to soften him."

"I'm not so sure," Pep said. "Here, take some notes." Handing me a pad and pencil, he began pacing. "You will start by telling of the stroke your father had which has kept him from working for two years. Your sister is still in the hospital recovering from her serious operation."

An hour later I had filled the pad. It was such a heart-rending tale as I read it back to Pep that tears almost came to my

Sid Perelman's *Brown Jug* cover memorialized for all time Quent Reynold's visit to Dean Randall's office.

eyes. The author, listening critically to his work, seemed pleased.

"Take it home and rehearse it until you've got it cold," he ordered. "And, wait, here's a nice trick. Tell him that only yesterday you went to confession and told the priest all about this. He made you promise to give it up and you agreed."

Although mature judgment suggests that Dean Randall was a good man doing a difficult job, he then impressed me as an authentic type from the works of Horatio Alger – the banker who takes delight in evicting a family on Christmas Eve. He waved us to our seats and began the ceremony with a recital of the indictment. His voice seemed to drip satisfaction, as though he enjoyed the dual role of prosecutor and judge. "Have you two anything to say for yourself?" he closed.

"Yes, Dean, I have," I said shakily, rising to my feet. "Of course, we had no idea you were going to call us in today, so naturally we are not prepared with any defense worth your attention, but if you would just give me a few minutes I would like to say —," and I launched into my tale of woe. After five minutes I knew I had the dean hooked. Within ten I, myself, was believing the lies I was uttering, and my partner was sobbing.

The dean took out a handkerchief and mopped his brow. I noted that his hands were shaking. Leaning back in his chair he said in a strangely hollow tone, "I don't want you to ruin your lives. You both have good marks and are due to graduate. You also have perfect records in Chapel. I am going to give you one more chance."

Our savior, who had been waiting for us, asked, in some anxiety, for the verdict. "It went well," I answered, "thanks to you, Pep." That evening we solemnly closed out the operation in the Delt house cellar with Pep as guest of honor. "Gentlemen," he said, raising a beaker of our rye, "to graduation!"

Although Kappy wrote for the literary supplement of the *Brown Daily Herald* and contributed to the book review page of the *Brown Jug*, most of his writing efforts were devoted to *Casements* (he was editor as a senior). The publication was inclined to be on the arty side, but it was an ideal vehicle for the students whose interests went beyond Composition 1-2. The magazine achieved a modicum of distinction once when the Providence police banned a particular issue because of a couple of risqué pieces. Sales on campus doubled overnight after the ban.

Kappy, whose main contribution to the magazine was poetry, had the following verse published in 1924:

Regret
Did you hear just now, gaoler,
    How sweet outside the children sang?
Perhaps tomorrow, they, I forgot—
    Tomorrow I must hang.
And if tomorrow I must hang,
    Aye, that's a sorry thing,
Because tomorrow I had hoped
    Again to hear them sing.

During his last two years in college, when Kap was toying with the idea of becoming a Latin scholar, he was a member of the Latin Club and became avidly interested in Latin poetry. One day Professor Clough suggested that perhaps someone in his class might try rendering some of Martial's poetry into English verse. "Well, of course it was Kap who did," Clough said some years back. "Next day he brought in a poem of Martial's and four different translations, all of them first rate. This was typical. He did four times beyond what was asked of him. This was his style as a student and what he was destined to do as a teacher and a friend."

None of this is to suggest that Israel Kapstein was a grind, living out the dream of his college years in the classrooms and the library. Far from it. He and Pep West were leaders in the formation of a club, the Rabelaisians, a title suggesting – in Kappy's words – "a wine, women, and song approach" to life. It was a shapeless sort of club – no officers, no dues, no admission requirements, and no set meetings. Whenever the men got together they discussed books and writers, had a few drinks, and showed off their wit – and occasionally some wisdom. Today Kappy admits that the members were about as Rabelaisian as a convention of choir boys.

"We enjoyed the sound of our own voices being cynical," Kap said. "It was a cheap cynicism. You could buy it for a nickel. Frequently we didn't know what the hell we were talking about. We didn't even do much carousing, except for putting away some bootleg stuff now and then. A bootlegger visited the dorms regularly and the boys would stash the stuff away, sometimes under the floor boards in the closets."

By the time Kappy graduated he was convinced that he wanted to be close to writing in some fashion. Publishing seemed the easiest route to that objective, and so he accepted an opportunity to work for Alfred Knopf at 730 Fifth Avenue in New York City, where he was a "utility infielder" for the firm for more than a year.

It didn't take Kappy long to make an impression on the boss. Being assigned to the textbook department, he did a quick survey of the mailing list and discovered that more than half the direct-mail material was coming back at a terrific expense. He sat down and wrote to every college and university in the country, asking each to send its latest catalogue, from which he then compiled an updated mailing list.

One afternoon, Mr. Knopf walked into the office waving a document in his hand and asking if anyone could read German. The deadly silence that followed was broken by Kap's voice answering in the affirmative. Knopf wanted a translation of a German publishing contract and wanted it bright and early the next morning. Actually, Kap didn't know very much German, but being an Ivy League graduate he did know how to find a German dictionary. He and the dictionary spent the night together, and a flawless translation was on Knopf's desk the next day.

After that, Kappy was the unofficial translator in the office. As time went by he also prepared indexes, wrote dust jackets, did proofreading, and was asked to read and criticize newly submitted manuscripts. It was excellent training for a man who wanted a career in writing.

For all his efforts, Kap was making the lordly sum of $20 a week. Things in the Big City did get better after six months. He was jumped to $30.

Meanwhile, Kapstein and Perelman were reunited on the top floor of a Greenwich Village flat on West 11th Street. There were two rooms, a bath, and a small kitchen. Supplied with the flat, at no extra charge, was the 6th Avenue El, on which trains would thunder by at regular intervals, breaking up conversations, not to mention an occasional cup and saucer.

In his talk at Kappy's retirement banquet, Perelman sketched a verbal cartoon of their life together in Greenwich Village:

"Put on your seven-league boots and knife through the clouds obscuring New York's rooftops. As you look through the skylight of this dingy apartment below you on West 11th Street, you see us reunited. By some alchemy that can never be explained, both of us had learned to read and write – not well, mind you, but enough to scratch out a meager living. Kapstein, using his new-found literacy, worked for the publishing firm of Alfred A. Knopf, and I, a freelance comic artist, for magazines that inevitably went bankrupt the moment they bought my drawings. Ah, those were halcyon days in the Greenwich Village of 1927. What if we often went to bed hungry, if there was no money to ransom our laundry or pay the rent? Were we down-hearted? Yes we were. We were miserable."

Kap admits that he and Sid lived close to the vest. But miserable? Never. They were young and healthy, and if they didn't eat as often as they would have liked, well, at least they fed well on hope. Though its former Bohemian glories were much diminished, Greenwich Village still had the atmosphere of an artists' colony. Poets in cloaks and capes and painters in paint-spotted pants were still around. Siegel's Restaurant served a filling bread pudding, sparsely dotted with raisins, for only 15 cents. So the two aspiring writers struggled, but survived.

Kappy had his impetuous moments, like charging a Brooks Brothers suit he couldn't afford and then limiting his lunch to soup and a roll for a month or more to help pay for it. When the weather was good, Kap walked from 730 Fifth Avenue at the junction of 57th Street all the way back to his flat at 11th Street, window shopping as he went and browsing in the book stores that dotted his path.

For entertainment there were movies for 35 cents, jazz in Harlem, or the speakeasies. Quent Reynolds had an in at a couple of speaks and took Sid and Kap on the town at least once a week. There were also some inexpensive nights at the Kenmore Hotel playing penny-ante with the night clerk – whose name happened to be Pep West. Pep didn't care whether or not he got caught. It was his hotel.

There are two versions of how Kappy came back to Brown. If you believe Kap, he received either a letter or a telephone call from Professor Benedict inviting him to join the faculty in the fall of 1928. If you believe S. J. Perelman, it happened this way:

"Kap and I used to sit up until four in the morning figuring out ways to improve our lot. Neither of us had the audacity to rob a bank or swindle an immigrant. For a while, we thought of becoming gigolos, but we didn't know any rich, elderly women to adopt us.

"It was a desperate situation that could only be solved by a miracle. And one day it befell us. There was a ring at the doorbell and a uniformed messenger handed me a telegram from Dublin. I had just drawn the winning number in the Irish Hospital Sweepstake. At practially the same instant another uniformed messenger appeared and handed Kap a telegram offering him a post on the English faculty of Brown University.

"Now comes the truly moving part. It was not until many years later that the truth emerged. I was the person sought for the teaching post and it was Kapstein who won the $36. So you see how a trifling clerical error can affect the entire course of one's life."

Regardless of which version you prefer to accept, the point is that Israel J. Kapstein never thought seriously of joining an academic community until Professor Benedict's offer came along. Like Perelman, Kappy had spent time in the West 11th Street flat hunched over the typewriter trying to write short stories. Several came off the assembly line, but none sold. Freelance writing has always been a risky business. That's one reason so many aspiring writers flocked to the colleges and universities in the 1930s. A job on the faculty gave them their bread and butter – and three months in the year to write.

Events moved swiftly for Kappy after his return to College Hill. There was the marriage to his childhood sweetheart, Stella Cohen (they met at Candace Street Grammar School), in June 1928, his master's a year later, the Ph.D. in June 1933, and the birth of his first child, Judith, a month after that. Jonathan was born in May 1939.

One of Kappy's first classes was a theme course under Professor Benedict. "He taught me a valuable lesson at our first weekly staff conference," Kap told me. "The junior members of the English department brought along the themes we had just corrected, and we sat around a large conference table reading, in turn, one of our corrected papers. 'Kapstein,' he said, when I had finished, 'I'm in general agreement, but didn't you notice in the first paragraph there was a break in the coherence of thought? And in the second paragraph he had a very long sentence in the middle and at some point or other he lost control of that sentence and forgot what the tense was?' He criticized the entire theme this way. The next time I went into that staff conference, I had gone over my papers much more thoroughly."

Kappy once said that he had begun his intellectual life by reading on his own. As a book worm "mas-

querading as a fat little boy" he gnawed his way with insatiable appetite through whatever reading matter came to hand. His companion in this bibliomaniacal orgy was Sid Perelman. The only difference between them, according to Kap, was that in the excitement of today's book he forgot the one he had read yesterday, while Perelman carried them all in his head and at a moment's notice could tell you what shenanigans went on in chapter three of *Eleanor Glenn*, which was written in 1907.

"Once one gets to be a reader, one also gets the notion of becoming a writer," Kappy says. "My first writing ambition was to become a poet. I made a little start in poetry while an undergraduate, but when I began graduate study the dream of poetry writing went glimmering. I found myself struggling with a new discipline, the discipline of scholarship, and the scholar in me finally shunted the poet aside."

The young instructor was working for his graduate degrees at a time when the German influence on graduate study and literature was still strong, though beginning to wane. The great German philologists of the nineteenth century had made literary study largely the study of language – its historical development, its structures, and its meanings. As a result, Kap found himself engaged in the close study of Old English, Old French, Old Norse, and Old High German, presumably, he says, "to prepare me for teaching the Old Englishmen, Old Frenchmen, Old Norsemen, and an Old High German."

Eventually, the scholar gave way to the teacher, and by 1933 Kappy was carrying a full academic load. At that point Kappy was convinced that he had come to his life's work – but he came to it at not much more money than he had been making working for Knopf Publishers in New York City. The average faculty salary in 1933 was only $3,111, and salaries at most colleges, including Brown, were frozen. Fred Astaire and Ginger Rogers danced "The Carioca" in *Flying Down to Rio* that year, Babe Ruth won the first annual All-Star game with a home run, and President Franklin D. Roosevelt was using the "fireside chat" to assure people that things were all right. But things were not all right. The world was sinking ever deeper into depression, the banking system had collapsed, men and women were selling apples on street corners for a nickel, and Hitler came to power in Germany.

"It was a world too massive, too fearsome to be ignored," Kappy says. "One could not pretend it was not there and go on with one's private life. The result of the world's pressure upon me forced me to respond to it in the way that a lifetime of absorption in literature led me to respond. Every moment that I could spare from my teaching and steal from my family, I gave to the writing of fiction. This was my response to the world I never made but nevertheless the world in which I was living."

Kappy ducked back to 1910 for his first literary success, a novelette called *The Song A Summer Evening Sings*. It was a nostalgic recreation of experiences common to that generation of Americans who grew up in those very pleasant days just prior to World War I. Spending long hours in the library stacks reading newspapers for the 1906-to-1908 period, Kap filled notebooks with hundreds of notes, of which he used only three. He admits to becoming "a wreck" in the actual writing process, which took more than a year.

Spurred to finish the story by the bait of a $2,000 short-story prize offered by a Boston publisher, Kappy drove the manuscript to Boston and personally handed it to the receptionist. "The rejection slip was back in Providence almost before I got home," he says.

A few weeks later the novelette was neatly packed and sent to a New York publisher, who promptly accepted it for *Story* magazine and sent Kappy a check that paid him about three cents an hour for his research and writing time. The piece was later published by Harper in an anthology under the collective title, *The Flying Yorkshiremen*, which became a 1937 Book of the Month Club selection. Kappy didn't get rich, but his story did bring him considerable critical acclaim.

"If I learned anything in the writing of that novelette," Kappy says, "it was that there is no harder job in the world than working with words. Back in my New York City days when Sid would be bent over his typewriter from morning to night, I'd hear a little chuckle out of him now and then. It wasn't that he was smiling at his own wit, but that he was happy at finding *just* the word he was looking for."

Kap's major opus, *Something Of A Hero*, took its title from perhaps the noblest but most aloof of philosophers, Santayana, who wrote, "The common citizen must be something of a saint, something of a hero."

Four years in the writing, this novel answered many of the questions crying out for answers in 1941: What is the meaning of democracy? How much does the individual owe society? What individual and group values can we live by? What is America and what ought America to be?

Kappy launched his novel of a small Midwestern city and its typical American citizens on the high tide of Fourth of July emotions in 1907. It was the era of Theodore Roosevelt, the Strenuous Life, the Square Deal, and resurgent patriotism under the Big Stick. Then the author skips ahead to July 4, 1917, with its war songs and war speeches. The youngsters we got to know in 1907 are now either in the Army or getting ready to go in. The third look is July 4, 1929, an era of high hopes and great expectations. The kids of 1907, the soldiers of 1917, are crowding their elders for a place in the sun.

Something Of A Hero is a microcosm of an American town as the early twentieth century rolls slowly away into history, but Kappy stays away from preaching. And he waves no flags. Fred T. Marsh, writing in the *New York Herald-Tribune*, said that Kapstein was "a story teller of considerable virtuosity" and added: "There are remarkable portraits from the life of this small city gallery – that strawberry blonde, the tin-horn crook, and the Armenian confectioner make a triangle that you are not likely to forget."

When *Something Of A Hero* shot high on the bestseller list in 1941, Kappy found his work in company with Hemingway's *For Whom the Bell Tolls* and John P. Marquand's *H. M. Pulham, Esquire*. The Literary Guild made it an alternate selection, England gave it rave reviews, and the novel was translated into Norwegian and Swedish.

"The book did well," Kappy says, "so well that it bought me a house. The theme – the odds of democracy maintaining itself, being a living force in the lives of individuals – was popular in the early 1940s when the world was engaged in a bloody war that put democracy on the line.

"Writing, any sort of writing, requires discipline," Kap continues. "You have to develop a writing habit, sitting down at your freest time of day and not getting up until you've written something. Some days you'll be bone dry. But there will be other times when your fingers touch that typewriter and the words are going to flow. Words meet words and ideas meet ideas. It's a wonderful feeling. It's also tiring. I'd work from 9 to 1 each day, but sometimes I'd be so carried away that I'd go back at it and work 'til 5. But the next day I'd be completely exhausted."

After *Something Of A Hero*, Kappy turned to short story writing and found a ready market for his wares in *Good Housekeeping*, *Collier's*, and other leading magazines. The short story is not necessarily easier to write than a novel; it's just different. To be effective, the short story has to be bound up tight, like the mechanism of a wrist watch. This usually means constant rewriting. Kap worked on one job over fifteen or sixteen times, polishing it with each go-round and not minding the time and effort because he sensed that this one was going to be something special. Just as he finished, after months of hard work, he got the idea for another short story, this one with a trick ending.

"I knocked that second story off in one sitting," Kap says. "No problems whatsoever. Then I sent them both off to my agent. 'I'm sending you a story that I've worked very hard on and which I'm sure will sell,' I told him, 'but I'm also enclosing something I banged out within a few hours. If you don't like that one, throw it in the basket.' In a few weeks I received a letter saying, 'The trick-ending story sold to *Collier's* for $1,200. I had your other piece out twenty-one times and nobody wants it.' You know, writing is such a crazy business."

But all this time Kappy was a teacher. He'd never cheat on that. By the 1940s he was teaching writing courses in the short story and the novel, a section on the Romantic Period of English literature, and his much-admired course on the modern American and British novel, for juniors, seniors, and graduate students. The undergraduates referred to it simply as "Kappy 172."

Professor Mark Spilka '49, chairman of the English department two decades later, took the 172 course and lives to tell about it. "The course was always crowded, about 200 students," Spilka said some years back. "One remembers the inevitable charts he drew upon the board and the passages he read from the novels. Kappy's lectures had wit and charm and were delivered with sardonic style. Most important to me was the sense they gave of a liberal conscience at work in the world of fiction. Also unforgettable is that long, *long* reading list he threw at us!"

There was a Kapstein style in the classroom. He was never inclined to baby his students. In fact, he liked to bait them, sometimes to the point of provoking anger. "When the emotions are stirred, education begins," he would say.

Kappy was particularly fond of his course on the Romantic Period. He didn't subscribe to the theory, popular at colleges in the early 1960s, of spending an entire semester trying to decide what some ancient author *really* meant in the middle three words of the fourth line of the second stanza of some obscure poem. He wanted his students to learn history and philosophy with their literature. And this was the accepted way of teaching the subject until this other foolish fad came along, ran its course, and died.

"One reason I enjoyed teaching literature is that if you want to do a good job you have to know so much besides literature," Kap told me. "You certainly have to have some notion of political movements when you consider that people like Byron, Shelley, and Keats were all political revolutionaries in their youth. In other words, to understand what the poets are saying, and why they are saying it, you first have to understand the age in which they lived. So you mix the pot, adding a touch of history and a touch of philosophy and maybe a dash of politics to your main dish and, you hope, when the semester ends your students have learned some literature but have also become better-educated individuals."

In the fall of 1936 a highly promising student scored well in the freshman placement exam, was assigned to an honors section, and found himself with nine or ten other classmates at a conference table presided over by Professor Kapstein. The student's name was E. Howard Hunt '40. He recently talked freely about Kappy to me.

"I saw him first seated at the end of our seminar table in University Hall. Jaw jutting. Powerful fingers drumming. Eager to begin. Effortlessly he dominated the room, involved my classmates and myself, and quickly brought us into harmony with his intent and purpose. I. J. Kapstein was obviously a man to soar with among the spheres of intellect. A man to play mumbly peg with on the green grass.

"Coming from a western New York public school, I was accustomed to grandmotherly teachers and was totally unprepared for a male instructor who was informal, Jewish, a hairy chested baseball enthusiast and camp counsellor, and seemingly knowledgeable of all things. Kappy's questioning had a gentle, depreciatory quality that diminished me to ant-size, but his own self-depreciation was a restorative leaven. Occasionally he'd insert the Garment District phrase, 'Such a gorgeous guy like me,' that startled me until I came to understand that my professor used slang and humor to puncture pretentiousness among students. That device showed us explicitly that Kappy was not just an austere Ivory Tower scholar but a man who had traveled the streets with a receptive ear and could grapple with life on whatever terms it chose.

"Once in discussing novel themes, Kappy remarked that he had always been interested in the common man's struggle for the necessities of life. I quickly said I had always been interested in the *uncommon* man's struggle for the luxuries of life – and that brought me a withering glare. Thereafter I refrained from elitist remarks, however jocular.

"Recognizing a superior being, I began to copy Kappy's manner of dress: brogues, wool socks, flannels, tweed jacket, button-down shirt, rep and challis ties. And while I was undergoing that external change I found that the mental and cultural stimulation I was receiving from Kappy was working needed changes in me. I was hypnotized by his persona, and for the first time in my life began to study in earnest and prepare for our seminar encounters. I wanted to please him, receive his approbation, and that desire marked a watershed in my life."

In time Howie Hunt became a baby sitter for Kappy and Stella, learning how to burp a baby while the Kapsteins enjoyed an occasional night away from home. There was always a sandwich in the refrigerator, a glass of milk, and sometimes a finger or two of Scotch. More important from Hunt's point of view was his unimpeded access to Kappy's library, which he tried to devour on the theory that if those books had made Kappy what he was, then he *had* to acquire their knowledge.

"In class and out, Kappy called me 'young Hunt,'" Howard continues. "It was a distinction I reveled in, for it showed he was aware of me. I was a swing trumpeter playing at most college and fraternity functions, and often saw Kappy and Stella, handsomely attired, among the dancers. His fondness for jazz formed another bond between us.

"That my professor, and by then, my friend, was a successful creative writer sharpened my own creative instincts and inspired me to write a novel for his course in my senior year. It was not a very good novel, but two years later, while in the Navy, I produced *East of Farewell* and at Kappy's suggestion sent it to an editor with whom he had worked at Knopf. Thus began my career as a novelist.

"After his son, Jonathan, was born I realized Kappy was spending hardly any time working on his novel, *Something Of A Hero*. When I remonstrated, he said, 'Look, young Hunt, I brought my children into the world. The least I can do is give them my time.' Responsibility. Not at all congruent with the stereotype of creative writers.

"I was then, and am now, overwhelmed by the vitality, the affirmative masculinity, the intellectual fervor of this man who was quite literally my first teacher. But he was much more than that. He was my guide to unexplored realms of literature, my companion in a great adventure of the mind, a friend and confidant without a gap of generations.

"In that era I could have easily drifted through four years of Brown in a haze of beer and Wellesley weekends. But in me Kappy saw more than I knew was there. He sparked the tinder, nursed the glow, and gained my everlasting gratitude."

Howard Hunt went on to become perhaps Brown's most prolific writer, with many of his spy thrillers written under a pseudonym. The list of men who studied writing under Kappy and then went into the field professionally is lengthy. It includes Burt Shevelove '37, who is perhaps best known for the musical comedy *A Funny Thing Happened On the Way To the Forum*; Charlie Mercer '39, who wrote a dozen novels, including the best seller, *Rachel Cade*; Jack Newcombe '48, associate editor of *Sport* magazine in its formative years and later London bureau chief for *Life*; and George Kennedy '41, executive head of Kiplinger Publications.

Kappy's popularity extended to the Pembroke campus, where he won "Favorite Professor of the Year" honors with monotonous regularity. In 1939 he was "married" to the entire Pembroke senior class in a ceremony with five bridesmaids attending. At his retirement banquet, the late Anne Byam O'Neil '41 said that the essence of Kap's charm was that he had something different for each student – encouragement for the shy, a curb for the excessive, a pin prick for the pompous, and a listening ear for the lonely. "He saw through all the college crises of heart and head," Anne added. "It was mostly soothing. Sometimes scolding. But above all – listening. Why do we all forget how much the young just need to be listened to!"

Actress Ruth Hussey Longenecker '33, writing from her home in Carlsbad, California, says that it seems like yesterday that she sat enthralled in Professor Kap-

stein's class. "To quote Shelley:

a sensitive plant in a garden grew
and the young winds fed it with silver dew.

And so did Kappy as he elucidated on the backgrounds, thoughts, and philosophies of the poets of the Romantic movement. Sometimes teacher and author become blurred into one. It was hard to tell which was which – until exam time when we were jolted from our reveries with such sticklers as this: 'Identify:

—Fair seed-time had my soul, and I grew up
Fostered alike by beauty and by fear.'

Give up? It's Wordsworth."

If a professor stays around long enough his former pupils may become his colleagues. And if he's very lucky one of his ex-students may become his departmental chairman. That's what happened to Kappy when Mark Spilka took over the chairmanship of the English department in the late 1960s. Spilka once said that Kappy was one of those enviable professors who moves with confidence through all academic assignments. "I once worked with Kap on making up a pre-

Kappy was a visiting professor in Saigon during the early 1960s.

liminary exam in the modern period. It took us about two and one half hours to pull together an effective and well-structured exam, and I marveled at the way he was able to pull feasible and imaginative questions alike out of the air with almost magical resourcefulness.

"Kap also happened to have a particular gift for articulate indignation. He could be more effectively, persuasively, and appallingly indignant than any professor I've ever known. Maybe that is the reason for his eternal youthfulness. He could get out of his system, with an amazing command of what he was saying, all those fed-up and outraged feelings which academic flesh is heir to. Also remarkable is the fact that after he had fought his fight and delivered his tirades – whether he won or lost – he would lapse into the most cheerful sweetness of mind and manner imaginable."

Despite the sweetness of which Spilka speaks, Kappy was frequently tormented in mind and heart over the time he was able to give to his three loves – family, teaching, and writing. With Kap, his family came first. His writing – and he had so much talent – eventually got short shrift. Right in the middle, not too far behind his love of family, came his respect for the teaching profession. It was not surprising, therefore, that during his last year or two on the job Kappy became extremely bitter over the drastic change in the attitude of the undergraduates. This was the start of the student rebellion, and Kap didn't like what he saw or heard. At his retirement banquet he spoke with candor about that period:

"In my maturity I came to know what every teacher comes to know – that teaching is not simply the communication of information and skills but the transmission of human values. Once this transmission becomes the teacher's goal he comes to know the agonies and exaltations of his vocation. He challenges himself in the classroom six to nine times a week, every time he delivers a lecture. He sweats before he begins, rejoices if he feels the current flowing back and forth between him and his students, comes out of the classroom fairly intoxicated if he has touched them alive or else overcome by self-disgust if he has failed. What he really seeks is not communication but communion. And out of such communion between student and teacher true education flows.

"So it is saddening to see on our campus today the violence that disrupts and destroys this communion. Such violence does not merely cut off entrances to offices, classrooms, and libraries, it cuts off the lines of communication between teachers and students, lines which are the prime reason for the University's existence."

Many of Kappy's colleagues felt the same frustrations, but most remained quiet. Kap spoke out in real anger and hostility. Since Kappy had long held the reputation of being an outspoken liberal, his stance both surprised and disappointed some of his liberal friends. A few years later he surprised them again when he stuck by Howard Hunt in the aftermath of Watergate.

It had become a tradition for the Kapsteins to visit the Hunts each year. They were good reunions, with talk of their shared love for fine fiction, reminiscences of days past on College Hill, or maybe some time in front of the TV watching a football game. There was a bond between the liberal Jew and the conservative WASP. And the tragedy of Watergate and Hunt's role in it didn't break that bond.

"One of the things that kept our friendship warm was that we recognized that our views were miles apart and we shied away from discussing things that might lead to an argument," Kappy said recently. "I guess you could say that our relationship is paternal, or grandpaternal. I do know that what developed over the years was almost like a family feeling. One of Howard's young children tied me to a chair one time to prevent me from leaving."

Hunt was grateful for Kappy's support through the difficult times and discussed the situation with me.

"Prying reporters interviewed Kappy about me, their assumption being that Hunt was an unlettered thug. They found it incredible that anyone could say a good word about me, and Kappy said many in my behalf. He was one of only a handful of friends who stayed loyally by me, supporting me during the worst period of my life, helping me to emerge whole from prison. Typically, Kappy honored his principles even though he absorbed criticism for doing so."

Those who know Israel J. Kapstein realize that as satisfying as teaching was to him, there were creative things that he could have done with almost as much satisfaction. He might have been just as happy as a writer or a sculptor or a horticulturist. As a writer he was something of an experimenter moved by an itch to try every kind of writing there is – poems, short stories, novels, plays for children, scholarly articles, translations, and a textbook.

Sometimes when he was hard at work doing the inescapable chores of teaching – correcting hour exams, reading term papers, grappling with final exams – he resorted to temporary relief. Close by in his study were sharp jackknives, a set of small chisels, a variety of sandpapers, and a piece of wood. At his feet were spread newspapers to catch slivers and chips, and with papers and pencils laid aside for the moment he sought relief from words by happily seizing a piece of wood to work on. In the simple, semi-abstract form he followed, Kappy became an accomplished sculptor. "If painting is for the eye and music is for the ear, then sculpture is for the hand," he says.

A man needs fresh air, and his body needs to be recreated. So, Kappy became a gardener. He never grows anything as mundane as carrots or cabbage. He grows flowers – perennials such as iris, peonies, and lilies and annuals such as zinnias, snapdragons, and marigolds. Who knows, some day, in tribute to his friend Wordsworth, he may put in a host of golden daffodils.

There are also those who claim that Kappy could have achieved a modicum of success as a billiards hustler if the cupboard ever became bare. But that's another story for another time.

These are some of the things Kappy might have done if he had not become a teacher. But he *was* a teacher, one who loved his profession and his college; and when the hour of parting came, the transition was not easy. Andrews Hall was hushed as Kappy came to the end of his speech and bid his goodbyes to those 400 friends at his retirement dinner:

"One feels the severance from a long familiar and long beloved life, severance from students and colleagues, from habitual comings and goings to one's office and to the libraries, from the walk to the classroom across the campus in all the seasons over all the years.

"Not that the campus is forbidden to me. I'm withdrawing on my own. I haven't been expelled. Just the same, I don't belong to the college now as I used to. At least I don't belong in the special way that put me at the center of the University's life. Now, at best, I must be an attentive observer rather than an active participant in her life. Does this hurt? Yes, it does!"

Kappy is 77 at this writing, still living at Dexterdale Road in Providence, still tackling the typewriter when the spirit moves him, and still carving a niche for himself with his sculpture. He and Stella enjoy the cold winter months, but they enjoy them from the comfort of Longboat Key on Florida's Gulf Coast. Their daughter, Judith, is associate dean of the Faculty of Arts and Sciences at Rutgers, and Jonathan is bureau chief of *Business Week* in Johannesburg, South Africa.

"I've been away from Brown for such a long time," Kap said last summer. "I'm even away from Providence for almost half the year. One hopes that people won't forget."

His long-time friend and colleague, Elmer M. Blistein '42, thinks they will not. "His ability as a writer is recognized by all who can read, his perception is honored by all who can think, and his wit is appreciated by all who can feel."

Chapter 7 🕮
Brown's ambassador of good will
for thirty-nine years

A healthy number of college professors can flash a Phi Beta Kappa key at the slightest provocation. But how many can also boast of once having caught the humming fast ball of a youthful Babe Ruth?

One who could was the late Wally Snell, former professor of natural history, chairman of Brown's Department of Botany, and one-time catcher for the Boston Red Sox in their glory days in the second decade of this century. For the better part of his years at Brown, Snell led a double life, dividing his time – and his loyalty – between the classroom and the athletic field.

As a botanist and a scholar, Wally Snell achieved international recognition. At one time he was generally considered to be the world's leading authority on boletus, a tubular stipulate mushroom. He also discovered several forms of mushrooms in the Northeast that were not thought to exist in that region.

These achievements brought Snell world-wide recognition. But the pipe-smoking, mild-mannered professor also took great pride in the fact that in his first twenty years at Brown (1920-40) he coached forty-seven athletic teams in baseball, football, basketball, and soccer and served as chief scout under two head coaches of football.

At some point during 1940, Professor Snell bid a fond farewell to the world of sport to devote more time to research and teaching. There were a few "thank-you"

dinners and a string of gifts, most of them cans of tobacco to soothe the hunger pangs of Snell's pipes. Then, early in 1943, Brown's athletic director, Tom Taylor '25, joined the Army. The powers that be looked to the botany department for Taylor's replacement. Suddenly, Wally Snell found himself leading two lives again.

It was much the same when Wally officially retired from the University in 1959. At his farewell party, Wally stood up, took a few puffs on his pipe, and said all the appropriate things, such as hating to leave the campus and how he would miss all his many friends and associates. Only with Professor Snell it didn't mean a thing. On Monday morning he was back at his desk on the second floor of Rogers Hall. It was business as usual.

The schedule Wally followed after his "retirement" was a model for how every man who wants to remain young and vital should chart his course in the autumn of life – provided, of course, that he has the strength, heart, and endurance of a Wally Snell.

He was at the office by 8 a.m., was back from walking the dog of his then associate, Esther Dick '31, '34 A.M. (who became Mrs. Snell on October 11, 1975, after the death of Wally's first wife), and had his pipe lit by 8:35. His retirement schedule included an eight-hour day, six days a week – except for those occasions when he "sneaked in" for a few hours on Sunday. "No damned interruptions on the Sabbath," he would say. In almost apologetic fashion, Snell would acknowledge that he cut his schedule back to four days a week during the summer months.

Esther Snell has an idea why her husband worked so long and so hard. "In the summer of 1970," she says, "Wally's most famous book, *The Boleti of Northeastern North America*, came off the press. Three months later some of the information in the book was outdated. Wally had to keep working just to stay even with all the changes that were taking place in the field that he loved so much."

The daily routine of Professor Snell didn't vary greatly until shortly before his death on July 23, 1980. He was ninety-one.

Walter H. Snell was born in West Bridgewater, Massachusetts, on May 19, 1889, the son of Alton and Clara Leach Snell. The family moved to Brockton a year later, where Mr. Snell went to work at the Brockton Public Market as a meat cutter. During his youth, Wally worked in the market after school and on weekends.

There were five children in the Snell family and all went to college, thanks to financial help from Grandfather Leach, a veteran of the California Gold Rush days of 1849. As a cabinet maker back home after his days on the trail, Leach produced equipment for the miners and made himself a small fortune. Most of Snell's boyhood summers were spent on the Bridgewater farm of his grandfather. Wally attributed his ability to spin a good yarn to listening to his grandfather tell tall tales while the old man sat in a rocker on the front porch during those long summer evenings.

"Walter had all the talent in the family," his brother Raymond wrote recently. "When he was in high school he started painting in water color and became so proficient that one of his teachers at Brockton High suggested he attend art school instead of college. He also began to play the guitar. He had no instruction, and there was no artist or musician in the family. He developed those talents on his own.

"It was the same with his athletics. He played a lot of sandlot baseball, and in the summer he played at Camp Durrell, a YMCA camp in Friendship, Maine.

His athletic talent must have come down through his father, but his competitiveness came from his mother. She was determined that her children were going to get an education. She seriously questioned whether high school sufficiently prepared students for college and encouraged his going to Andover."

Mrs. Snell was deeply religious, went to church twice on Sunday, and kept an especially tight rein on the Sabbath activities of her young children. The boys were allowed to take a short walk – strictly for exercise – but there was to be no ball playing on Sunday. Sometimes Wally beat the rules. He would meet friends while on his walk, one of the boys would bring along a football or baseball, and the gang would get together in an empty field for a quick game.

At Brockton High, Snell played a year of both football and soccer, was captain of the basketball team, and attracted special attention for his skills as a baseball player. He was the regular Brockton High catcher for four years and captain his last two seasons. He also ranked number one in his class academically.

Wally once recalled for me that there were advantages to being a good baseball player in the Brockton area in the early years of this century. "Amateur baseball was on the rise, Sunday afternoon games drew good crowds, and the managers were able to make sure that their players had a little jingle in their pockets at the end of the day."

Because of his exceptional skills as a student and baseball player, Snell was offered a scholarship to Phillips Academy in Andover, Massachusetts. He was captain of Andover's first undefeated basketball team and played two more seasons of baseball. He also won the Latin and German Prize and received the highest honor at the Academy – the Yale-Andover Cup, given annually to the best student-athlete.

At that time Andover was a prep school for Yale, with the overwhelming majority of the senior class heading for New Haven, maybe 10 percent for Harvard, and the balance matriculating at schools such as Brown, Dartmouth, Princeton, or Amherst. Traditionally, the winner of the Yale-Andover Cup continued his education at New Haven. Wally Snell caused something of a furor on campus when he announced on Commencement Day that he was heading for Brown.

"I was all set to go to Yale," Wally said a few years ago. "Signed, sealed, and almost delivered. Even went to New Haven with some Andover friends in the spring of 1909 and picked out my room. But things happened and I decided to make the switch to Brown."

Basically what happened was that Snell was friendly with two Brown students from Brockton – Ken Nash '12 and Art Staff '11 – who were prominent members of the Brown baseball team. They worked on Wally, arguing that Lenny Burdette, also a talented catcher, had gone from Andover to Yale the previous year and might have the receiver's job nailed down. It was a good argument, for Snell had been forced to play right field his first year at Andover while Burdette worked behind the plate.

"There was quite a commotion when Walter switched from Yale to Brown," his brother Raymond wrote. "He was such a good athlete that there was even some talk about him getting paid to make the switch. Of course that was nonsense."

Snell entered Brown in 1909 and played one year each of football and basketball and four years of baseball at a time when Brown was regularly rated among the nation's top collegiate teams. He captained the Bruins his senior season and was a two-time All-America choice. He was president of his class for two years, won his Phi Beta Kappa key as a junior, and was awarded the Sigma Xi key after he was graduated.

The 1911 football team, on which Snell was an alternate fullback, finished 7-3 under Coach Edward North Robinson '96. Captained by the fiery Bill Sprackling '12, a three-time Walter Camp All-America quarterback, the Bruins lost only to Harvard, Yale, and Carlisle.

Snell had vivid memories of the Carlisle contest, which was played on Thanksgiving morning at Andrews Field off Camp Street, the home of Brown football from 1899 until the Stadium was constructed in 1925. Some 5,000 fans (a complete sellout) paid $1 each to watch Sprackling go up against one of the finest football players the country has ever produced, the big Indian, Jim Thorpe. Coached by Pop Warner, Carlisle had a 10-1 record coming into the game and were 11-1 when they left after a 12-6 victory.

"Thorpe was immense," Snell said a few years ago. "I was backing up the right side of the line late in the game when Jim headed in my general direction. He ran right over our right end and zeroed in on me. He was built like iron and, gawd, what legs. But I put his ankles right together and dropped him. When you tackled Thorpe you felt the impact from the tip of your toes to your scalp."

Snell was a starting guard on the basketball team when it went down to New Haven to play Yale during the 1910-11 season. Just before the game a Brockton student at Yale introduced Wally to the man he would be playing against. The name of the Yale forward was Bob Taft, later the Republican Senator from Ohio. The late William P. Burnham '07 recalled the situation some years back.

"After the game," Burnham wrote, "Wally's friend said to young Taft, 'Well, how did it go?' 'All right, I guess,' Taft replied, 'but that young Snell is the toughest Christian I ever played against.' Snell's reply to the same question was, 'Taft had a bad habit of intentionally sticking his finger in my eye.'"

Baseball had been a major sport at Brown since the 1890s. In 1896, the Bruins went through the season 20-4 and then defeated Chicago, the Western title holder, in the best-of-three series for the intercollegiate championship. During Snell's four varsity seasons, Brown had a 69-21-2 record, won an Eastern title in 1912, and was ranked second nationally to Yale in 1913.

The late Harry Pattee '06, who was coach during the Snell years, once described Wally as "a stylish catcher who could handle pitchers well, throw with accuracy, and hit for a high average." He also said that Snell was completely fearless, whether it was in blocking the plate, running the bases, or chasing a foul ball.

Shortly before he died, Bill Burnham recalled the day he first saw Snell. "Wally was catching against Princeton at Andrews Field in 1912. It was the first of the ninth, two out, and a count of three and two on the batter. The Brown pitcher threw a high, hard one that the hitter fouled off the bare hand of the Brown catcher, who jumped high in the air and yelled: 'Romulus, Remus, Darnation, Galumpus, Jupiter Priest.' Rather astonished, I asked a friend what was going on. 'Oh, that's Wally Snell,' he replied, 'and that's his special brand of profanity.'"

College baseball players were not allowed to play summer ball, although most of the good ones did, using an alias to hide their identity. The penalty for being caught was severe – loss of eligibility for a full season. Wally couldn't resist the opportunity to play during the summer, but he took special precautions. "For one thing, I played in the summer leagues that were a long way from home," he once said. "Also, I kept my mask on from the time I walked on the field until I left the park after the game. That way, no one could recognize me."

One June day back in 1913, Captain Snell was catching his last game for Brown, the traditional wrap-up contest against the alumni. Daff Gammons '98 was at the plate, and Eddie Eayrs '16 was pitching. Daff fouled off a pitch, and the ball smashed Wally's thumb. The injury couldn't have come at a worse time. He had been signed by the Philadelphia Athletics of the American League and was due to report to Connie Mack, the A's manager, later that week.

When he learned of Snell's injury, Mack sold the catcher's contract to the Boston Red Sox. This was at the beginning of a great baseball era in Boston. The club finished fourth that year but moved up to second in 1914 and then won the American League pennant and world championship in 1915, the first of three World Series titles in the next four years. The team was managed by Bill Carrigan, had Smokey Joe Wood and Dutch Leonard as pitchers, and featured the finest outfield in the game at that time in Duffy Lewis, Tris Speaker, and Harry Hooper.

"Wild Bill Carrigan, one of the toughest players in baseball, was the first-string catcher," Wally told me in a 1972 interview. "Right away, I knew I wasn't going to see too much playing time. But Carrigan could handle players, run a team, and was tops on strategy.

"The layout of Fenway Park was different then. The bullpen consisted of nothing more than a few benches in center field. No one ever hit the dead ball that far in those days so we were seldom disturbed. If a player was still suffering the effects of the previous evening's entertainment, the Fenway Park bullpen was a nice place to catch some shuteye. In left field there was an embankment about 10 feet high sloping up toward the wall. We had a substitute outfielder who never mastered the art of climbing that hill for a fly ball. One day someone hit a vicious liner that took two hops and went right through this fellow's legs. The ball continued up the embankment, with our man giving honest pursuit. Then a funny thing happened. The ball hit the wall, shot back down the incline, and went through the left fielder's legs again. He drew two errors on the same play."

Snell's early days with the Red Sox were pleasant enough – good pay, pretty fair food, the best of hours, and nothing to do but get into uniform, sit on the bench, and watch a big league game every afternoon. His major league debut came when Carrigan sent him up as a pinch hitter. On his way to the plate, Wally asked Harry Hooper what he should look for from the pitcher. "Go for anything you can reach," was the only advice he received. Nick Culp was hurling for Cleveland that

day and he got two quick strikes with roundhouse curves. Rule number one for pitchers is always throw a rookie the curve ball. The third pitch was also a curve, but Wally drove the ball past the lunging second baseman, Nap Lajoie, for his first major league hit.

Bill Burnham saw Snell catch several times that summer. On one occasion, he watched him put on quite a demonstration of how to throw a runner out at second base. "Between the games of a double header some of the Red Sox and New York Yankee players had contests at running the bases, throwing from the outfield, that sort of thing," Burnham wrote. "Wally was involved in another one of the activities, accuracy for throwing from home plate to a bushel basket that was set on second base. Of his first ten throws, eight landed in the basket."

In the spring of 1915, Snell went South with the Red Sox for spring training in Hot Springs, Arkansas. It wasn't the best of springs for the Brown All-American. Ultimately, he was cut from the roster and shipped to Toronto of the International League just before the team broke camp. It was during spring training in 1915 that Snell first met Babe Ruth, then a rookie left-handed pitcher with the Red Sox. "The Babe was a completely irresponsible kid," Wally once told me. "He ate too much and drank too much beer, but, oh, what ability when he stepped on the mound and fired that heavy fast ball into my glove. Everyone in camp knew that the kid was going to make it big, but none of us dreamed that his success would come as a hitter instead of as a pitcher.

"Money never stayed in the Babe's pockets very long. He'd get his spending money on Friday and by Monday morning he was broke again. The Babe would come back to the boarding house with boxes of brightly colored silk shirts, sport shoes, and other things he was never going to wear. We figured he was trying to make up for all those years in the Baltimore orphanage.

"There wasn't a mean bone in Ruth's body, but he could sure do some crazy things. One evening after supper the players were sitting on the front porch of the boarding house when Babe came riding up the center of the street on a bicycle that was almost completely dwarfed by his hulking form. He looked comical as hell riding back and forth in front of the players, ringing the bike's bell, and wearing a grin a mile wide.

"One of Babe's problems was that he never knew when to stop his shenanigans. When some of us got to the park the next day there was Babe, in uniform, riding the bike around the base paths, and cutting up the dirt pretty good. Carrigan gave a real dressing down to the Babe, who just stood there, head down, taking it. Whenever he got caught at anything, Babe was like a repentant child – for about ten minutes. Then he was the same old fun-loving Babe again."

After playing for Toronto in 1914 and for Rochester of the same league the following summer, Snell spent a year with Manchester of the New England League before deciding that it was time to forget baseball and get on with his life's work. The broken thumb had never healed properly and remained a handicap, especially when he was batting. But Wally never expressed any regrets. "There are other things in life besides baseball," he told me one afternoon. He paused, and added: "But it sure would have been fun to have caught the Babe in the major leagues."

Snell had returned to Brown in the fall of 1913, both to further his education and to kill time while waiting for another baseball season to start. His undergraduate major was in biology, but he took graduate courses in a different field – botany. It didn't take long for Wally to decide that he preferred plant to animal pathology. He moved along rapidly in his new field, was an assistant to Professor Harlan T. York in botany in 1914-15 and again in 1915-16, and earned his master of science degree in 1916.

As a botanist, Snell found his special interest centering on trees and fungi, particularly the blister rust that was taking its toll of the white pine forests in the Northeast. Because of this interest, Snell decided to do further graduate work at the University of Wisconsin, which reportedly had the most progressive group of plant pathologists in the country. Its department of botany and plant pathology was intensely field-oriented and so Wally spent the next several summers in the redwood country of the Pacific Northwest on the payroll of the United States Department of Agriculture's Bureau of Plant Pathology.

While he was working for his Ph.D., Wally coached football, basketball, and baseball at Milton College, a little Seventh Day Adventist College just barely in reach of Madison. "I'd get in my flivver and go out

there every afternoon," Wally said. "It was fifty miles of bad roads down and fifty miles back. Very few athletes. Almost no equipment. And I'd get home late and have to sit down and study when I really felt like going to sleep. My pay was $100 for the year."

If Wally Snell received a bad break (in more ways than one) on his chance for a major league baseball career, things could hardly have fallen more neatly into place when he went looking for a job. In February 1920, Professor York left to accept an offer at West Virginia University. He was making $1,500 a year, and Brown refused to grant him a $300 raise to match his West Virginia contract.

"Brown couldn't dig up $300 for Professor York, but when President Faunce found himself without a botany department, he suddenly located the money to pay me and an assistant $1,800 each," Snell recounted. "In 1920, I thought $1,800 was a lot of money."

Immediately after returning to Brown, Snell started his research on the fungi that infect forests and destroy timbers. His summers were spent in the Adirondack Mountains studying the white pine blister rust as assistant pathologist with the New York State Conservation Commission. As far as Wally Snell was concerned, his academic life had begun and his association with sports had ended. However, things didn't work out quite that way.

The catch was that the botany department was then housed in Maxcy Hall, and Wally's laboratory overlooked old Lincoln Field, now known as the Lower Campus. Lincoln Field had been the home of Brown football and baseball until the construction of Andrews Field in 1899, and in 1920 it was still the site of afternoon pick-up games. Every time he heard the crack of a bat meeting a ball, Wally would look up from his work to see what was going on. It wasn't long before he found himself doubling in brass, coaching baseball as well as teaching botany.

"Harry Pattee was still the baseball coach when I came back to Brown," Snell said. "He didn't have much material and he didn't want to take the job again unless Brown gave him more than a one-year contract. Well, old Doc Marvel [then Brown's athletic director] wouldn't have given his mother more than a one-year

Coach Snell, right, in the dugout at Andrews Field in 1923 with second baseman Myron Ruckstull '28 and Professor Hugh Robertson '19.

contract. Harry suggested I should take the job if it were offered to me. So, I found myself back in baseball again – on a one-year contract."

Snell coached the varsity baseball team from 1922 to 1926 and the freshman nine from 1926 through 1939. He coached varsity basketball in 1921-22 and 1922-23 and the Cubs from 1926-27 through 1934-35. He was identified with football from the fall of 1921 through the 1939 season, coaching each afternoon and scouting a future opponent each Saturday.

The best baseball player Wally ever coached was Irving "Bump" Hadley '28, who spent sixteen years in the American League with the Washington Senators, St. Louis Browns and the New York Yankees, and compiled a 161-165 lifetime record. The Lynn, Massachusetts, native was 49-31 as a starter and reliever with the great Yankee teams from 1936 to 1939 and had a 2-1 World Series record with the Bronx Bombers.

The late Fred M. Knight '28, sports writer for the *Boston Globe*, gave Snell credit for the development of Hadley from a thrower into a pitcher during the big right hander's year-and-a-half at Brown. "Snell worked with Hadley in the cage at Lyman Gym every day for three weeks in January of 1926," Knight once wrote. "Until that time, Bump had been utilizing only his powerful arm to get his great speed. But Wally and his assistant, Eddie Eayrs, another veteran big leaguer, persuaded Hadley to make a few changes. In two weeks' time they had him putting his whole body behind every pitch. He joined the Senators that spring and a year later was one of the bright young pitchers in baseball with a 14-4 record and a 2.85 earned-run

average. Bump always claimed that Coach Snell was responsible for much of his early success."

As a coach, Wally Snell preferred to show a player how to do something rather than to explain it verbally. One afternoon he was standing at home plate showing the squad how to square away and drop down a bunt. "What happens if the pitcher throws at your head?" one exceptionally bright Brown player asked. "You tomahawk the ball," Coach Snell replied, holding the bat vertically to illustrate his point. "You hold it like this and when the ball comes at your head you simply bring the bat down in tomahawk style and line a base hit right up the middle." Then, looking toward the pitcher, he yelled, "Fire one right at my head and I'll show you what I mean." Unfortunately, Wally's "tomahawk" was a bit rusty that day and the ball plunked the coach squarely over the left eye. Wally went down like a shot. As the players crowded around, he sat up. "It didn't work just right that time. But do you see what I mean?"

After the 1926 season, Jean Dubuc was brought in as varsity baseball coach and Wally took over the Cubs. It was a bitter disappointment at the time. Bert Schwartz recalls the moment. "Wally was sorely hurt by the move, but his only remark to me as we sat on the bench at Aldrich Field was: 'I will help him all I can.' As a teacher in the classroom or on the athletic field he was superb. As a human being who won every student's respect and affection, he had no peer. Today, in my seventy-third year, I still miss him. He didn't just teach botany; he instilled his love of nature in the hearts of everyone who was privileged to know him."

There were only a few occasions when Snell would talk about his days as basketball coach between 1921 and 1923. That's because the games were played in Lyman Gym, where a running track over the corners of the court and pillars on the playing surface made each home game something of an adventure.

When Snell accepted Doc Marvel's offer to help out with football in 1921, he started a nineteen-year affiliation with a sport he loved almost as much as baseball. In his early days Snell worked under Reggie Brown, one of the premier scouts in football history. After Tuss McLaughry replaced Edward North Robinson as head coach in 1926, Snell became chief scout.

From 1926 to 1935 Wally coached the Pollywogs, the name given to the twelve or so players each year who were ineligible. "The chief function of the Pollywogs was to learn the plays of the upcoming opponent and run them against the varsity," says John J. McLaughry '40, captain of the 1939 Bruins and later Brown's head football coach. "Wally was very good at this job because he kept up the enthusiasm of these men with his quiet, homey personality. The ineligibles had no reason to stay out there all season – except their love of football and their respect for Wally."

Football scouts were not privileged people back in the 1920s and early 1930s. There was no seat for them in the press box and no baconburgers and coffee at halftime. They sat in the stands in fair weather or foul, protecting their notes against the elements as best they could. Frequently a scout had to buy a ticket to get into the stadium. Yet the scout was a very important part of the game. There were no film exchanges because few colleges took game films until the mid-1930s.

Every fall Snell would see Harvard and Yale play two or three times each. "Wally would come to our house Sunday mornings," John McLaughry said. "He'd give my dad [head coach Tuss McLaughry] a very rudimentary verbal report, stressing the tendencies of the upcoming opponent and the formations we might see. Remember, this was back when teams ran the single wing, double wing, short punt, and other formations.

"Wally was very good at picking out the weaknesses of individual players, even those of All-American caliber such as Larry Kelley, Yale's Heisman Trophy winner in 1936. He reported to my dad, and later to the squad, that Kelley tended to be a free-lancer who went where his spirit took him. So in 1936 Wally and my father worked out an eight-man defensive line, which was unheard of in those days, and prevented Kelley from getting out to run his pass patterns. As a result, a very average Brown team held one of Yale's best teams to a 14-6 score.

"The squad always looked forward to Wally's Monday afternoon scouting report," John McLaughry continued. "He talked fast, holding his pipe in one hand, and using both arms to illustrate the point he was making. He was held in such regard by our players that they could go out with the tools he had given them and do the job."

By early 1940 Wally Snell retired from athletics for a second time to devote all his time to education. His place of eminence as one of the world's foremost mycologists was drawing a close line around his time and energies. Wally was through with sports. This time he was certain of it. Nothing could bring him back. But something did.

The 1925 football coaching staff. Left to right: J. W. Albright, Reggie Brown, Coach Edward North Robinson, Spike Staff, and Wally Snell.

WALLY WAS ALL-AMERICAN COLLEGE CATCHER IN 1913 AND HAD A SHORT MAJOR LEAGUE CAREER BEFORE HE FOUND HIS NICHE IN LIFE

BOOOT TIT, LAD

HE COACHED ALL SPORTS AT HIS ALMA MATER INCLUDING SOCCER

I HAD 'EM IN THE FUTILE YEARS

HE WAS A FOOTBALL SCOUT AND A GOOD ONE

AND DURING WORLD WAR II HE WAS ATHLETIC DIRECTOR

PROF. WALTER SNELL, ONE OF BROWN'S MOST BELOVED AND FAMOUS SONS IS RETIRING (TO A DEGREE)

FOR A MAN WHO HAS SPENT HIS LIFE PROTECTING FORESTS HE HAS BURNED A LOT OF LUMBER LIGHTING THAT PIPE

FRANK LANNING

"Our vice president, Jim Adams, had spoken to me about the possibility of athletic director Tom Taylor leaving to go into the service," Snell told me. "Then Jim walked into my office in Rogers Hall [the botany department moved to Rogers Hall in 1938] one morning and said, 'Tom's gone, Wally. You're it.'

"This room isn't big enough to hold all the problems I had in that job. There was nothing but problems. One year we started the baseball season with six bats. Coach Eddie Eayrs finally found a few more by going around to drug stores in Centerdale and Arctic. We also couldn't buy baseballs. We had eighteen balls for the entire season. Fortunately Eddie and I knew George Weiss of the New York Yankees, and he sold us some baseballs.

"Travel was also a problem during the war years. You couldn't hire a railroad car to take a team to New York. Couldn't even charter a bus to take us down to URI and back. Since so many Navy V-12 men were on our baseball team, we did get a Navy bus to take us to Kingston one day. The only trouble was they weren't

allowed to wait and bring us back. No other bus was available, so the entire Brown team had to hitch hike back to Providence."

Perhaps Athletic Director Snell's biggest problem was finding accommodations in New York for the 1944 football team after the Biltmore Hotel had cancelled a long-standing reservation forty-eight hours before the game with Columbia. He called every hotel in New York City, with no success. Everything was booked tight. Then he remembered that some Brown alumnus was connected with the Statler chain. But Wally couldn't recall his name.

"Miss Dick was taking dictation, and I was walking around that long table in the athletic director's office trying to pull that name out of the air," he said. "The only thing I remembered was that he used to sing a bawdy song at fraternity parties, and elsewhere upon request. Several hours later the song came to me. It was called *The Ballad of Shark Tooth Sholes* and included a line about this guy meeting his girl and repeating his original sin. And with that I remembered the name –

Walt Smith, class of 1921, and a Theta Delt.

"So I called Walt, told him about the jam we were in. 'I'll throw out fifty people immediately and you'll have room for your party Friday night,' he said. They had bunks in some of the rooms, but at least we had a place to stay. If Walt hadn't come through for us, we'd have had to take the early-morning train out of Providence, get to Baker Field at noon, play the game, and then get the 5:30 train coming back with all our men still in uniform."

Wally Snell left no doubt in anyone's mind that he was somewhat less than enthusiastic about accepting the job of war-time athletic director, especially since he had to drop everything right in the middle of a semester and move out to Marvel Gym. Esther Snell, who went with Wally to the Gym, comments on this phase of his life: "I think Wally knew that in trying to run a department he would face unbelievable wartime problems. But he loved his University dearly and he would have done anything in the world for Brown.

"At one point, Wally was getting extremely nervous because it really was a morning, noon, and night-time job. Plus the fact that he was still teaching his course on campus. One day he seemed different and I asked him what had happened. 'I had a session with myself last night,' he said, 'and I decided that nothing was going to give me ulcers.' After that he calmed down – somewhat."

There was a very thin staff at Marvel Gym during the war, and this sometimes caused a problem at the football games. Occasionally, the athletic director did everything but sell the programs. One day he took on that job, too. It was the game with Holy Cross in 1945. The Crusaders had a fine team, one that was to end up in the Orange Bowl. Gas rationing was lifted earlier that week and the Holy Cross fans came pouring into Providence from Worcester and other spots in Massachusetts. Instead of the anticipated crowd of 8,000 or 10,000, Brown ended up with a sellout house of 20,000, with others outside literally screaming to get in.

"The lines were backed up more than a block," Esther Snell says. "Nobody had time to make change at the ticket booths because the people were pushing and shoving so hard. I actually saw women wearing high heels climb on the hoods of cars and then jump the high cyclone fences to get into the game. Little kids were digging holes and going under the fences. The whole system eventually broke down, and, right in the middle of this chaotic situation, half of our ticket sellers quit. Wally and I ended up selling both tickets and programs."

Early in 1947, Snell came back to the botany department, and Paul F. Mackesey '32, a former football captain, replaced him at Marvel Gym. Snell had one parting comment. "Paul," he said, "on opening day next fall I'm going to get into my car, drive down Elmgrove Avenue, thumb my nose at Brown Stadium, and just keep driving."

Vice President Jim Adams had picked the right man for a very difficult job. Snell kept the sports program afloat during the war years, established a new policy at Brown of setting blocks of tickets aside for the undergraduates, and paved the way for the return of the minor sports after the war.

He also brought something else to the affairs at Marvel Gym that had never been there before. The late Barney Madden, sports writer for the *Providence Journal*, commented on this in the 1946 Thanksgiving Day program, which was dedicated to Professor Snell: "Thanksgiving Day originally was one on which thanks were given for the harvest, and so it is today for any and all affiliated with Brown athletes, for they surely appreciate the harvest of friendship and goodwill that has been gathered for Brown by Wally Snell, not only from the collegiate fields but from the press, the radio, and public as well. Wally Snell has been described by countless observers as 'a great guy.' Self-effacing, deferential, quick to help, he has spread the gospel of Brown on such a fundamentally sound basis that during his three years as Athletic Director the University's reputation was enhanced immeasurably, her friends multiplied, and her debtors – for favors graciously granted – made legion."

From 1947 through his retirement as Stephen T. Olney Professor of Natural History twelve years later, Professor Snell finally found himself free to give full attention to his botanical interests. At various times he taught general botany, mycology, forest pathology, and dendrology. But it was his research and his writings that brought him international acclaim. He had been identified with the blister rust eradication work since 1916 and was a ranking authority in that field. He also had done much original work on wood decay and termites, with one piece of writing in that area requiring ten years of research. His main work, however, on leaving athletics was the boletes, a group of tube mushrooms. In this field, he was then the world leader.

"One of the loneliest jobs is to be a pioneer in a certain field because there's no one who can help you," says Hubert J. Dyer, professor emeritus of biology and earlier a member of the botany department. "Wally was a descriptive mycologist, and, in dealing with the boletes, he raised all sorts of crazy problems that he had to thrash out for himself. Various people had taken a stab at this field and stayed at it long enough to bow out gracefully after they published a paper. Wally remained on the trail of the boletes all his professional life."

During the twenty summers following his doctorate, Dr. Snell was assistant forest pathologist for the New York State Department of Conservation, and it was during those years that he completely reorganized, corrected, and extended what was known about the blister rust disease of white pines in the Adirondack Mountains. "When Wally finished, he left no room for further fundamental work in that subject," according to Professor Dyer. "Without question, he gave us our modern picture of this problem, which is so at variance with the vague and often incorrect understanding of it which characterized earlier years."

Basically, what Snell discovered was startling evidence that it was the European black currant, not the red and white, that brought about significant infection of the white pine by *Cronartium ribicola*. Since federal agents had been ruthlessly eradicating red currants for years, Wally was greeted with a stony silence when he first brought his new evidence to the attention of that department.

Locally, he worked with the New England textile mills, which were troubled by fungus infestation not only of the mill timbers but also of fabrics. His studies with a home-made high-humidity test cabinet and test cultures led to isolation of several kinds of wood-rotting fungi and the development of experimental methods for the study of their comparative wood-destroying potential as well as the comparative effectiveness of counter measures. These were pioneering studies in

the 1920s in a field in which the future extent and importance was scarcely realized until the Quartermaster's Corps encountered jungle rot on a massive scale in the South Pacific during World War II. While doing research in this area during the '20s, Snell had noticed one particular fungus that killed other fungi or bacteria. The genus of that fungus was penicillium. Snell wrote a paper on this discovery but never had the time to make revisions needed before publication would be possible. His research was quite similar to that done by Fleming in his discovery of penicillin in 1928.

"It seemed that Wally was on the road to the discovery of penicillin at about the same time that Fleming was doing his work," Esther Snell says. "When Wally read of Fleming's discovery he was momentarily annoyed, but annoyed at himself because he hadn't had time to refine his research paper and get it published. This could be attributed to the fact that he was trying to work two jobs every day, one on campus and one on the athletic fields."

During one particularly wet summer in the Adirondacks, Professor Snell came upon an exceptionally big mushroom that he doubted was known on the North American continent. To make sure of this, he needed the whole plant and time to study it. He couldn't just ignore his job, which was about forty miles away, so he watered the mushroom each day, went about his business, and returned to water the mushroom again, following this routine until he had time to study it properly. By that time, Wally estimated that he had driven more than 1,000 miles to and from the rare mushroom, which was a bolete. "The effort was well worth it," he would say later, "because my find turned out to be the first authentic discovery of that particular species in North America."

Along about 1920, in that same region, he had started his career-long attack on the hitherto intractable problem of identification of the boletes, a special kind of mushroom that has myriad tiny tubes on the underside rather than gills. It is from these tubes that spores fall to the ground, to be borne away at the wind's whim to start more mushrooms elsewhere. Some are delicious. Some are poisonous.

At one point Snell had about 3,000 dried specimens, most of them from the Northeastern United States, but some from Europe and India. At that time they comprised the largest collection in the world. Early in his research Wally decided to make a hobby of identifying the boletes, and he went looking for a book to take up

Dr. Snell and Professor George L. Church work in the greenhouse.

the mountain to use as a guide. He discovered only two books on the subject, one published in 1889 and the other in 1911, and both completely inadequate. That's when he decided to write his own book.

Some forty years later, the product of all that research was published as *The Boleti of Northeastern North America*. The book, written by both Wally Snell and Esther Dick, is considered the definitive work in the field and has been purchased by mycologists around the world. A most important feature of the book is the seventy-two colored plates containing more than 400 figures, reproduced from original watercolor drawings by Snell from fresh specimens in natural size. It was the first account of the boleti from any of the sections of the United States and Canada that is completely illustrated in color.

There were two other major works in Snell's career. In 1936 he wrote a dictionary of some 3,000 mycological terms, and twenty-one years later, he collaborated

with Esther Dick on *A Glossary of Mycological Terms*, a dictionary of 7,000 such terms. Both proved to be indispensable reference works.

Wally Snell spent the summer of 1939 identifying specimens for Harvard and the Universities of Michigan, California, and Tennessee, among others. These institutions had gathered bolete specimens but never had anyone to identify them. Michigan's supply, for example, dated to 1903. He also became something of a prophet in his home state, working with citizens' groups as well as the state government on such things as fighting Dutch elm disease and chestnut blight.

In 1934, when a committee was formed in Rhode Island to combat the Dutch elm disease, Professor Snell was its first chairman. He was also a long-time president of the Audubon Society of Rhode Island and the Rhode Island Horticultural Society. On the national level, he was a charter member and vice president of the Mycology Society of America.

For many years Snell was in great demand as a toastmaster at civic, University, and athletic banquets. He combined a relaxed, home-spun delivery with the special knack for telling a story. But although Wally enjoyed telling a good story, he was a man who believed firmly in the economy of words in his daily life.

Professor Dyer recalled an incident when a rather garrulous student visited Wally to seek advice on whether or not he should go into the teaching profession. The student waxed poetic for four or five minutes, telling how much he enjoyed the course in botany. When he finished, Professor Snell took the pipe out of his mouth and said, "Thank you very much." Gushing onward, the young man recited the litany of his own virtues and his obvious qualifications as a budding botanist. "Well, that's interesting," was Snell's reply to that soliloquy. Getting the floor back, the student explained in detail that although he felt himself a born teacher he was concerned about the lack of money in the profession. Sucking on his pipe, Wally said, "Teach for love, son. Marry for money." The meeting between professor and student had lasted some twenty minutes and Wally Snell had uttered fourteen words.

"One of the notable things about that little department of ours was that there was no aura about Wally Snell," Professor Dyer says. "No brochure was handed out telling what his landmarks were. His door was always open if one of us needed help, but Wally wasn't the sort of man you sat around with exchanging little corkles of information. We worked together many years, but it wasn't until I read his obituary that I learned he was a Latin scholar, a Greek scholar, and a former catcher for the Boston Red Sox. The man just didn't talk about himself.

"The thing I *did* learn about Wally right off the bat was that he had the patience to work with people who needed help. He never robbed the slower students of their self-esteem. That's very important in a teacher."

It's possible that the botany department had no brochure extolling Snell's virtues because none was needed. His personality spoke for itself. George Church, professor emeritus of botany at Brown, recently said that when he came from the Harvard Graduate School to Brown with the possibility of joining the staff the first person he met was Professor Snell.

"I was so delighted to find a man so radiant with energy, friendliness, and humor that I agreed then and there to join the Brown faculty, even before I visited the laboratories in Maxcy Hall," Professor Church said. "As it turned out, life for me in Maxcy offered a lively tempo, particularly when I heard Wally rapidly charging up the stairs for an 8 o'clock morning class. He was, of course, vigorous in body, with muscles kept in tone by daily exercises in the gym. Equally vigorous was his mind as he directed a full schedule of teaching and research that frequently extended to seven days a week."

It's certainly no secret that Wally Snell's trademark was his pipe. He smoked constantly (although he never inhaled), rotating three or four pipes a day. And he was as meticulous in cleaning the pipes as he was in pursuing his research on the boletes. He had fifty pipes, each one with a curved stem, and he lighted them with old-fashioned kitchen matches.

Professor Snell had one other weakness. He truly enjoyed the chocolate sundaes he could get at McDonald's, a drugstore on Elmgrove Avenue. Wally wasn't interested in nuts or whipped cream. He just wanted chocolate ice cream, hot fudge, and marshmallow. And McDonald's made the best sundaes in Rhode Island, according to Snell.

When McDonald's closed about 1968, I sent a sympathy note to Wally, which drew the following response: "Instead of calling a press conference, Jay, I will make an announcement through you that the world is waiting for. I have the chocolate sundae situation licked. I am making them myself and they are as good as McDonald's. Now I can settle back to a peaceful and satisfactory old age."

Wally married Adelaide Elva Scott on October 25, 1913. The couple had three sons: Walter '39, an Annapolis architect; George '41, retired vice president of Memorial Hospital in Pawtucket and a resident of Bristol; and Donald, who was killed while on active duty with the Merchant Marine on September 29, 1942. After the death of Mrs. Snell in early 1975, Wally married his long-time associate, Esther Dick.

Esther first met Wally in 1927 when she was a freshman in his botany course. She worked for him as an undergraduate and then stayed on as a research associate in the department. "Working for Wally was an exciting experience," Esther said recently. "He had a brilliant mind. He knew something about everything and a great deal about many things."

One of the points Esther Snell stressed was that her husband never felt he was too old to acquire a taste for something new. "Between teaching, research, writing, and publishing papers, Wally had very little spare time," she said. "When he did find a few free moments, he painted. As a result, serious music was one of the things for which he never cultivated a taste. But after we were married and he realized how much I loved music, he started to listen carefully to the Boston Symphony and other music and began to ask all sorts of questions. The next thing I knew he had the house filled with books on classical music. It was important to him that he should acquire a taste for this music, not only to please me but also because he became curious about the subject and wanted to learn as much as possible about it."

It's safe to say that Wally Snell had an open mind on most things. There were two exceptions. He would never climb into an airplane, and he had the greatest disdain for male ballet dancers. "I'm afraid he just drew the line on young men in tights hopping around on the stage," Esther said. "I could never get him to a ballet."

When Wally was a young man first working in the Adirondacks, he found a dog frantically running around in circles with porcupine quills sticking out from head to tail. He spent the next two hours pulling out the quills, one by one, and for the rest of that summer that dog never left Wally's side. Through most of his lifetime Wally had a dog for a pet. This is why it was so ironic that it was a dog bite that led to his death.

"We were on vacation in New Hampshire during Labor Day weekend of 1979," Esther said, "and Wally took our dog, Tinker, out for a walk. When they came back, both were bleeding from bites inflicted by a large dog who attacked Tinker. Wally's cut was on his finger. Osteomyelitis set in, and the finger was removed in July of 1980, several weeks before he died. He took so many antibiotics in an effort to cure the infection that his system was weakened to a dangerous degree. On top of which, it's quite a shock to go into the hospital and have a finger removed at age ninety-one."

When they held a Memorial Service in Manning Chapel for Wally Snell, it seemed appropriate that organist Bill Dinneen started the program by playing "Ever True to Brown." The comments of several speakers that day reflected the respect and admiration for Wally on the campus. "Wally Snell had that quality of character in the old-fashioned sense which we don't hear very much about these days," said Professor Richard T. Goss, dean of biological sciences. "He had a

wit, somewhat irreverent, I suspect, most of the time. He was at one and the same time a generalist and a specialist in an era when we are mostly specialists. He was a specialist in his own love of nonvascular plants, but he was also a generalist in the sense that he had other interests – his athletics, his books, and his ability as a water-color painter."

John Rowe Workman, profesor of classics, said that Professor Snell's headquarters were not in the Blue Room or the Faculty Club or the long exhausting faculty meetings in the Corporation Room of University Hall talking into the night about curriculum revision, but in his research laboratory, and added: "In his highly effective and quiet way he pursued his own thing, like the subject of his research, an effervescent thing which only his talent and personality and modesty combined to make for him and for Brown University an international reputation."

The text of Chaplain Charlie Baldwin's talk that day was, "In My Father's House There are Many Mansions." As I was walking out, someone sidled up to me and whispered, "I wish Charlie had slipped and said, 'In My Father's House There Are Many Mushrooms.' Wally would have liked it better that way."

The Sock and Buskin board assembled on stage for this picture. Standing, from left, Professor
Ben Brown and Edward L. Herrick '29. Seated, from left: Gilmore O. Bush '28, Francis B. Armington '28,
Leslie T. Chase '28, Franklin Gamwell '29, Rufus C. Fuller, Jr. '19, and Professor Tom Crosby.

Chapter 8 🎗
Two men of extreme pride
who lived on the same stage

With an interesting blend of respect and familiarity, Tom Crosby was always called and frequently referred to as "T.C." He was of the old school – charming, courtly, impeccably dressed, and generous with help and advice. In appearance, he looked every inch the part of a tragic actor. He had a mantle of white hair, furrowed brow, and sad, penetrating, deepset eyes. Crosby was first and foremost a man of the stage. Whenever he was in class, on campus, directing a play, or doing one of those readings for which he was so famous, the thespian in him was always close to the surface.

His pupil and eventually his succcessor in Brown theatre was Ben Brown. On the occasions when students would meet with Ben Brown in the Faunce House Theatre, at the Brown Faculty Club, or over drinks at the Spaghetti Place on Mathewson Street in downtown Providence, it was always an exciting adventure. His relations with students were informal and casual. While directing a play, however, Brown was a stern taskmaster who demanded perfection. He could be the very essence of charm, or he could fly into a towering rage in an instant and stalk off in his wounded pride. Most people loved Ben Brown. Some disliked him strongly. None who knew him failed to form an opinion.

For more than half a century these two men *were*

Brown theatre, with Professor Crosby serving as director of Sock and Buskin from 1901 to 1920 and Professor Ben Brown following from 1921 until his death in 1955. The two men had much in common. Both were bachelors, both had a deep abiding love for the theatre, and both were extremely popular with the students. Yet, in some areas they were as far apart as two people could be. They argued frequently, sometimes bitterly. They were men of extreme pride living on the same stage, each one fighting for his own identity in the small college community that was Brown in the 1920s and 1930s. Yet, from the devotion and diverse talents of these two directors came the foundation of today's impressive theatre arts program at the University.

Born in Newport, Rhode Island, on August 8, 1870, Thomas Crosby, Jr., was the son of Thomas and Martha Winslow Crosby. He attended the local schools, worked summers for his father, and was graduated from Rogers High School. He once said that his early interest in the theatre was stimulated by the many road companies appearing at Newport summer theatres. There is a story, possibly apocryphal, that when he was only ten, Crosby borrowed some tools from his father, built a crude set, and put on a play in his home, taking all the parts himself and asking that his friends and relatives pay a dime to see the production.

As a boy he frequently dreamed of his first appear-

ance on a professional stage, standing next to a world-famous actor and taking curtain call after curtain call. As luck would have it, that's almost what happened. It seems that during his freshman year at Brown in 1890, Crosby won the role of a lowly spear carrier in the Providence Opera House production of *Julius Caesar*. The star of the show was the famous Shakespearean actor, Edwin Booth. Just before the conclusion of the final act, Crosby's toga became snarled on Caesar's bier, which occupied dead center stage. This predicament left the Brown freshman with the dubious option of departing the stage without his toga or sticking around for the curtain calls. Booth received seven "calls" that night and so did the immobile Crosby, his face turning a deeper crimson each time the curtain went back up.

After earning his master's degree from Brown in 1895, Crosby taught briefly at Worcester Academy and at the University Grammar School, located in the old Supreme Court building on Benefit Street. Then, in 1898, he headed for New York City, studied at the Stanhope-Wheatcroft Dramatic School there, and made a favorable impression on the famous Minnie Maddern Fiske, who offered him a part in her next play, *Becky Sharp*.

Crosby's interest in the theatre was sharpened by the acceptance he was getting in New York. There were those at the time who felt he had all the qualities needed to become a distinguished professional actor. His parents, however, did not share Tom's enthusiasm for the stage.

"Tom was not from a social family," says Professor Robert W. "Pat" Kenny '25, who studied under Crosby and then served with him in the English department. "His father owned and operated the amusement park and roller coaster at Newport's First Beach, a landmark until the 1938 hurricane washed it away. But the Crosby family had social aspirations and tried to discourage their son from a life on the wicked stage, as it was then referred to in many circles, including the social circle.

"The story goes that the family applied sufficient clout to have Tom appointed to the Brown faculty in the fall of 1900 as professor of public speaking and coach of the debating team. In deference to his parents,

Tom accepted the appointment. But he left the stage with more than a little regret. This isn't to say he was unhappy with the life of a college professor. Tom thought social. He had absorbed the Newport gentility. He dressed well and had excellent manners. He was invited to social parties back in Newport when he was a Brown student, and, as a professor, he became a favorite of the Providence East Side set. But I always felt that Tom had left a part of himself on the New York stage."

Crosby was an innovator, a person who wouldn't accept the status quo. In his first year of teaching, he established a course in public speaking that reflected contemporary usage and contrasted greatly with the formal courses in oratory and elocution then found in nearly every college curriculum. The course became an immediate hit, and in his long association with the University, Professor Crosby won the enduring devotion of hundreds of Brown men, whom he inspired to respect the King's English and to pronounce the native tongue sincerely, correctly, and without affectation.

Recently, Francis B. Armington '28 talked with me about that course and about the verbal twister Crosby prepared for his students. "All in the class were expected to memorize and recite to the satisfaction of the instructor an essay called 'Exercise in Pronunciation,' which started like this: 'Gentlemen, I present this idea. I believe it is the duty of our newspapers not at all to provide literature for the family but to record generally happenings of society for the whole people. In a measure, fellow citizens, we are all students of the history of our own times....'

"Any one who so far forgot himself as to say 'ex-uh-cise' or 'gennulman,' or 'ideer' had his knuckles figuratively rapped. The whole thing was a marvelous compendium of words usually carelessly pronounced."

One of Crosby's students was the late Joseph F. Reilly '13. Many years later, writing in his column, "Smoke Rings," in the *Brockton Enterprise*, Reilly recalled that experience: "I decided to have a go at Tom's public speaking rodeo in my junior year. It was not the intent of the course to run a group of Daniel Websters off the assembly line. Instead, it was advertised as a help in thinking and speaking before a group. Scholastic grades were earned in proportion to your improvement. The veriest tyro shared the same opportunity to win an 'A' as did gifted members of the varsity debating team. Tom gave us the business on posture, breathing, gestures, and enunciation. Once in swing, the course was a lot of fun."

Crosby was also rare among his contemporaries in American universities in his recognition that literature did not stop in the middle of the nineteenth century. Professor George Pierce Baker of Harvard, later of Yale, was one of the few who shared Crosby's view. There was a growing restlessness on the part of college students in the pre-World War I years prompted by a desire to study the poets and writers who touched *their* lives. Young women at Radcliffe had actually petitioned (in vain) for courses that dealt with current authors, contending that their college education helped them feel a little bit at home in every world except their own. Finally, over the protests of many senior members of the Brown faculty, and amid much bitterness, Professor Crosby was allowed to introduce into the Brown curriculum courses in modern drama, modern essay, and modern poetry.

Paul F. Mackesey '32, former alumni executive officer, recently told me about Crosby's famous course in the modern drama: "He was a delightful gentleman with a deep, mellow voice and with those famous pince-nez glasses with the black ribbon hanging down.

As a senior, Crosby, right, played Ponce deLeon in the Hammer and Tongs production of *Florida Water*. Arthur C. Stone '97 was Minnie He He.

Frequently he'd use those glasses as a prop, taking them off and looking at you under his brow.

"Even though class attendance was compulsory in those days, Tom Crosby never took roll. He didn't have to. No one would have thought of missing his class. I can still see him sitting on the edge of his desk in the first room on the left in Sayles Hall. His play readings were a complete show in themselves, with T.C. playing all the parts with his usual wit and charm. It was like going to the theatre. At the end of the hour, his performance was frequently greeted with foot-stomping, a traditional sign of approval at Brown in those days."

For many years, dramatic talent at Brown was centered in an organization called Hammer and Tongs, which presented an annual student-written operetta. During his undergraduate days, Crosby had taken part in one of these productions, playing the role of Ponce de Leon in a gem called *Florida Water*. When Hammer and Tongs went under financially and passed from the scene in 1897, Brown was without a theatre group.

Early in 1901 a number of students, led by Russell W. Richmond '02, came to see Professor Crosby, asking that a new theatrical group be created. Crosby relished the opportunity and immediately went to work signing up students, arranging for a place to stage his plays, and raising money. Within six months, Sock and Buskin was formed. The "Sock" in the title is symbolic of the footgear worn by the Greek comedian, and the "Buskin" refers to the high-laced sandal worn by the Greek tragedian. The goal of the new organization was to produce one play each year rather than an operetta.

The first effort was *Our Boys*, produced in the spring of 1902 as part of the annual Junior Week (something akin to today's Spring Weekend), a period of relaxation before final exams. Since there was no location on campus where plays could be produced, Crosby had made arrangements to use the Providence Opera House, a lavish if somewhat ornate building constructed in 1871 on the present location of the Outlet Department Store. The emphasis each year was on light material with strong box-office appeal: *The Cool Collegian*, *The Rivals*, *Charley's Aunt*, and *Private Secretary* were typical of the fare offerred.

Given the circumstances of these productions, it should have come as no surprise that there was an inordinate amount of extra-curricular student participation during the performances, most of it emanating

The 1902 cast of *Our Boys*, seated from the left: Jackson, Schloss, Hoffman, Winslow, White, Daggett, and Richmond. Standing: Buxton, Calder, Blanding, Currier, Professor Crosby, and Rich.

from the upper balcony where the undergraduates traditionally gathered. One night hundreds of streamers were thrown from the balcony and college cheers were rendered. Hoots and howls frequently echoed through the large hall, and it was not at all uncommon for pennies and flour bombs to be aimed at the actors. One night things got so out of hand that Professor Crosby felt compelled to step before the curtain and ask the students kindly to refrain from hurling flour bombs at the performers. The undergraduates quickly obliged. They tossed the bombs at Professor Crosby instead – all in good fun, of course.

The inclusion of Pembrokers (technically the Women's College in Brown University at that time) as female cast members was still thirty years away when Professor Crosby formed Sock and Buskin. Writing some years back about this period, the late Francis J. Brady '16 had this to say: "No giggling, gurgling Pembrokers were allowed to upset our serious devotion to the 'drammer.' Men such as Billy Lynn, Charlie Berry, Paul Howland, and many others flitted abut the stage

with mincing steps. They spoke in dulcet tones, in a clear falsetto or a warm alto, but not without occasional discordant husky cracklings. Dresses would get caught underfoot, straps would slide bewitchingly over shoulders, and the audience would appreciate the artistry of the realism."

As might be expected, the local press had some fun at the expense of the "female" cast members. One *Providence Journal* theatre critic described an actor in a woman's part as "looking very well, but when 'she' spoke the bass voice was startling, and when 'she' walked it reminded one of a baseball player trying to make first base."

Alice Fuller recalls an incident involving her husband, the late Rufus C. Fuller, Jr. '19: "One night while Rufus was in rehearsal for his role as Raina in *Arms and the Man*, I stopped by the theatre to have a word with him. There was the man of my life in the wings, a pink-cheeked ingenue, leaning against one of the props and puffing on a foul-smelling cigar."

Between 1901 and 1919 Sock and Buskin produced

one full-length play each spring, usually for one performance only. Supplementing this effort were trips to nearby towns in Rhode Island and Massachusetts where Sock and Buskin "shed the inspiring light of culture in the by-ways," as Professor Crosby said.

These off-campus trips to town halls and high school auditoriums weren't without their hazards. One night the back wall of the "room" on stage caved in just as one of the actors was standing in its doorway. Tom Crosby was proud of his pupil that night. The door frame escaped hitting the actor but left him standing among the rubble – still reciting his lines.

Tom Crosby had a good, biting sense of humor, which verged on the barb but was never intended to hurt. He was all business, however, when it came to working with his performers. He had a rare talent for dramatic interpretation and a strong interest in developing a similar ability in his students. He was an expert in the eighteenth-century way of strutting and fretting. He knew every face patch, every flip of a snuff box, and every whiff of a lace cuff, all a part of powdered-wig-and-hoopskirt drama.

Francis Brady summarized Tom Crosby's teaching style this way: "What a thrill it was to sit at rehearsal and watch Professor Crosby work. His pedagogical technique was simple. It involved no lengthy exhortations for us to search our souls for some spontaneous emotional spark. 'No, no, this way,' the master would say, and we would imitate the inimitable. We would reflect and modulate, pause and stress, speed up and slow down, rehearse and rehearse, play and play, until we became the very incarnation of the saints and sinners, the swaggering vagabonds and timid souls, the colonel's ladies and Judy O'Gradys, the subtle knaves and men of honor of whom the authors had dreamed."

A number of Sock and Buskin performers of that era stayed with the theatre after graduation, some becoming drama teachers in the public schools, others joining or forming community theatre groups, and a few making the grade professionally. W. P. "Billy" Lynn '10 appeared on radio and in operetta, made a dozen films, and was featured as Edwin Throwbridge, the greeting card and racetrack con man in the 1935 long-running Broadway comedy, *Three Men On A Horse*.

Tom Crosby apparently wasn't adverse to stretching the rules on occasion to help students. Joe Reilly illustrated this point in his newspaper column: "The first baseball game of the season was a week away, and I was three points shy of eligibility after a game but losing effort with geometry. I approached Tom and informed him that I couldn't get a make-up exam until June and asked if he would send over to the registrar's office right away a final passing grade for my course with him. Tom fixed me with the look Hamlet reserved for his father's murderer, held the gaze for a few long moments, and then broke out in a gale of laughter. 'Your request is so preposterous and is powered by such unmitigated gall that I'm going to grant it,' Crosby said.

"Then Tom set two conditions. 'Joe,' he added, 'you must promise to attend every class to the year's end and you must agree to knock in a flock of runs.' I did the former, but on one particular afternoon I had trouble with the second request. The next morning a note was in my mail. 'Your posture at the plate yesterday was excellent, your gestures with the bat vague and inconclusive. Even your protest to the umpire on that called third strike was unconvincing. I shall expect a better performance against Yale next Saturday.'"

Tom Crosby became something of a legend at Brown and was also considered the dean of amateur stage in Rhode Island. In the winter of 1909, Robert P. Brown, owner of the Talma Theater, which later became the Providence Boys Club on South Main Street, proposed that Crosby start an amateur players group for his theatre. Working with Mrs. Daniel Webster and Mrs. William M. Weeden, Crosby planned the organization subsequently known as The Players. The first production was *The Liars*, given in December of 1909, with Professor Crosby as Sir Christopher Deering and Mrs. Webster as Mrs. Crespin.

In the decades that followed, The Players, with Crosby as its director, became recognized as one of the outstanding amateur dramatic groups in the country. Crosby's specialities, both as an actor and a director, were the famous eighteenth-century comedies, *She Stoops To Conquer*, *The Rivals*, and *The School for Scandal*. While he was attempting to develop experienced actors

Mrs. Samuel Nicholson, Paul Howland '10, Tom
Crosby, and Lawrence Lanpher '23 head for Barker
Playhouse.

in Providence, Crosby frequently had to double as an
actor in his own productions, which allowed him an
opportunity to display his acting talents on a state-wide
basis.

When Jessie Bonstelle's stock company came to Providence for a lengthy stay just after World War I,
Professor Crosby was invited to appear in a number of
its productions at the Opera House. In one of his appearances he played Sir Peter Teazle to Jessie Bonstelle's
Lady Teazle in *The School for Scandal*. Crosby also took a
number of the youngsters of the Bonstelle troup under
his wing. One whom he helped was Ann Harding,
who became a leading lady on the stage and later in
Hollywood.

Crosby was active in summer stock for many years.
His direction of Eugene O'Neill's *Ah, Wilderness!* (in
which he also played the role made famous by George
M. Cohan) won him praise from the New York critics
in the summer of 1936.

Over a glass of wine at the Brown Faculty Club, Pat
Kenny talked with me about Professor Crosby. "Tom

was most happy when he was in front of an audience.
He was a great actor, one who could get a lot of mileage
out of his looks, especially by rolling his large and
striking eyes. He was very distinguished looking, with
a manly appearance."

Professor Crosby had that elusive quality called
charm. A brilliant conversationalist with an urbane
wit, he was in great demand by the social set as a fourth
for bridge. Readings were very popular in the first few
decades of this century, and T.C. was frequently invited
to any number of East Side homes to read from the
classics. Considered a most eligible bachelor, Crosby
was eagerly pursued by ladies of society – but always
managed to avoid their rush.

Crosby was also a *bon vivant* and an expert spinner
of yarns, with many of his best stories spun late at
night in the Senate Pub, which was in the basement of
the Flatiron Building at 10 Weybosset Street, now the
home of Amica. The Senate Pub was the best bar in
town, a gentleman's bar located in the banking and
business district. Along about midnight most every
evening, usually sporting top hat, white tie, and tails,
Crosby would glide into the establishment for his mint-
julep nightcap. His instructions to the bartender when
he placed his order were always the same: "Danny,
put your heart into it."

Tom Crosby's closest friends were Harry Barker and
his vivacious wife, Sarah Minchin Barker. Tom served
in regal splendour as best man at their wedding. Harry
Barker had money in the bank and time on his hands,
and the theatre was his toy. He liked to play around
backstage doing creative work, especially with scenery.
He was a late riser and didn't mind working on scenery
until three in the morning. Some of Harry's student
apprentices, those with 8 o'clock classes, did mind.
Harry also was very active with Players, especially as a
producer.

His wife, Sally, was an extremely beautiful and
talented actress with a lilting voice. She had a charming
personality both on and off the stage and was much
beloved by all those who knew her. She and Tom had
one thing in common, beyond their love of theatre. As
a young girl, Sally had aspired to be a professional
actress, but deferred to her parents and settled down
in Providence.

The Barker apartment on Benefit Street became a
home away from home for Tom Crosby. He called it
his club and used it as such, often dropping in after
rehearsal to relax with a drink and some quiet conver-

sation. Harry and Tom would sit up into the early hours of the morning discussing aspects of the current Sock and Buskin or Players production. "Listening to them was a thrill," Sally said. "Two men talking with such intensity and depth about one love – the theatre."

Sally Barker and Tom Crosby played opposite each other in a number of productions at The Players, and became fast friends. "I always thought Tom remained a bachelor because he was in love with Sally and she was a married woman," Alice Fuller said. "They had a very special friendship."

Despite this friendship, Tom took Sally to task one night backstage at Barker Playhouse. "We were appearing together in *The First Mrs. Fraser*," Sally told me in the summer of 1981 from her room at Hallworth House on Benefit Street. "Tom and I were on stage, but I didn't have that many lines at one particular point and I nervously toyed with the doilies on the arm of the chair in which I was sitting. When the curtain came down he turned to me. 'Sally Barker,' he said, 'if you ever try that trick again in my scene I'll put you across my knee.' I think he meant it.

"In all our years together on the stage, I only saw Tom fluff his lines once. Going home that particular night with Harry and Tom, I said, 'Fine show, Tom, but what happened in the second act when you went off?' And he said, somewhat stiffly, 'Mrs. Barker, I did not go off. It was just that I looked down at my shoes and one was black and the other was brown.' He was so meticulous about how he dressed that this little thing was enough to throw him off."

After Harry's death many years later, Sally bought the property at the corner of Benefit and Transit Streets, converted the building on the site into a theatre, and named it Barker Playhouse in his memory.

When Tom Crosby retired in June of 1939 his public speaking class gave him a box of cigars, and his drama class applauded his final reading for a full five minutes. Aside from the theatre, Professor Crosby's chief interest had been sketching and water color. In retirement, he quickened his painting pace and enjoyed another showing or two at the Art Club. Like many people who are growing old, Tom Crosby feared that his mind wouldn't stay alert during his retirement years. So, he took on the mental discipline of learning Spanish. He also stayed close to the theatre, doing both acting and directing with The Players.

Unfortunately, a stroke slowed Crosby in 1944. Then, on August 23, 1947, he suffered a heart attack in his

The 40th reunion of *Our Boys*, from left: Tom Crosby, Colonel G. Edward Buxton, Judge Russell W. Richmond, and Professor William G. Hoffman.

apartment at 261 Benefit Street. The next morning, after a leisurely breakfast in the hospital, he put his head on the pillow and died.

Crosby's last association with Brown theatre had come in the winter of 1941 during the celebration of Sock and Buskin's fortieth anniversary. Thirty-five Sock and Buskin alumni gathered at the Faculty Club in late January for dinner and to listen to T.C. provide anecdotes on the early days of theatre at Brown. It was a pleasant evening, made more so when the group later went backstage at Faunce House Theater and viewed the collection of cast photos dating to the days when Brown men made themselves up to be beautiful women. Crosby delighted the group by not only remembering the names of each cast member but also by recalling the part each played and whether or not the actor had done a good job.

Among those returning for the evening were three alumni who appeared in *Our Boys*, the first Sock and Buskin production: Col. G. Edward Buxton '02, Judge Russell W. Richmond '02, and William G. Hoffman '02. It was an evening of reminiscences, one that cried out for a tape recorder.

Two weeks later, Crosby made his final appearance on the Faunce House stage as Nathan'l Berry in the alumni production of *Shore Acres*. This particular role had been very close to Tom since 1893, when he had seen it performed by its author, James A. Herne, an innovator who ushered the naturalistic movement into our theatre, in a first-season performance at the Providence Opera House. The late Leslie Allen Jones '26, a member of the theatre staff, recalled Crosby's 1941 interpretation in an article written for the *Brown Alumni Monthly* in 1951:

"Although we did not suspect it then, Tom Crosby was playing his last role on our stage. The old gentleman, Nathan'l Berry, is closing up for the night in the Maine kitchen where the final act is laid. He picks up his candle and goes slowly about the set – kicking the rug against the door to keep out the chill of the winter night and closing the damper on the stove. Then he comes to the newel post of the stairs and stands there. And the audience was so quiet you could have heard a program drop – caught in the magic and mystery of the play – wrapped up in the mantle of Tom's playing."

Among those caught up in the magic of Tom Crosby's final Brown performance was his successor, Ben Brown. Down through the years people have tried to compare these two men. Sally Barker has her memories and spoke of them candidly with me: "Each man was extremely popular with students, but they were popular in different ways. I would have said students revered Tom Crosby. They were more chummy with Ben.

"Of course, Tom was by far the superior actor of the two. He was superb on any stage and in any role. I happen to think that Tom Crosby was also a wonderful director. But he didn't want to do much with the technical end of the theatre. And if you're going to be a *great* director, I've found out, you've got to know something about what goes on backstage. Ben was also a good director, although he wasn't keen about backstage

work either."

Alert and in good health at age ninety-one, Sally Barker recalled that Tom and Ben had very different personalities: "Tom was a calm man, and I guess you could say that Ben had a very short fuse. They just didn't belong to each other, and yet, down deep, I think they were fond of one another. Tom always thought of Ben as his protégé, and eventually that can become somewhat grating on the protégé.

"It's so very long ago, but I remember that Tom had a great love for those big Emperor grapes, which were quite expensive and were sold only at the Chase Market on the East Side. Tom loved them, but he wouldn't pay the price. Well, Tom and Ben would get into one of their periodic disagreements and wouldn't speak for several days. Then Ben, to make things up, would go to the Chase Market, buy a very large bunch of Emperor grapes, and take them to Tom as a peace offering."

Lois Lindblom Buxton '43 was a friend of Tom Crosby's and a Ben Brown leading lady who turned down an offer from Hollywood. She recently described the strong points in each man's directing techniques:

"Both got the most out of what they worked with. Tom was more adept at producing plays with broad-based humor, while Ben was more interested in making his audience think. If there was any other difference it would have been in style. For example, if a male was playing a female role, Tom could get up and *show* the actor how he should cross the stage. Ben wouldn't do this. If he had tried, he would have been ludicrous. But Ben could get the same result by *telling* the actor how it should be done. He made his actors *think* the role."

Henry C. Hart '35 and Lois Lindblom Buxton '43 in the 1956 alumni production of *The Road to Rome*.

Benjamin Williams Brown was born in Danielson, Connecticut, on December 1, 1897, a direct descendant of Roger Williams. His first theatre experience came at age five when his father took him to see *Uncle Tom's Cabin*. A few years later Mr. Brown's barn behind the home became Ben's first theatre. He once told of producing *Robin Hood* there when he was only eight. Some of the boys in the cast had a merry old time swinging on ropes from one hay loft to another until their parents found out about it and gave the hook to the young actors.

As an undergraduate, Ben took part in Sock and Buskin, acted as a reader for the Glee Club, earned his Phi Beta Kappa key, and worked as a reporter for the *Brown Daily Herald*. He was in the infantry's officer training school at Petersburg, Virginia, when the Armistice was signed in 1918. Ben's main love through college remained the stage, so much so that during his sophomore year he left Brown to join a vaudeville act. He was on the Keith Circuit for six weeks, returning to college only after the act folded.

Later, Ben had more extensive and rewarding experiences with the professional theatre. He was a juvenile with the Albee Stock Company in the summer of 1919, played two seasons with the Jessie Bonstelle stock company at the Providence Opera House, directed summer stock, and appeared with The Players.

While working for his master's degree ('21 A.M.), Ben taught at Deerfield Academy and then joined the Brown faculty in 1921. His appearance relieved Tom Crosby of his directing duties and allowed him to concentrate on his courses in public speaking and the modern drama.

Ben Brown's immediate contribution on joining the Brown faculty was to change Sock and Buskin from a dramatic society presenting one production a year into an organization that was active throughout the academic year, offering an assortment of dramatic delights ranging from Greek tragedies to Shavian comedies, from Dunsany's symbolism to Arnold Bennett's realism.

The thirty-four years of Ben Brown's directorship was a period of great change. There was the construction of a new theatre, the merging of Sock and Buskin and Komians (the Pembroke theatre group), the birth of Brownbrokers, and the establishment of the now-traditional Alumni Show as a part of Commencement Weekend. Through it all, there was never any question of who was in charge, and there was little doubt that whatever was tried would succeed.

In switching from one production a year to a full theatre season, Ben Brown was joining the Little Theater Movement, which had been spreading throughout the country for several years. For Brown undergraduates, the "Little Theater" was the second floor of what was then called Rockefeller Hall, more recently known as the Art Gallery in Faunce House. A temporary stage was erected, and the Sock and Buskin organization obtained lighting equipment, scenery, drapes, and furniture. The facilities were modest, but they constituted a home for Sock and Buskin at last and brought the productions from downtown to the campus.

The experimental theatre on the Brown campus was an artistic success but a financial disaster. Terence's *Phormio* drew only fifteen undergraduates on opening night in 1921. This was disappointing but perhaps not surprising. Audiences of the Roaring '20s were seeking escape in the theatre at the very time when Ben Brown was switching over to message plays, most of which lacked popular appeal. In order to make money to support the experiments, Brown decided to send the shows on the road. By the mid-1920s at least one major production each year was being designed specifically for presentation off campus – meaning anywhere from Bristol High School to Wellesley College; from Uxbridge, Massachusetts, to Cranston, Rhode Island.

The income from these shows promoted by Professor Brown served Sock and Buskin well until the early 1930s when the program was cancelled due to the Depression. In 1933, Sock and Buskin became Sock and Buskin, Inc. (it's now called Friends of Brown University Theatre, or FOBUT) when a group of men, at Ben's urging, formed a corporation to help raise funds through membership dues and through proceeds from a relatively new venture called the Alumni Show. The original corporators were: Ben W. Brown '19, Fran Armington '28, Leslie T. Chase '28, William B. Farnsworth '17, Rufus G. Fuller, Jr. '19, Theodore L. Sweet '22, and S. Everett Wilkins '24.

The first Alumni Show, *Ghosts*, had been produced in 1926. Two years later Harry Barker staged *East Lynne*, the first of a long series of nineteenth-century revivals produced by the alumni.

During this period, Tom Crosby, Ben Brown, and Rufus Fuller became known as the Great Triumvirate. It's fair to say that without these three talented but diverse individuals pulling together, Sock and Buskin might not have survived. Fuller, a Providence man, had gone into the family business, Fuller Iron Works, after graduation, but Brown theatre remained his main hobby and interest in life. Although a very good character actor and a highly successful director, Fuller had but one role in this triad. He kept his two partners in tow financially.

"Tom and Ben were perfectionists and were quick to spend money on sets, costumes, and properties," said Alice Fuller. "Sometimes they spent money they didn't have. This is where Rufus stepped in. He looked after the front of the house while his two artistic partners did their thing backstage."

The day after Commencement in 1931, a strange procession wended its way from Rockefeller Hall to Rogers Hall. Janitors were seen carrying Elizabethan benches, lengthy columns, and bulky platforms. Several custodians bounced jauntily along the walks carrying Roman spears on their shoulders, stopping now and then to take a playful stab at an elm or a fellow custodian. Early in September, the same procession formed again, this time moving from Rogers to the theatre's new home in Faunce House.

Thanks to John D. Rockefeller, Jr. '97, Rockefeller Hall had been extended to include a new 360-seat theatre. Rockefeller's only stipulation when he made the gift was that the entire building be named in honor of his old friend and Brown's former president, Dr. William H. P. Faunce.

Ten years of living in cramped quarters in the Art Gallery and operating with inadequate facilities ended in June of 1931 with the alumni production of *Uncle Tom's Cabin*, featuring Ben Brown in the title role. Dedication of the new theatre came that fall. The play was *The Merchant of Venice*, and the stars were the late Thomas A. Chapman '34 as Antonio and Gerald L. Brown (Bronstein) '32 as Shylock.

The move to a modern theatre brought Sock and Buskin new prestige and added support. The subscription list jumped from about 200 in 1930 to more than 1,200 by the 1940-41 season. In that same period the number of students participating in the theatre rose from twenty-five to 125.

Ben Brown played a major role in another change of

Before Komians was formed in 1901, Tom Crosby (back row) coached the annual Shakespearean play produced by Alpha Beta at the Women's College. This 1900 production was *Twelfth Night*.

the 1930s, the decision to merge Sock and Buskin and Komians. Founded at the Women's College in 1901, the same year that Sock and Buskin had its start, Komians operated in an assembly room in University Hall until Sayles Gym was built in 1906. By 1927, Komians had moved into the new Alumnae Hall, where a real stage and permanent equipment were available. Like Sock and Buskin, Komians struggled through its early years. Women were forced to play the male roles with the added handicap of being forbidden by the University to wear men's costumes. After a performance of *The School for Scandal*, the *Providence Journal*'s theatre critic commented about the men in the cast appearing in "skirts and peek-a-boo waists."

Sally Barker took over as director of Komians in 1920 and stayed on for sixteen years, a period of professional growth in which the group did three major plays a year. Ruth Hussey Longnecker '33, later a Hollywood actress, was one of Mrs. Barker's prize pupils in Komians.

Efforts to merge Sock and Buskin and Komians had been made in 1925, 1928, and 1933, all with no success. Ben Brown, Sally Barker, and Rufus Fuller favored the move. Dean Margaret Morriss of Pembroke was strongly opposed. Her feeling was that the women wouldn't have so many opportunities to secure important parts, which was probably true. She also felt that women would not have the same opportunities to work backstage, which turned out not to be true.

It was agreed in 1931 that impersonations would be

dropped and that women guests from off campus would be invited to fill all Sock and Buskin female roles. Pembrokers still were not welcome. Finally, after many years of talking and planning, Komians and Sock and Buskin joined hands at the end of the 1940-41 season.

Another major event in the history of Sock and Buskin took place in the spring of 1938 when the University, at the urging of President Wriston, set up a Committee on Dramatic Productions and appointed Ben Brown as its director, with full responsibility for stage presentations at Brown and Pembroke. It was the first time in thirty-seven years that the title of director was officially used to define the work done by Tom Crosby and then Ben Brown. Despite his new title, Professor Brown remained a member of the English department. It was to be another forty years before the Department of Theatre Arts would be created.

Between 1942 and 1945, Ben was on a leave of absence to serve as first assistant manager for the American Red Cross in the North Atlantic region. While Ben was away, the task of keeping Sock and Buskin alive fell to Leslie Allen Jones '26 and Janice Van de Water. Jones was the man in charge of the design and construction of sets for all Sock and Buskin productions, serving as a volunteer under Ben Brown from 1931 to 1942, at which time he was appointed to the faculty. He was also the man Ben called on to cover for him by taking an early morning class when the previous evening's entertainment lasted a bit too long.

Miss Van de Water (she later married Sevellon Brown III, an editor and publisher of the *Providence Journal*) had a strong background in speech and an academic interest in Shakespeare. The Barnard College graduate (her M.A. was in drama at the Teachers College of Columbia University) had a sense of style and was a superb director of stylized drama. She also had a good eye for detail and served as a technical director, rather than as an acting director à la Crosby and Brown. Her first meeting with Ben Brown was one she will never forget.

"My interview," Janice says, "was with Dean Morriss, Professor Hastings, the woman I was to replace, and Ben. We met for lunch at the Brown Faculty Club in May of 1940. I remember we were all concerned because France was falling, and Dean Morriss asked that a radio be left on during lunch so we could hear the latest news from Paris and London. There were hard feelings between Ben and my predecessor, and

they bickered back and forth across the table all during lunch while I was being interviewed. I couldn't believe it! Life at Brown, I thought, was certainly going to be interesting."

It certainly was interesting one night when Janice had a run-in with J. N. "Skip" Stahley, Brown's head football coach. One of Ben's theories was that football players made good actors because they were accustomed to tight discipline and they knew how to move. As evidence of this theory Ben liked to point to Jay Fidler '43, a large, handsome lad who, in the fall of 1942, was a starting tackle on Stahley's team while also playing the role of Prospero in Sock and Buskin's *The Tempest*.

"During dress rehearsal one evening," Janice told me recently, "Coach Stahley came storming into the back of the theatre. 'Where's Fidler?' he shouted. 'He's on stage,' I replied. 'He can't be on stage. I want him,' the coach countered. So I opened the door to the theatre, and at that very moment Jay Fidler, in costume and makeup, was giving Prospero's speech, eloquently, with lights on him and the house all dark. 'There he is,' I said. 'If you want him, take him.' The coach glared at me. 'Tell Fidler if he misses another skull session he's off the team.' And with that Mr. Stahley vanished into the night, slamming the door behind him."

When Ben Brown returned in February 1945 he picked up his courses in nineteeth-century drama and play production and once again took firm control of Sock and Buskin. He also resumed his role as a campus celebrity and quickly fell back into his old rituals. One of these was sharing a drink or two after rehearsal with a few students or a faculty member. Ben's favorite spot remained the Spaghetti Place on Mathewson Street in downtown Providence. Al Saglio, the owner-manager, developed a devotion to Ben, who ate at the Spaghetti Place nearly every night, and always in elegant fashion. Reportedly, as soon as Ben walked in the door the bartender mixed the "Ben Brown Special" – a martini decorated with an anchovy. He also liked his Scotch, but *always* with warm water.

Dr. Bertram H. Buxton '40, one of Sock and Buskin's most distinguished actors, recently recalled some of those evenings at the Spaghetti Place. "After the final performance of each play, Ben would hold open court down there. Gale Noyes of the English department would usually be along, and members of the cast and other students would crowd into the booths in Ben's immediate area. Toasts would be lifted to the play and to individual members of the cast and then Ben would stand up and give a parody of the reviews of the play carried in the *Providence Journal* and the *Brown Daily Herald*.

"To be at the Spaghetti Place on these occasions was like going to a lecture on the theatre. Ben would discuss the history of the play we had just completed, when it first came to Broadway, and the merits of the performances of its stars. The students would just sit there spellbound, and Ben would be in his glory. Since he was a bachelor, Ben's family was his students. We loved him and he returned our love. It was a happy arrangement. To many of us, Ben Brown was the Mr. Chips of Brown University theatre."

The Spaghetti Place was also where many of Brown's theatrical seasons were planned. It was a tradition at Brown for students to have a say in the selection of plays. But Ben would sometimes bend that tradition a bit. The Sock and Buskin board inevitably would wrangle about the selections for the coming year for a month or more. Then Ben would take two or three members of the board to the Spaghetti Place and there, over good wine and under poor lighting, the upcoming Sock and Buskin season would be planned. At the next meeting of the board, Ben would say, "Gentlemen, we've been procrastinating too long. It's time we came to a decision." At which point one of his downtown cohorts would say, "I think we should do such and such." Beaming, Ben would pound his desk and shout, "That's a splendid idea," and the program would be voted through.

Janice made a number of trips to the Spaghetti Place with Professor Brown. "The Saglio brothers saw themselves as the Sardi's of Providence," she said recently. "They cultivated theatrical personalities, such as the acts from Fay's Theater, a vaudeville house just a block or so away. I was there one night when the trained dogs act came in. The dogs sat at a table with their little dishes and their jeweled collars. I asked Joey, the waiter, if dogs were permitted to eat in a restaurant. 'They're very clean dogs,' he said, shrugging his shoulders.

"You would meet quite an assortment of people in there – magicians, singers, dancers. The bill at Fay's Theater changed each week so there was a constant flow, which made life rather interesting at the Spaghetti Place. Sometimes the actors would be putting on or taking off their makeup while they ate. It was most unprofessional, but they were always in a hurry."

Shortly after World War II, there was a feud betwen two strippers who were working in different nightclubs outside Providence. One used doves in her act and the other used snakes. The basis of the feud was that each claimed the other didn't have the physical dimensions publicly advertised. The snake stripper, who was a frequent visitor to the Spaghetti Place, was particularly proud of her bosom. One night, Al Saglio thought he'd have some fun, and so he brought the stripper to the table of the distinguished professor. She sat there, pouring out her troubles and explaining how the dove stripper was giving her the put-down, saying that her breasts were not up to snuff. The more she talked, the more irate she became over the injustice of it all. "She even says I wear falsies," she blurted out. With that the snake stripper grabbed Ben's right hand and thrust it down inside her dress. According to several eye witnesses, Ben is reported to have responded to the situation admirably. "Yes, my dear," he muttered, "they are yours and yours alone. And they are magnificent."

This same lady brought her snakes to the Spaghetti Place one Sunday afternoon. They were in a long box with a grill at one end, presumably so they could breathe. The bartender said he thought the snakes were hungry, although he didn't explain how he knew this. But then he didn't have to explain the Thorne Smith atmosphere of the Spaghetti Place. Al Saglio got on the phone immediately and called the Bronx Zoo in New York City to find out what snakes preferred for lunch. A hush fell over the crowd as everyone waited for the answer. "Snakes eat mice," Al Salgio finally announced in rounded tones worthy of John Barrymore at his best. "There should be plenty of mice in *your* kitchen," Ben Brown thundered from a spot well beyond Saglio's reach. After much discussion, the group finally decided that snakes would prefer spaghetti, since it ought to go down easily in snakes. It was just a typical Sunday afternoon in the Spaghetti

Ben Brown wore the laurel crown when he was named "Favorite Professor" by the Pembroke senior class in 1940.

Place.

If Ben Brown played hard, he also worked hard. He certainly brought a professional approach, a discipline, to Brown theatre. It was understood that you came to rehearsal on time and that if you missed a rehearsal for any reason other than illness you were automatically out of the cast, even if you were the lead. Ben also insisted on the curtain going up on time, saying that it wasn't fair to people who arrived on schedule to delay the curtain for those who lingered over a second or third martini at a pre-theatre party.

Jay Fidler is among the Sock and Buskin alumni who have vivid memories of Ben Brown's well-orchestrated rehearsals. Each night the director would watch from a different seat in the middle of a darkened theatre. The cast, however, always knew precisely where he was because even the dim stage lighting would pick up his glasses and his shiny head.

"At some point in each rehearsal," Fidler says, "Ben would erupt from his seat and come striding down one of the aisles, and from either a spot in front of the proscenium, or up on the stage, he'd tell you what he was thinking, why you should change your interpretation or movement. Sometimes he became exasperated when he thought lines should have been committed to memory – and weren't. And during such moods he'd run his hand, fingers widespread, from his forehead over the top of his baldness to the rear of his head – a characteristic Ben Brown gesture."

Time was not important to Ben Brown during rehearsals, which would sometimes last until the early hours of the morning. The cast worked on scenes until it had them right. And at the end of each rehearsal every player sat on the stage in a semi-circle as Ben went over, in turn, the praise, the criticism, the suggestions each weary player would take back to the dorm. "These sessions were lectures on the theatre," says Lois Buxton, "If you took part in one, it stays with you forever."

An incessant smoker, Professor Brown sometimes used his cigarette as a pointer to emphasize the salient elements of one of his rehearsal lectures. "Ben would distinguish between timelessness and timeliness," according to Joseph R. Weisberger '42, now a justice of the Supreme Court of Rhode Island. "He would analogize a play to a symphony. One of his most frequent messages went something like this: 'The timing of a line of dialogue in a play is not significantly different from the timing of an instrument in a symphony orchestra. Unless the cymbal crashes precisely at the point where it is required by the music, it were better that it had never crashed at all. If a line is not spoken precisely at the point that dramatic impact requires, it were better that it never be spoken at all.'"

The lovely Hollywood star, Ruth Hussey '33, visited Sock and Buskin in 1941.

When the character interpretations, the achievements of the proper rhythms, the movement about the stage were all so wretched as to defy Ben Brown's ability to give constructive directions for their remedy, he would utter his most scathing evaluation of a rehearsal – namely that it was "beneath criticism." This was the comment cast members feared most of all.

Ben Brown was a man of many moods, and it was always easy to tell what mood he was in by his voice. If he gave you a breezy, "Hi, boy," you knew that his mood was good. He could also give out with a roar that could be heard through the theatre. Then his voice would lash out like a whip, sometimes bringing tears to a leading lady's eyes. There was a third mood, one that elicited sympathy. He'd clutch his side and in a soft voice would say, "If I were in better health, if it weren't for this liver, I could stand up to this."

Geoff Riker '54 was eleven when he first worked under Ben Brown. He was playing a street urchin in a play that starred his older brother, Joseph Riker '47. "I was shy, unsure of myself, and was having trouble with a street dance," Geoff Riker writes. "Ben stopped rehearsal, made everybody wait – including my much respected brother – while he personally did the dance and then asked me to imitate. My recollection is that I was so aware that this very important man had stopped everything to help me avoid making a fool of myself that I could not fail to do exactly what he wanted. And when I did – and Ben applauded – that little fourteen seconds of business was set in concrete for the run of the show."

When an actor or actress began to develop certain skills in a role, Ben Brown had a knack for letting that person know that there was still more in the part than the individual had discovered. But he would never restrict the ways in which the actor developed the role. It was more a matter of guidance than of laying on specifics and rules. His standards were higher than those of many professionals. And it was understood that no Sock and Buskin actor expected to be thrown a cue after dress rehearsal.

"Serious and intensive work was the hallmark of Ben's direction," says Til Mason '35, "and the cast could see improvement happen before its very eyes. This was a testimony both to the slave driver and the slaves. The result was that most actors got the feeling that 'I must be better than I thought I was.' This is important in the theatre."

One of the few things Ben wouldn't tolerate was the casual approach to theatrical productions. On more than one occasion he closed down a rehearsal, shouting, "When you're ready to work, we'll work." Ben Brown was a man you wanted to please. Sometimes the reward for doing so was *not* being chastised. And that was enough.

For many years, a Ben Brown tradition was the annual May strawberry breakfast he gave at the Brown Faculty Club for senior members of Sock and Buskin. While frequently dealing with undergraduates on what essentially was a peer basis – whether at the Faculty Club or the Spaghetti Place – Ben was always able to retain an authority position and to command respect. "Ben would lead the discussion but would always give to the articulated thoughts of his students kindly and considerate attention," Judge Weisberger writes. "Every student thespian in Sock and Buskin was treated by Ben Brown as a comrade. He never talked down to us but always responded as though we were fellow members of the faculty."

In the classroom, Ben tried to shock his students by taking a position that would be unexpected. He'd come in one morning praising Shaw's *Arms and the Man* as one of the world's great plays. A few days later he would mention the play again, this time referring to it as one of the author's lesser works. If the students wanted to cater to the teacher's taste on an upcoming exam, they had to go further than his lectures.

If pride is a sin, then Ben Brown was a sinner. He was temperamental, difficult to get along with at times, and he seemed to grow more imperious as he grew older. As a director, he always gave himself full credit on productions, but was far less generous for staff members who worked under him. Make no mistake about it, Ben Brown *was* Brown University theatre. He operated there with the same majesty as he did on Commencement mornings when, like Tom Crosby before him, he led the Procession down College Hill carrying the mace.

No one worked longer at close range with Ben Brown than Leslie Allen Jones. Some years back he wrote of the "genius" of the man, but also noted that Ben had his warts:

"Unasked he wrote the preface and helped me find a publisher for my first book. He was gleeful about the illustrations I did for his book. Once I remember he came to the house with a Mexican blanket he had bought for me in Mexico City. He held me spellbound with his account of the great stained-glass curtain in that city's opera house. About a year ago I was to go into the hospital for a minor operation. The night before, he called to wish me well. It had been three weeks since I had seen him, yet he remembered.

"We worked well together because each of us respected the other's professional ability. We never had words over a set. Once, however, I spoke my mind in his office over policy. He was black-browed and snorting when I left. When I met him on campus the next day he was his most charming self. 'I think,' he said, and proceeded to give me back my idea as his very own. The truest thing he ever said about himself was one evening when we were alone in a dressing room: 'You know (and here a smile) I'm not sure I would recognize the truth if I said it.'

"He was child-like. There was his childish, petulant voice. It was a deep mumble, and it demanded soothing. Things hurt. I was to put them right immediately. Sometimes that was absolutely easy, for the wrong

was in his own mind only. Again, it was not easy – or possible – but in a day or two the mood would change and the wrong had never been.

"He was arrogant and willful at times, wrapped in his own delusions, and many people could not understand him. He liked that and went out of his way to shock and confound his own academic colleagues. I was not always his defender. He would bruise the undergraduates, who would then come to me bewildered at having discovered clay feet in their idol. And sometimes it was my good fortune to make them understand his sweet childishness. For he was gentle of heart."

When the occasion called for it, Professor Brown could be a fighter. One colleague recalls that once in a fight, Ben always went for the jugular. Early in his career he took on Nelson Jones '28, a popular campus figure who was in charge of activities in Faunce House. Ben wanted to reserve the new theatre exclusively for

At the opening Convocation in 1946, Ben Brown carried the Mace, followed by Chancellor Henry Sharpe and President Wriston. Also seen in the picture are Sam Arnold and Pat Kenny.

rehearsals and productions. Nelson Jones felt that the theatre was fair game for movies, lectures, and various other student activities. Ben Brown won this one on a knockout.

In 1942 he locked horns with the curriculum committee in a long and bitter battle over whether or not a course in play production should be added. Many faculty members felt strongly that there was no place for courses in theatre in a liberal arts college. Again, Ben Brown was the winner, but some of the scars from this battle remained for years.

Professor Brown had a catholicity of intellectual interests. He read widely and voraciously, not only in the field of English literature but in history, economics, and the sciences as well. He could talk persuasively and interestingly on almost any subject that might be raised.

Throughout his career, Ben Brown investigated the theatre in most European countries. He studied in 1925 at the University of Touraine, worked under Max Reinhardt in Salzburg in 1927, and later haunted the Shakespeare Festival at Stratford-on-Avon. After a sabbatical in Russia, during which he stayed in Moscow and studied the nationally supported theatre, he returned home and wrote *Theater on the Left*, a brilliant recap of what had been happening on the Russian stage since the Soviets took over. He later wrote *Upstage, Downstage*, a book on acting and production techniques.

Ben was equally interested in what was happening to theatre in this country, never missing an opportunity to see plays in Boston and New York. He often boasted that in 1936 he took in twenty-nine of the thirty-three new productions on Broadway. Because of his knowledge of theatre and his enthusiasm for production of drama, Ben Brown became widely sought after for summer work on college campuses, as a reader, and as advisor to the New York State Board of Education in organization of dramatic work in public schools.

"Theatre-in-the-round, in the experimental stage in Europe during the late twenties and early thirties, intrigued Ben," Francis B. Armington told me. "I am certain that if facilities at Brown could have been adapted to that form of presentation, Sock and Buskin under his aegis would have been a pioneer in this country.

"For Ben was an innovator in the theatre, never content to stand still, never hesitating to bring an old play back to life with a new and up-to-date interpretation, presenting Shakespeare in modern dress, searching out the best in experimental theatre. He made extra-curricular theatre so challenging, so exciting, so fascinating that many a graduate chose it as his life's work, not through his academic learning, but because of Ben's contagious dedication to the theatre."

At some point in his life, Ben became a disciple of the Stanislavski method of acting. Walter Covell '38, a Sock and Buskin alumnus, recalls: "One of the Alumni Shows in which Ben appeared was directed by his good friend and Brown roommate, Rufus Fuller. Well, Ben liked to establish his background as the character in the play, including where he lived, what he had for breakfast that day, what books he read, and so forth. Then, on trying to hit on a motive for his entrance, he asked Rufus, 'Where do I come from in this scene?' 'Out of the wings, you damn fool,' was the reply."

Although he was not a witty man, Ben Brown had a good sense of humor and could appreciate amusing situations, which for some reason or other, he found himself in more often than not. "One cold winter day Ben and I finished grading exams and headed downtown for lunch," Janice Van de Water Brown says. "The sidewalks were covered with ice and the two of us slipped and fell directly in front of the Deke House on College Hill. Sitting on a piece of ice with a dignified posture (which is not easy to do), Ben turned to me, sprawled beside him, and said, 'I'm afraid, Janice, that they'll never believe in the Deke House that we are cold sober.'"

Socially, Ben was an asset at any party, from a clambake to a formal wedding. He was a good conversationalist and made the person with whom he was talking feel that he or she was the most important human being in the world. He read poetry beautifully and usually could be persuaded to give a reading spontaneously. Once, while visiting Rufus and Alice Fuller, he tore down the portieres to create the proper atmosphere and costume and then to everyone's delight gave a stirring rendering of "If Villon Were the King of France."

There were invitations to dinner, for which Ben was grateful. Once, however, he did make a complaint. "People always feed me chicken or steak," he said. "Sometimes I'd give my eye tooth for a good bowl of home-made beef stew." One night not too long before his death, Ben visited Sally Barker. "He sat slouched in a chair staring at nothing in particular," she recalled last summer. "'Sally,' he said, 'I'm lonesome.' You can't be lonesome with all those wonderful kids you have with you, I told him. Still staring straight ahead, he said, 'I'm tired of pinning up diapers.'"

Over the years, Ben Brown was always more than willing to toast a friend. And he made many friends. By the early 1960s, Les Jones had to take over more and more of Ben's early-morning classes. "I'm not an alcoholic," he'd quip, "just a heavy drinker." A coffee cup in his hands on the way to his lips would shake violently, to the point where one expected the brew to splash on the table. But it never did. He got into a row with Janice Van de Water Brown one night at the Spaghetti Place when she reminded him that he was not supposed to drink. "I intend to die the way I have lived," he shouted at her.

Having no family of his own, Ben Brown hated the holidays, especially Christmas. After the Christmas break in 1954, he didn't show up for his classes, nor did he appear at the Spaghetti Place for his favorite martini. On January 5, 1955, a colleague, Professor James O. Barnhill, went to Ben's third-floor Athenaeum Row apartment on Benefit Street and found him lying on the floor with a three-day growth of beard. He had suffered a stroke, and he died in the hospital a few days later without regaining consciousness. He was fifty-seven. Even in death there was a parallel with Tom Crosby, who had lain helpless in a hotel room after a stroke in 1944.

In writing the memorial minute, Professors Elmer M. Blistein '42 and the late Charles H. Philbrick II '44, colleagues in the English department, called Ben an actor "both in reality and in metaphor" and added: "He was always a man whose chief role was his own life. The range of his emotions was never confined. He could be a King Lear in the regal outrage at the perversities of the world which he never made but which he nonetheless held dear; he could be a Horatio in his wise counsel or gentle consideration, or a Hamlet in his unwearied advice to his players; he could be a Mercutio in his volatile fancy, his wide-faring humor, his deep compassion, and his charming companionship. For him these were not merely parts to be assumed for an occasion and discarded. They were as much a part of him as they were a part of Shakespeare, and we use these terms to speak of him because they were the terms by which he lived and worked.

"Were we to follow the language of Shakespeare, we might call Ben Brown an *original*. He belonged to what seems to be, unfortunately, an ever-declining group of true individualists. He was, in the best sense of the word, a *character*, a legend at Brown while still alive."

Chapter 9 🕬
Life for him was his research and his graduate students

When members of the Brown faculty and administration decided to have an eightieth birthday party for Charlie Kraus in 1955, Provost Samuel T. Arnold '13 brought the news to the man they called "The King" in the chemistry department. "It's safe to assume that some of the speakers may drone on a bit," the provost told the stoop-shouldered little man with the gray hair, goatee, and bristling mustache. "If anyone wants to stay until 3 a.m. telling stories, I'll keep up with them," Kraus shot back.

Kraus had been keeping up with the world for quite some time. He gained international fame in 1923 when he developed a process for producing tetraethyl lead economically and in quantity, thus making possible "high test" or ethyl gasoline. He is credited with much of the research leading to the use of Pyrex glass and the mercury lamp. He was also deeply involved in the Manhattan Project, which produced the atomic bomb that ended World War II, and his work on the conductivity of hydrogen chloride in water received attention around the world.

The Brown scientist also devised simple methods for extraction of the role element "germanum," resembling silicon, from germanite ore. His research resulted in yields of the element four times as great as those elicited through previous methods. Kraus was also credited with the invention of a vacuum-tight seal widely used

in the manufacture of ultraviolet lamps and with the first successful method of lining steel containers with glass.

In 1948, Kraus received the Navy's highest civilian award, the Distinguished Public Service Award, for his part in the development of synthetic rubber during World War II and for the development of the Navy Rebreather, an oxygen-breathing apparatus for aviators.

The record also shows 246 published papers, five honorary degrees, seven medals and citations, membership in the National Academy of Science, and the presidency of the American Chemical Society. Professor Kraus was one of the most eminent chemists of his era. But in typical Kraus fashion he reached this position through unconventional means. His undergraduate major was in electrical engineering, his master's was in physics, and it wasn't until he started work on his Ph.D. that he took courses in chemistry.

Charles August Kraus was born in Knightsville, Indiana, on August 15, 1875, the youngest of five sons of John Henry and Elizabeth (Shaefer) Kraus. Charlie Kraus didn't remain a Hoosier for long. Legend has it that his father went to western Kansas, took a train to the end of the line, walked another mile, and then staked out a two-homestead lot near a town called Hays City. He built a home, laid out a farm, and then brought his family to Kansas.

Kraus had vivid memories of his boyhood, living in a sod house and watching his father break the rugged soil with a plow. He once recalled that the plains at that time were swarming with buffalo bones, which settlers collected for shipment to dealers in Boston, where bone charcoal was used to take the color out of crude sugar.

According to Betty Kraus Hartline, her father conducted his first experiment when he was only seven. "The family was in its second home, a roomy cottage, by that time," she told me. "My dad set up three cans in an upstairs bedroom, one filled with kerosene, one with turpentine, and the third with something else. He was about to put a match to things when his mother walked in and put a paddle to him! This didn't discourage Dad. He was going to find out why some fluids burned and others didn't. So the next day, while out in the pasture tending the cows, he conducted his little experiment."

Since no school was then available, Charlie Kraus received his first education in the kitchen of his home from a young woman from Cape Cod who came to Kansas and conducted classes. Charlie was a bright student right from the start and there were plans to send him to a seminary. The high school principal intervened, however, explaining to the family that the young man's interest was in science, and so he was sent to the University of Kansas.

"Like many other German immigrants, the Kraus family had a great respect for learning and did not oppose Dad's ambitions," Betty Hartline said. "My grandfather worked hard all his life and lived to be ninety-seven. Three of the sons stayed on the farm and became prosperous, and I know that my father's capacity for work and his desire for excellence were shaped during those early years on the farm. I remember asking him once, 'Wasn't Kansas beautiful when you were there?' His reply was, 'We were so busy working we didn't have time to notice.'"

Kraus entered the University of Kansas in 1893 at a time when it had a remarkable record in the training of chemists. But the university can't claim too much credit for turning Kraus into the brilliant chemist he became. His training during those years was in electrical engineering, and he often boasted that the only formal course in chemistry he ever had came during his freshman year. He also visited lectures in organic chemistry given by Professor Edward C. Franklin, but he didn't even audit the course. The visits were strictly for his own enjoyment, but they helped form the basis for a friendship with Franklin that continued through the years.

There was some evidence, even in his days back on the farm, that Charlie Kraus was a young man who would go through life doing things his way. This independent spirit surfaced while he was at the University of Kansas; he refused to take some required course that he found completely objectionable. As a result he didn't graduate with his class, being forced to wait a year until a special ruling freed his diploma.

But that year was a profitable one for Kraus. With time on his hands, he began, in collaboration with Professor Franklin, the monumental work on solutions in liquid ammonia to which both men eventually devoted such a large amount of their scientific attention. This work continued for another year while Kraus held an assistantship in physics. "At that point in my life, degrees and semester hours meant very little to me," Kraus once wrote. "The pot of gold at the end of the rainbow for me was the opportunity to do investigative work."

After spending a year in the department of physics at Johns Hopkins University, Kraus returned to the University of Kansas for two semesters and then accepted an instructorship in physics at the University of California, where he spent three years. The first three weeks, though, were the toughest. It seems that the physics department did not favor research at that time, and Kraus without research was like a soap opera addict without a TV set. It didn't take Kraus long to find a friend in the person of Professor Edmond O'Neill of the chemistry department, who created a corner in his lab for Kraus to call his own.

I t was in this poorly lighted laboratory, and in spite of a heavy teaching schedule, that Charles Kraus gained his first public recognition. According to one of the stories Kraus used to tell, Svante A. Arrhenius, director of the Nobel Institute for Physical Chemistry in Stockholm and a former Nobel Prize winner, visited the campus of the University of California, but refused to meet with the president of an institution that did not accord greater recognition to a man of the caliber of

In the lab at Clark University in 1917.

Charlie Kraus.

Whenever Kraus looked back on his life, he had nothing but fond memories of 1904. During the winter of that year, the prominent physical chemist G. N. Lewis visited the University of California while on his way to accept a post in the government laboratories in the Philippine Islands. On the recommendation of Professor Franklin, he looked up Kraus, became extremely impressed with him, and wrote to Professor A. A. Noyes, who was then just starting to build up the research laboratory of physical chemistry at MIT. That fall, Kraus accepted an assistantship at MIT and, at the same time, began a new phase of his life.

It is possible that never before in the United States had there been gathered in one place such an outstanding group of physical chemists. There were men such as G. N. Lewis, Tolman, Keyes, Whitney, Sosman, and Washburn. Some thirty years later most of the eminent physical chemists of the country had either been in that group or trained by men who were.

At that time, the Ph.D. examinations at MIT consisted of four six-hour and one three-hour written tests. What the department really was looking for, however, was exceptional ability in the field regardless of whether or not one had in his head a large amount of miscellaneous material. Kraus completed the work for his doctorate, took the exams, but had little interest in taking the doctorate. When he talked about this in later years,

Kraus was evasive, noting only that some subterfuges were necessary in order to make him accept his degree in 1908, the year he was appointed a research associate in physical chemistry.

Kraus stayed at MIT through 1914, finding there a haven highly conducive to research. Most of his attention during his decade at MIT was devoted to a study of the alkali and alkaline earth metals dissolved in liquid ammonia. Starting in 1907, he wrote a series of articles dealing with this subject that appeared in the *American Chemical Society*, articles that are still regarded as classics in the field. In short, Kraus was able to study a metallic system, composed in part of a non-metallic constituent, which by the addition of ammonia, would pass to one that was truly electrolytic in its properties. He demonstrated that the more dilute solutions ionize to give the normal positive metal ion and the negative electron, the latter probably being associated with large amounts of ammonia.

The acclaim with which these experiments were received can be attributed to the unusually fine manipulative skill of Kraus, especially in designing and constructing glass apparatus. G. N. Lewis, in his work with Kraus on the measurement of the standard electrode potential of sodium, writes in his text on thermodynamics: "The discovery that ethylamine had approximately the desired properties was due to the investigations of Kraus, and it was his extraordinary experimental skill which made it possible to obtain for the first time the electrode potential of a highly electropositive metal, and with a constancy and reproducibility exceeding any that has hitherto been obtained with any electrode of solid metal."

In 1914, Professor Kraus left MIT to become professor of chemistry and director of the chemistry laboratory at Clark University in Worcester, Massachusetts. During the decade that followed, he was practically the graduate division in chemistry, giving almost all the courses and directing all of the research work. Clark offered ample freedom and opportunities for research, and Kraus took advantage of the situation. He continued his work on solutions of metals and did advanced work in this general field.

By the time Kraus settled down at Clark University, he was married and the father of four children: Charles Newton, Philip, Douglas, and Mary Elizabeth, better known as Betty. On June 11, 1902, he had married Frederica Feitschans, who had been one of his students at the University of Kansas. They had corresponded for a year and then she went to California to marry him.

"Dad came from a pioneer farming culture in which all the German immigrant families hung together," Betty Hartline said. "His rigid views toward women were formed there – and they were centered on the old German ethic – *kinder, kuchen, kirke*, or child, cook, and church. I'm afraid this view colored his domestic relations. My grandmother on my mother's side was an educated woman who studied in Vienna and later taught languages and was in charge of teacher training in Springfield, Illinois. Being brought up in this environment, my mother became quite independent. You might even say she was an early feminist. So from time to time there was a clash of strong personalities between my parents.

"Still, we had a pleasant childhood, especially at Clark University, where our home was on one end of campus and Dad's chemistry lab was on the other. I still have fond memories of small groups of graduate students coming to dinner on Friday evenings. During World War I, I recall my father planting a war garden in our back yard. He never approved of wasting money, especially on things such as fireworks, but Mother, with her independent streak, saw to it that we had some sparklers and pinwheels to light on the campus each Fourth of July."

Betty remembers the family routine as being quite rigid. "Dad would get up early each morning, ring a bell to let Mother know he was out of bed, and then sit down to the same breakfast day after day – bacon, eggs, toast, and coffee. Immediately after breakfast he'd head for his lab, return home for dinner, and then right back to the lab again. He was so completely wrapped up in his science that he couldn't extract himself from it. Obviously, he didn't have much time for his family – except for the trips to the farm."

The Kraus farm was in Princeton, Massachusetts, about ten miles from Worcester. In the early years the family took a local train from Worcester, got off at Brooks Station, and then walked the two miles to the farm. Later they bought a Marmon and made the trip by car. Mrs. Kraus and the children spent the summers at the farm and Charlie came out whenever he needed a vacation, always bringing his graduate students with him.

"Although Dad and I went fishing occasionally in Worcester, took walks looking for chestnuts, and played a card game called Skat, we saw more of him at the farm than anywhere else," Philip Kraus told me recently. "He was completely relaxed up there. Dad was a great farmer and loved to dig in the dirt. He was especially proud of his potatoes and corn, and he kept all the neighbors well supplied."

Every August Kraus would invite all of the people from the lab to a "corn roast" on the farm. There was a large stone circle near the corn rows and guests would gather round and cook corn, steaks, and potatoes while Charlie Kraus walked around the circle barking out instructions. "Because Dad was the youngest member of his family he got pressed into working in the kitchen when he was a boy," Betty Hartline said. "He certainly considered himself quite a cook and had strong ideas on how a turkey should be stuffed, a bread pudding should be cooked, or a corn roast should be run."

Considering his complete dedication to science, it's not surprising that Charlie Kraus could never be coaxed out of the house to attend a movie or a dance. He did, however, enjoy a violin concert, although he didn't play the instrument himself. Betty recalls one particular evening when she went with her mother and father to Mechanics Hall in Worcester to see Fritz Kreisler in concert. "I was studying the violin then and the evening had a special meaning for me."

Charlie Kraus became a celebrity during his last few years at Clark through his role as a pioneer in the development of ethyl gasoline. The story goes back to 1916 when Thomas Midgely, Jr., working at General Motors Research Laboratory, started research on the problem of preventing engine knock.

In 1922 Midgely had discovered the anti-knock properties of tetraethyl lead. But no satisfactory method had been devised to make the unfamiliar chemical compound in large quantities at a reasonable cost. That's when Kraus, who had been appointed a part-time consultant to Standard Oil in 1921, was called upon to work out a practical method for the preparation of the alkyl compound on a comparatively large scale. Joining Kraus on this phase of the problem was Conrad C. Callis, who was working for his Ph.D. under him at Clark. By early 1922 Kraus had made tetraethyl lead with an apparatus that he and Callis had designed and built. Then they tried out the compound in automobiles and were more than pleased with the results.

"DuPont had begun to manufacture the compound by the bromide process, the best process then known," Kraus once said. "It had the disadvantage, however, of requiring bromine, which was both scarce and expensive. We knew there was no sense in fooling around with the more expensive iodides or bromides. So, it was full steam ahead with ethyl chloride."

On February 2, 1923, the first public sale of ethyl gasoline was made at a service station in Dayton, Ohio. On that date only seventy gallons was pumped into the tanks of a few curious motorists. One of the odd things about the two men associated with the development of ethyl anti-knock compound is that neither was trained as a chemist. (Tom Midgely's background was in mechanical engineering.) Yet, both eventually won national recognition in the field of chemistry and both served as president of the American Chemical Society.

According to Harold R. "Jerry" Nace, professor of chemistry at Brown, Kraus put a patent on his discovery: "The story we heard was that Kraus had a royalty agreement that every pound of tetraethyl lead that was sold for seventeen years would bring him a fixed amount. I do know that at one time DuPont was making 12 million pounds a month. Yet, if you asked Dr. Kraus, he'd say that he didn't have any money. Some people at DuPont say he did receive a handsome royalty. Others say he lost most of it in the crash of 1929."

Kraus left Clark in 1923 when a new administration changed the character and the direction of the university, which had been especially strong in chemistry, physics, and biology. He did some lecturing at Brown that year and then, in 1924, he accepted an appointment from President Faunce to join the Brown faculty as research professor of chemistry. In an unusual move, Kraus brought his twelve graduate students with him. One was Warren C. Johnson ('25 Ph.D.), who became chancellor of the University of Chicago, and another was Gordon Teal ('28 A.M., '31 Ph.D.), later executive vice president of Texas Instruments and a former member of the Brown Board of Fellows.

Although Brown was one of the very first institutions in the United States to award the Ph.D. degree, the University had not expanded its graduate school. And Kraus, at that point in his career, had shown that his chief interest was in research and in the systematic training of graduate students. His first home at Brown was in Rogers Hall, where all graduate study in chemistry was to remain for fourteen more years. The facilities were inadequate and financial support was a sometime thing, but Kraus immediately set out to expand graduate study at Brown.

In his Faculty Minute written shortly after the death of Dr. Kraus, Professor of Chemistry Robert Cole touched on this point: "The many years of the work of Kraus at Brown not only produced classic investigations of solutions of electrolytes, they also coincided with the emergence of Brown as a university in fact as well as name. Graduate study at Brown is now accepted and commonplace as an essential function, but it was not so when Kraus began. It was largely through his efforts and a few others that it became so. That there were very stormy periods of battle with the administration is clear from records and recollections, but he and his worthy adversaries gained a mutual respect and understanding.

"Whatever the circumstances of their work, some forty Ph.D.'s who did their research under Kraus remember him as a great teacher and educator in the best sense of the words. This was not because of his lectures, which were brilliant but infrequent. Kraus felt that courses should be few and rigorous, but he was also convinced that preliminary or general examinations were an abomination, and that a student learned best by accomplishment in the testing ground of the laboratory.

"Examinations in this area were unscheduled, of almost daily frequency, and searching. That Kraus was a master of his philosophy is attested by the product. His students had widely varying aptitudes and interests, but after his training they shared a confidence in tackling difficult problems, and a proper mixture of respect and affection for 'The King' who helped them realize their potentials."

President Wriston, shortly after his installation in 1937, paid a visit to the rag-tail facilities used by Kraus and the other Brown chemists in Rogers Hall. "I will never forget that first look at our meager facilities for chemistry," Wriston said. "It seemed to me that I had never seen so much done with so little."

Some contend that the efforts of Kraus to build a better chemistry department at Brown were carried out with imagination, skill, and the good sense never to become department chairman. He and Bob Chambers '09 and Sam Arnold '13 would get together once a year to select a chairman. And it was always a 2-1 vote for Chambers, with Chambers casting the lone dissenting vote. "Kraus and Arnold ganged up on me,"

Chambers said, shaking his head, after one of those meetings. "They did it to me again."

Chambers was a mild-mannered man, Kraus was – well, not known for his sweetness of disposition. But the two men got along just fine. Chambers ran the Metcalf Chemical Laboratory, which was constructed in the mid-1920s after a major gift from Senator Jesse Metcalf, and Kraus was lord and master of his research lab in Rogers Hall. In fact, the two men teamed to raise some $500,000 from Senator Metcalf for the construction of a modern research laboratory adjacent to Metcalf lab.

The new lab (Metcalf Research Laboratory) was dedicated in 1938 as a feature of the annual meeting of the American Chemical Society, held that year on the Brown campus. It was a gala occasion, with former President Herbert Hoover among the guests. The lab was described as one of the most complete in the country, and Kraus was installed that day as president of the American Chemical Society. The brick colonial building contained sixty-one rooms and, at the time of dedication, housed a scientific library of 50,000 volumes on the third floor.

Charles Kraus had placed his faith in research before it was the fashion. At the dedication of Metcalf Research Lab, he said, "The philosopher's stone, for which alchemists sought so ardently and vainly of old, has been discovered by modern science – it is research. Through research the innermost secrets of nature are being disclosed, the elements have been transmuted, and the span of life has been lengthened."

Kraus played a key role in the design of his new laboratory and, in the process, had his first run-in with Henry Wriston. As designed by Kraus, the top floor of the building would have been a dorm for his graduate students. But Kraus lost this battle, and it was the start of a tempestuous relationship with the Brown president. "Kraus was furious with Wriston," Professor Cole told me recently. "He figured that he had raised most of the money for this new facility and had spent the better part of a year designing it to his specific needs and then this new president came along [Wriston was installed in February 1937] and spoiled his plans.

"About a year later they clashed again. This was when the Faculty Club was located in Andrews House, the beautiful building that is now the Brown infirmary. There was no drinking in the Faculty Club then, but Charlie, who liked a nip before lunch or dinner, got around the rule by visiting a crony who lived on the third floor of the Faculty Club. Well, in 1939 Wriston turned the building into an infirmary and shifted the Faculty Club to its present location on Megee Street. There was still no drinking allowed in the new club, nor were there rooms for this crony to live in. So Charlie resigned in a huff and joined the University Club."

According to Cole, Kraus got back at Wriston in his own fashion. He would never march in the Procession on Commencement Day, knowing how much it bothered Wriston when full professors sat out this festive occasion. But the cruelest blow of all was that Charlie would always be on the landing at the top of the front steps of the University Club and would lift his martini in a mock toast when Wriston marched along Benefit Street leading the Procession.

"Once he settled in at Brown, Dad's life was his lab," Betty Hartline said. "As a result, his home became less and less a part of his life. In retrospect, I guess you could say that Dad was a man that men appreciated. His greatest enjoyment came when he was with his colleagues or his graduate students.

"When we got to Providence, he did take an interest in our preparatory work. For one thing he forbade us to take chemistry in high school, simply because he didn't think it was taught well enough. He stressed that we should build up our background for chemistry by taking loads of physics and math at that age."

Philip Kraus said that he took one course with his father. "Dad warned me in advance that I wouldn't get any special favors. He was right. I didn't."

Betty Hartline '31 acknowledged that having a Charles Kraus for a father did not make for an easy childhood. "Here was a parent who had a distinguished career, and all his children felt a step or two below Mount Olympus. Maybe it was rebellion. Maybe we were saying that he had too much of a one-track mind. Certainly there was a revolt among us in not getting involved in the same intense pursuit of science as father did."

Mrs. Hartline, who lives in Hyde, Maryland, taught at Bryn Mawr for three years, took care of her growing family, and now is involved in conservation work. Her husband, Keffer Hartline, is a research biologist who won a Nobel Prize. Philip Kraus '31, of Wilmington,

Delaware, served for many years as a chemist with the DuPont Company. Douglas Kraus '34, of Kingston, Rhode Island, is professor emeritus of chemistry at the University of Rhode Island. The late C. Newton Kraus '31, who lived in Warren, Rhode Island, was a prominent ham radio operator who in 1957 won the Navy's Distinguished Service Award for keeping radio contact between Navy men at Operation Deep Freeze in the Antarctic and their families in Rhode Island.

Professor Lee Clapp, who was hired by Kraus, said that The King put Brown on the map as far as chemistry was concerned. "He won all the important medals of the American Chemical Society – The Gibbs Medal, The Nichols Medal, Richards Medal, and The Priestley Medal, which is the highest honor the society can give. So, he had an international reputation, especially in electrolysis, electric chemistry, and liquid ammonia in chemistry. I think it's safe to say that he was regarded so highly because he was the first to do anything of note in these fields. He was a pioneer, one whose active scientific life began during the period when physical chemistry was becoming established as a definite branch of chemistry.

"Probably the one thing that helped Kraus obtain such stature in his field is that he didn't pay any attention to the other duties within the department. He stuck strictly to chemical research. He never attended a faculty meeting or even a chemistry staff meeting. One year he served as president of Sigma Xi at Brown and never showed his face at a meeting. He spent his entire life driving hard in one direction, and he knew that direction quite well. In my long life in chemistry, I've never seen anyone to compare to him."

Kraus expected the same dedication from others. This especially applied to his graduate students. His entire life revolved around his research and his graduate students, and he was disturbed if he didn't find his students working in the lab when he arrived at 8 o'clock each morning. He had a theory that students didn't learn anything from books. They learned from getting into the lab and working on it. So, Kraus taught as few courses as possible. He'd always be listed in the catalogue to teach a course, but it usualy petered out long before the semester ended. Courses, after all, were just a waste of time to Kraus.

Charlie Kraus ran his research program and his graduate students with an iron hand, perhaps unparalleled in Brown's history. Few of his students had the audacity to get married while they were working under Kraus and the few who did take the time to marry did so with fear and trembling. Edward Koubek ('64 Ph.D.), professor of chemistry at the United States Naval Academy, came to Brown long after Kraus retired but heard stories about The King constantly. "One saying that came down from the Kraus era was that he expected his graduate students to work an eight-hour day – eight hours *before* dinner and eight hours after dinner. There were also stories about how he conducted oral exams. Apparently one of the requirements for the student taking his orals was that he bring along a bottle of Bushmills [an Irish whiskey Kraus loved], some ice, and a few glasses. Then when the questions from the faculty members ended, everyone could sit around and have a party. It became a chemistry department tradition over the years."

When Kraus lectured, he never read from notes. He talked from his own experience in the lab. Some students felt Kraus was dictating from Heaven when he lectured because he tended to pontificate. But they were never turned off because that was his style and – he was Kraus. He was a very good speaker and had a strong voice that belied his slight frame.

Kraus was known for being highly protective of his graduate students. Professor Nace recently discussed this with me: "I can remember one graduate student who came up for his Ph.D. oral exam. His experiments were magnificent because Kraus had told him what to do, but after a few minutes it was obvious that the student really didn't understand what he had done. Well, the questioning from the professors got heavier and heavier, and the student became more and more confused. At this point Kraus took over and helped his grad student answer the questions. Two young faculty members then tried to take Kraus on, and he just chewed them up into little pieces. And the grad student passed. Kraus would stand no interference from anyone with his students."

No women were allowed in the Metcalf Research Lab except the secretaries. The wives of many of the graduate students were scared to death of Kraus and wouldn't have thought of setting foot in the building. That was his domain – the entire building.

Right after World War II Kraus wanted a graduate

Kraus considered the lab his personal domain.

student from the West Coast, a man named Wagner. There was a hitch, however. Wagner was married and would come only if his wife, Juanita, was also accepted. "The idea of a woman doing research in chemistry in *his* lab really boggled the mind of Charlie Kraus," Professor Cole said. "But he agreed to go along with what he considered a radical experiment. Several years later he sat in on Juanita's Ph.D. oral exam, and when it was over he had a messenger boy come in and present her with a dozen red roses. This was typical of his style. You never knew what to expect." After that, Brown took women graduate students in chemistry regularly.

It was no secret on campus that Charles Kraus liked to take a drink. Henry Wriston once said that Kraus was the inventor of that modern weapon of war – the dry martini.

"With all the stories about his drinking, I never saw Dr. Kraus when he wasn't in complete control of his faculties," Professor Nace said recently. "He knew what his metabolism was and he drank accordingly. Every noon he would head down to the University Club and consume three martinis. Then he ate an enormous lunch. He couldn't have weighed much more than 100 pounds.

"At 5:30 he'd head back to the University Club. This time he drank Bushmills. He'd have three or four on the rocks before dinner, eat a large meal, and then head home to do some serious drinking. This went on like clockwork, day after day, and we all wondered how he could do it. But he was never the worse for wear and his research never suffered."

Each fall Kraus would invite the new members of the department to his home to introduce them to the staff. "His rule on these occasions," Professor Clapp said, "was that you couldn't leave until the ice in your drink melted. And he didn't want you to stay much longer than that either."

The joke around the chemistry department was that Kraus had a better supply of liquor in his cellar than did most liquor stores on the East Side. One night his son, C. Newton Kraus, rushed in the front door. "Dad, I need some Creme de Menthe," he said. "White or green?" Kraus asked. "Green," Newt replied. "Go to the northeast corner of the cellar," Kraus said. He knew exactly where everything was kept.

Back in the early 1940s President Wriston had a reception and buffet at his home each fall for the faculty. The pre-buffet beverage was always punch since Wriston didn't tolerate liquor in his home. And each year Professors Kraus, Chambers, and Cross, all of whom enjoyed something more fortifying than punch before dinner, would visit the University Club and drink about as much as they could safely hold without disgracing themselves at the reception. One year, largely in deference to the chemists, Wriston decided to relax his standards on liquor, and when Messrs. Kraus, Chambers, and Cross arrived at the president's home, the first thing they saw was a long table spread with bottles of the choicest whiskey. Wriston never could understand why Kraus and company didn't avail themselves of this spread.

As Professor Nace told me last fall, Kraus was a wonderful man to be around. He was opinianted to the extreme, but he was also willing to listen. And although he had a hot temper, he never held a grudge. "Kraus was a staunch Republican and almost all of the other department members were Democrats," Nace recalled. "Well, the arguments that raced up and down the halls of Metcalf Research Lab during the 1952 presidential campaign between Eisenhower and Stevenson were pretty bitter at times. The day after the election Kraus called a meeting of the department. We all thought he was going to come in and gloat.

Instead he arrived with Bushmills and soda and then gave the most wonderful speech you ever heard. The King said that all was forgiven and the department should close ranks. I still have a wire recording of that speech. It's a classic in statesmanship."

Kraus was a gregarious man who loved good company and intelligent conversation. He and President Keeney were good friends, perhaps because they had so much in common. Both were extremely independent and both enjoyed relaxing over a drink or two. Kraus was also close to Sam Arnold, his colleague in chemistry and later provost of the University. In this case you couldn't have found two men who were more opposite. Sam Arnold was a genial, mild-mannered man who never took a drink in his life.

At one time the University Club had a small dining room just off the main dining area. Kraus was the center of attraction in this room, and the men who ate with him from time to time called themselves members of the Rover's Club. There were many friends, some from the downtown business district, who could hardly wait to see him each noon.

"Dr. Kraus would talk about anything under the sun – except chemistry," Professor Nace said recently. "Literature, philosophy, religion – fine. Kraus loved to argue. One day he and Senator Theodore Francis Green got into a heated discussion over religion. I really thought for a minute that they were going to come to blows. But they stopped short of that.

"There was a certain magnetism to Kraus," Professor Nace continued. "He had friends all over the country, people who thoroughly enjoyed being in his company. Every so often the annual meeting of the American Chemical Society would be held in Atlantic City. One year I attended with Spike Coles [Professor James S. Coles, later president of Bowdoin College] and Bob Cole. Kraus had gone down before us. As we went on the Boardwalk the next morning to head for Convention Hall, we spotted a table set up under an awning. On the table was a good supply of the best liquor money could buy, an ice bucket, and some tall glasses. And there sat Dr. Kraus. He had set up shop for the day. As his friends came along they would sit down for a chat and a drink."

Kraus traveled to meetings all over the country. But he wouldn't fly. And he never drove a car after a lab accident nearly cost him his eyesight during his Clark years. In 1934, while he served as field secretary of the National Research Council, he surveyed graduate instruction in the fields of physics, chemistry, and math – and he traveled the breadth of the country by train.

Some members of Brown's chemistry department rejoiced when they heard that Kraus was going to be traveling for the better part of a year. "Most members of the department got along with Kraus by staying away from him," Professor Clapp told me. "He had mellowed by the time I came to Brown," Professor Nace said, "but we all feared him. He could hurt people with his tongue and with his actions. There were many outstanding people who left the department just because they could see that they weren't going to get anywhere under Kraus. Sometimes he would take a dislike to a person simply if he parted his hair the wrong way. Kraus was no Orphan Annie. He was The King. And you did it his way or else!

"I was lucky," Nace added. "He took a liking to me. One evening when Mary Alice [Mrs. Nace] and I were at his house he was complaining that he couldn't get smoked sausages for breakfast anymore. Well, Mary Alice came from Somerset, a small town in western Pennsylvania where smoked sausages are made. We placed a phone call, and a few days later I presented Kraus with three pounds of smoked sausages. You'd have thought I had brought him a box of diamonds."

Kraus made his share of mistakes in judging people, partly because he was quick to put down anyone who wasn't marching to his tune. During the Clark years he took a dislike to a bright young physics professor and thought his ideas were whacky. Today the Goddard Space Center is named after that man.

Then there was the case of Lars Onsager, a brilliant Brown chemist who didn't have a Ph.D. degree. Kraus looked past the degree and hired Onsager, who proceeded to do some brilliant work at Brown. Eventually Onsager got on a topic Kraus felt was a waste of time, and Kraus told him so in no uncertain terms, telling him he'd better get back into things in which Kraus had an interest. Onsager's work was on the theory of irreversible processes, work that some forty years later won him the Nobel Prize. It's interesting to note that when Onsager was dropped by Brown during the Great Depression it was Kraus who got him a position on the Yale faculty.

Throughout his life Kraus delighted in poking fun at importance, including his own. "Becoming emeritus is just a technicality," he said. "The only difference is that you do your work and don't get paid for it." He also liked to say that it was easy to arrive at distinction. "All you have to do is outlive your contemporaries." He'd say this in such a way that the listener would tell him it wasn't true in his case and would then cite all his unique achievements. And Kraus would bask in the praise.

Professor Nace recalled that Kraus had a sly sense of humor and, when in one of his good moods, would sprinkle his conversation with dry, witty comments. "Odd things amused him, too. There are three maple trees on the sidewalk outside of Metcalf Lab, and Kraus, Sam Arnold, and Bob Chambers would each select a tree in September and place a bet as to which one would have the last leaf on it. The two losers would buy dinner for the winner. So in late fall these three eminent scientists would sit by the window all day waiting for those last few leaves to fall."

When he was in his seventies, Kraus became interested in long-range weather forecasts. On Saturday afternoons in the fall he'd sit by the radio and tune in football games all over the country. By doing this for several weeks he'd get a pattern of the jet stream and the high altitude wind currents. Along about December 1 he'd make his forecasts. In that era of far less sophisticated weather reports, Standard Oil of New Jersey actually based its oil deliveries on the predictions sent to them by Kraus.

At his 80th birthday party, on August 15, 1955, Kraus received congratulations from Professor Frederick T. Keyes, seated, outgoing President Wriston, incoming President Keeney, and Professor Robert Cole.

Although he had little time for hobbies, Kraus did love to play Skat, a free-wheeling German card game for three or four people. "Dad and I played this game by the hour on rainy days at the old farm," Philip Kraus said recently. "He thought it was a very superior card game. It did provide many options and even someone with a poor hand had a chance to do something. I know for a fact that all his graduate students had to learn Skat. Some said it was a prerequisite for graduation."

Kraus was always proud of his war record. During World War I he directed research for the Chemical Warfare Service and acted as a consulting chemist for the Federal Bureau of Mines. His contributions during World War II were far more significant. In addition to assisting in the purification of uranium salts for the atomic bomb research carried on in the Manhattan Project, he also discovered the use of potassium peroxide as a way of absorbing carbon dioxide in a submarine, thus liberating oxygen and allowing the subs to stay under water longer than was previously possible.

After his retirement Kraus kept coming back to his office on the second floor of Metcalf Research Lab, located between the stairs and the departmental offices. One of the interesting items in that office was a table with a brass rail along the bottom matching the one in the University Club. But no man as dedicated as he was to science could ever retire, and if his pace in his later years slackened, it was only to that of ordinary human beings.

Along about 1950 some colleagues thought it would be a nice idea if a portrait of Kraus hung in Metcalf Research Lab. While sitting for the portrait in oils, Kraus gave the artist a course in chemistry in return for a detailed explanation of the technique of portraiture. Knowing that the painting would be exposed to chemical fumes, Kraus provided the artist with special varnishes and plastics which, with an aluminum backing, forever sealed the portrait from the effects of moisture, dust, and fumes.

That same year the graduate students had a party for Charlie Kraus. "They asked Charlie in advance if he would be willing to give an off-the-cuff talk," Bob Cole said. "I happen to know that he spent half a day preparing those 'off-the-cuff' comments. He poked fun at everyone from the top administrators of the University to the junior members of the department. He didn't spare anyone. The next day some of the

grad students came by and played back the tape of his talk. Kraus listened quietly, puffing on his pipe. 'Well, what do you think?' one of the students asked. 'I've been misquoted,' he said, getting up and leaving the room."

On his ninetieth birthday, his family and some of his colleagues, past and present, threw a party for Kraus, who settled in an upstairs bedroom like a bearded lion holding court. Early on in the proceedings Donald Hornig, then scientific advisor to President Johnson and later president of Brown, started to reminisce about the good old days at Metcalf Research Lab. Kraus cut him short. "I don't have time to look back," he said. "There's too much in the future to be thinking about." He then went into a detailed explanation of his research in liquid ammonia and liquid bromine. It was a memorable get-together. Kraus turned ninety and got a new piece of research started all in one day.

In January, 1967, Kraus suffered a broken hip and was confined to the Jane Brown Hospital. Betty Hartline recalls visiting her father there: "I was chatting with him, trying to get as much of the family history as possible," she said. "But at one point a soft look came over his eyes, and his mind seemed to stray for a moment from the subject at hand. 'The thing about science,' he said, 'is that it is so much fun.' I think it's safe to say that my father was an honest person who allowed people to think independently but didn't always allow them to act independently."

Jerry Nace also paid Kraus a visit. "He was propped up in a hospital bed with a gown on, but with his vest over it and his gold watch chain showing. 'How would you like a drink?' was his opening remark. He reached down to his bedside table and out came a bottle of Bushmills. He rang for the nurse. 'Bring us some ice,' he barked. Well, she did. 'Now put some in that glass.' The nurse bristled, 'I'm not here to mix drinks for you two bums.' And she stalked out."

A Brown alumna, Frances Fascitelli Yates '47, took care of Kraus during his hospitalization. "He had everyone on the floor on edge," she told me. "One day I became exasperated at something he did. 'Professor Kraus,' I said, 'you're driving me to drink,' 'Well, in that case, help yourself,' he replied, pointing to a bottle of Bushmills on his night stand."

Six months later Charlie Kraus was dead. And life at the Metcalf Research Lab would never again be quite the same.

Chapter 10 🖋
He wrote about the super-natural but never used a ghost writer

The last time I saw Curt Ducasse he was a frail man of eighty-five striding across the College Green with more determination than agility, reminding me of a motorcyclist from a 1925 silent movie with his tinted goggles, fur cap with ear flaps, and long leather gauntlets, all as protection against the chill of an early and typically windy spring afternoon. He had three years left before starting his "great adventure" – as he liked to refer to his death – and yet it was difficult to reconcile the sight that met my eyes that morning with my memory of the dapper, vigorous, and immaculately dressed professor of philosophy who graced the Brown campus when I first arrived in the summer of 1943 and who was once described by a colleague, Vince Tomas, as "a symphony in blue."

We had never been close, usually exchanging just a nod of quick recognition, but no one associated with Brown between the arrival of Curt Ducasse in 1926 and his retirement approximately thirty-two years later could possibly be unaware of the key role he played in the life of the University. He was an unusually produc- tive man and an exceptional teacher of philosophy on both the undergraduate and graduate levels. His curios- ity was constant and penetrating, and he retained to the end an open mind on controversial issues of inter- est. He served as acting dean of the Graduate School from 1947 to 1949 and, in 1945-46, he played a leading

role in the creation of Brown's new curriculum (known for twenty-five years as the "Ducasse Curriculum") with its emphasis on distribution requirements. This curriculum was in force until Ira C. Magaziner '69 and Elliot E. Maxwell '68 led the student drive for another new curriculum in 1968.

You cannot pinpoint the exact date when Ducasse retired. The University records say 1951, members of the philosophy department prefer 1958, and then there are those who claim that the slight affable pixie of a man never did retire but, like the Old Soldier, merely faded away. Suffice it to say that Professor Ducasse made more farewell appearances on the campus than did Madame Schumann-Heink in the opera centers of the world.

Curt Ducasse was a kindly, soft-spoken, gentle per- son who was very much in control of himself. There were never any insecurities. He stood 5'8", weighed perhaps 150 pounds, and had a faraway look in the large blue eyes that dominated his thin face. Articulate and precise in his speech, he carried the trace of a French accent that was slight, yet discernible and beautiful. When he spoke, there was a tendency toward quick gestures that suggested pent-up energy.

Through most of his Brown years, Ducasse was one of the best-dressed men on campus, even to the point of being considered sporty. He was always concerned that this would match that. His trademark was a tweed jacket, corduroy pants, and soft shoes or short boots. And there was always that French blue shirt, back in an era when most American men were still wearing the traditional white.

Ducasse was fond of wearing a green cellophane eye-shade. "He'd be sitting at the head of the seminar table back when I was a student of his," says Professor Tomas, "and I thought that perhaps he should be dealing a poker hand rather than discussing philosophy." For a while, a seersucker suit and sneakers became a familiar campus combination. When he was acting dean of the Graduate School, Ducasse once appeared at graduation wearing Keds, purple socks, and yellow trousers underneath his academic robe.

A man with an international reputation in philosophical circles, Ducasse published widely, was in great demand on the banquet circuit, and was known for provocative statements on any and all subjects. He liked few things better than keeping students, colleagues, and especially members of the press off stride. At one moment he could lead a detailed discussion of his widely acclaimed book, *The Philosophy of Art*, and then quickly switch the topic to cats, a subject of great importance in the life of Curt and Mabel Ducasse. He would suggest that if his listeners would delve deeply into the annals of French crime they would certainly find a gentleman named Ducasse. An ancestor, perhaps? The world's first cat-burglar? He would smile wisely but never say. However, he walked the campus with a decidedly cat-like gait, wrote letters to his wife addressed "Dear Cat," and kept a series of well-fed and much adored felines at their Riverside home. On one occasion when a cat died while Ducasse was on a business trip, his wife put the animal in the refrigerator until her husband's return so that the couple could conduct proper burial ceremonies.

Ducasse had a particularly strong interest in paranormal phenomena, an interest that went back to his boyhood in France when his mother took him to a clairvoyant in a desperation move to cure the partial deafness that resulted from a case of mumps. For an hour the clairvoyant riveted the twelve-year-old Ducasse to his chair, holding him in a spell that was not broken until his death seventy-six years later. When lecturing on the paranormal, Ducasse would be especially careful to perform the true function of a philosopher and raise more questions than he answered. He would bring an audience to the edge of its seats by asking: Is there some form of life after death? Can the dead communicate with the living? Is it possible for bodies to rise and float unsupported in the air? Are ghosts real or figments of the imagination?

This interest of Ducasse in paranormal phenomena was not forgotten when Provost Merton P. Stoltz and Chairman Reginald Archambault of the Department of Education met in University Hall one summer afternoon in 1975 to decide on a name for the handsome red brick building at 159 George Street that had just been assigned to education. Two names were discussed that day – Ducasse, whose course on philosophy of education had been one of the most popular at Brown, and Alexander Meiklejohn '93, former dean of the College, later president of Amherst, and author of an important book, *Education Between Two Worlds*.

At one point, the provost joked that it would be financially advantageous to name the building after Ducasse because the University could then use telepathy and extra-sensory perception to communicate, thus saving the cost of telephones. When the moment of decision arrived and Meiklejohn won out, it is reported that a very strange thing happened. Five books quickly fell from the top shelf of a Victorian bookcase which, until that moment, had been standing comfortably and unobstrusively in the corner of the provost's office.

"I'm not sure things happened quite that way," Professor Archambault chuckles. "But, it does make a good story. To be perfectly accurate, however, I think it was *four* books that fell."

Curt John Ducasse was born in Anhoulême, France, on July 7, 1881. His parents were Jean Louis Ducasse, a sea captain, and Clementine Theoda Ducasse, the daughter of a German painter. After attending schools in France and spending a year at the Abbotsholme School in Staffordshire, England ("Compared to English boys he has more brain than body," the report card said), Ducasse had thoughts of becoming a civil engineer. These plans were shelved in 1900 when, at age nineteen, he was struck by a sudden case of wanderlust and abruptly left for Mexico. During the next six years the young Ducasse lived out of a suitcase, going through seven jobs and developing what he

Ducasse on the middle horse.

termed "dangerous skills" as a hypnotist.

His first stop was in Mexico City, where Ducasse became a "human elevator" in a dry goods store, carrying bolts of cloth up and down four flights of stairs six days a week. To earn extra money, he doubled as a watchman, sleeping each night on a counter in the store.

During his Mexico City days Ducasse started to read about the powers of hypnosis. Before long he was conducting experiments on a young Mexican (Ducasse spoke Spanish and so no interpreter was needed) who worked in the same dry goods store. The man was neurotic and had been hypnotized before, a fact which left Ducasse wondering whether his subject was easy to hypnotize because he was neurotic or neurotic because he had been hypnotized. When it reached the point where he could call his subject on the phone and give him post-hypnotic suggestions and commands, Ducasse became alarmed and decided that his venture into the field of hypnosis had gone far enough.

"There are extreme dangers in a practice which enables one individual to control another," Ducasse once told Winfield Scott of the *Providence Journal*. "Some people did not agree with me about this. They say, 'Oh, you cannot make a man commit a murder unless he is naturally a murderous character.' But the trouble is that the hypnotist can disguise his suggestions to the patient under the hypnotic spell. Thus, you see, with his actions and thoughts entirely controlled by the hypnotist, the hypnotized person may easily reason

that putting arsenic in lemonade is a service."

After several months in the dry goods business, Ducasse worked for a window glass firm before deciding that the only way to make money was to go into business for himself. Buying a stock of Mexican lace, Ducasse went to New York City and opened a lace shop on Fifth Avenue. Business was booming in New York City in the early years of this century, but not for young Mr. Ducasse. He was flat broke in six months.

Staying in New York and utilizing his ability to speak Spanish, Ducasse found a job handling the Spanish correspondence for the G. Schirmer Company, a music publishing house. He translated their catalogue into Spanish and then was sent back to Mexico as a sheet music salesman. This venture hit a sour note when he was robbed of his wares one afternoon just outside Mexico City. "The irony here is that the bandit probably couldn't even read," Ducasse once said, shrugging his shoulders in resignation. At this point, the French vagabond headed north again, back to New York City, this time to serve as a stenographer in the foreign department of the Mutual Life Insurance Company.

Even the pictures of Ducasse had supernatural qualities.

Through these early years, Ducasse retained his curiosity about hypnotism. In February of 1906, he was present at two attempts at regression to the past through hypnosis. Dr. Morris Stark, a New York physician, conducted the experiments on a young woman who was familiar with the idea of reincarnation and who understood that the doctor would attempt to make her regress to a time prior to that of her birth. In one session, the subject, in a regressed state, claimed she was the wife of a high official of the Roman Empire; in another she was an Egyptian personality. In both sessions, the woman painted a vivid verbal picture of the land in which she lived and of the people with whom she associated. Ducasse recorded her comments in shorthand, retained the typescript of his notes, and used the material in a chapter ("The Past Through Hypnosis") of his 1961 book, *The Critical Examination of the Belief in a Life After Death*.

In the late spring of 1906, having decided that the insurance business was not for him, Ducasse went to Seattle, Washington, where he became secretary to the chief engineer of the Oregon and Washington Railroad. This job lasted only until September, when, having received a legacy from his family, he decided to end his vagabonding days and return to the classroom. At age twenty-five, with advanced standing because of his European schooling, Curt Ducasse entered the University of Washington. He was graduated in 1908, received his master's a year later, and became an American citizen in 1910. The young Frenchman entered Harvard as a University scholar, studied under Josiah Royce and Hugo Muensterberg, two of the leading philosophers of that era, and earned his doctorate in 1912.

During the next fourteen years, Ducasse held the successive positions of assistant professor and associate professor of philosophy at the University of Washington. In 1924, he served as chairman of a committee that organized the Pacific Division of the American Philosophical Association. That same year he gained wide recognition with the publication of his first book, *Causation and the Types of Necessity*. To celebrate this success, Ducasse and a colleague, Professor Guthrie, climbed to the top of Mount Rainier, enjoyed a healthy portion of a bottle of brandy, and then buried the bottle. When he was in Seattle some twenty years later, Ducasse looked up Guthrie. They climbed the mountain again, dug up the same bottle, enjoyed the contents for a leisurely moment, and reburied the bottle. Today,

Enjoying a picnic in a forest near Seattle.

somewhere near the top of Mount Rainier, there is a brandy bottle, still with some miles left in it, just waiting to be rediscovered.

Professor Ducasse came to Brown in 1926 as an associate professor of philosophy, was appointed a full professor in 1929, and succeeded Professor Walter G. Everett as chairman of the department the next year. From 1932 until his retirement, he held the Romeo Elton Professorship of Natural Theology. In 1961, Brown conferred an honorary degree on Ducasse, citing him as a professor whose "inquiring teaching has stimulated generations of students to see and sometimes to find."

From the very start, it was obvious that in Curt Ducasse, Brown had appointed a professor whose voice would be heard beyond the campus. A man of courage and integrity, he constantly spoke out on issues of the day. In a lecture on art history shortly after his appointment to the faculty, he told his class that "the most that can be said of the contents of museums is that they constitute documentary history of the tastes of museum directors."

Ducasse was frankness personified also when addressing the American Philosophical Society in 1939, the year of his presidency. "Philosophy," he said, "has still not advanced past the question, 'What is philosophy?' and is advancing more slowly than the natural sciences."

In 1940, Ducasse joined with John Dewey and Alfred North Whitehead, both former presidents of the American Philosophical Society, in supporting Bertrand Russell in his dispute with City College of New York. The British philosopher had just been hired to teach a course on logic, but his appointment was cancelled after public outcry because of his views on free love and marriage. On the same day that the Catholic Daughters of America roasted Russell, Ducasse wrote to Dr. Sidney Hook, chairman of the Committee for Cultural Freedom, claiming that "a more competent or more distinguished philosopher for the position could not have been found."

Ducasse also told 100 women who were members of the High School Teachers Association of Providence what he thought of the art of cosmetics. "Woman," he said, "is the animal with red cheeks. Woman's cheeks are red when she blushes, and she blushes when she is ashamed of herself. Woman, furthermore, is the animal that beholds herself in mirrors. She is the animal that is not satisfied with merely living her life, but, in addition, is capable of and insists on watching herself do it."

After noting that it was only natural that physical fascination should be an aim figuring conspicuously in our attempts at self-embellishment, Ducasse brought up the subject of cosmetic art. He admitted that powders and creams, skillfully applied, of course, may to some extent endow the "most promising surface" with the "skin you love to touch," and then he went through the litany of female artifice unflatteringly.

"Take finger nails, for example," Ducasse continued, as a number of the women quietly slipped on their gloves. "When a lady stains her finger nails in such a manner that they resemble the claws of a tiger ripping up a sheep, we cannot plausibly suppose the lady intends to make anyone believe that the bright crimson color is just the result of vigorous good health. And if *red* finger nails, why not blue, and yellow, and gold? And why not gold eyebrows, or gold ears, or golden lips? And how about golden wigs?"

Ducasse could deliver a lecture such as this to a potentially hostile audience and still survive because he employed the light touch. Even when making his most scathing criticisms of the manner in which women used cosmetics, Ducasse let a smile flirt with his lips. He always retained this charming quality of the plebeian, ready with simple humor and gentle slang – in French or in English – to endear himself to businessmen, physicians, psychologists, philosophers, – or teachers – who welcomed his knowledge, his wisdom, and his simple humanity.

The fact of the matter is that, while Ducasse took his work quite seriously, he was always able to look at

himself, and even his profession, with balance and perspective. This is evident in the preface to his 1944 book, *Art, the Critics, and You*, in which he wrote: "The artist and the philosopher are two men regarded by the general public with a certain bewilderment, compounded of respect and mistrust, mild scorn and envy, impatience and wonder. The philosopher is popularly conceived as an impractical being, so deeply plunged in abstract thought that he does not even see where he walks and cannot recognize his wife when he meets her at the train unless he takes along a photograph."

In addition to having some fun with the philosophy of aesthetics, as he did in his talk to the teachers' group, Ducasse made some significant contributions in the field. In fact, some critics felt that at one time he was the foremost aesthetician in this country. Ducasse was especially effective lecturing to large groups of art students and others, where he always stressed that "art is a necessity, not a luxury," and that "there is something of the artist in all of us." He also wrote about the philosophy of art in two books and in countless articles.

His most famous book on the subject was *The Philosophy of Art*, a 1930 publication that enabled Ducasse to take his place among the great philosophers of the world. The book devastatingly attacked a number of conventional views of the nature of art and beauty and set forth in vigorous and convincing fashion a radically individualistic philosophy of art. He maintained that there are no binding canons of beauty; that there are no authorities in matters of aesthetic worth; that art is not the creation of beautiful things but the objectification of feelings. His most daring contention back in 1930 was that art has no connection with beauty.

"When Professor Ducasse wrote *The Philosophy of Art*, he wrote the standard work on the subject," says Professor Tomas. "It is probably the clearest, most fully developed, and most ably defended version of the emotionalist theory of art and aesthetics appreciation that has been written."

Fifteen years later, Professor Ducasse wrote the aforementioned follow-up, *Art, the Critics, and You*, a book for the layman that was a declaration of independence of taste in matters of art. Ducasse especially deplored the fact that people are inclined to distrust their own tastes and are in awe of certain types of critics who use a jargon of their own and regard themselves as high priests of mysteries into which only a few are, or can be, initiated. This results in what Ducasse termed "flock following" instead of independent selection. It causes one book, which is praised by the critics, to sell in the hundreds of thousands while another book of equal or higher merit perishes in the publisher's storerooms. It causes everyone to rush to the "hit play" while another play of equal merit closes at a loss after only a few performances.

Reviewing the book in the *New York World-Telegram*, Burton Rascoe, a noted theatre critic of that day, described the work as "a revolutionary treatise on the nature of art and aesthetic appreciation" and said: "Dr. Ducasse rightfully comments that the professional critic is not an authority over your taste. His true role is that of a helpful guide to your exploration of the arts."

Curt Ducasse also had an international reputation in the field of paranormal phenomena. In 1954, at age seventy-four, he chaired a meeting in Cannes, France, of twenty of the world's leading philosophers, who met to compare notes on psychic phenomena. They were there to discuss things of the mind and spirit that they didn't understand but felt might exist.

Although Professor Ducasse had a lifelong interest in paranormal phenomena, he was never dogmatic about the questions philosophers and theologians have debated for years. He consistently stressed that he was guided only by "the passion to know the truth" and added that "in the presence of novel facts, the truly scientific attitude is neither the will to believe nor the will to disbelieve, but the will to investigate."

It was never easy to debate Ducasse on any of the challenging questions he raised, for he was the master of parry and thrust. He also happened to be a highly skilled logician. The members of his discipline recognized this by electing him president of the Association for Symbolic Logic, an organization of pundits dabbling in what Ducasse described as "the algebra of logic."

It was Ducasse's contention that we should not automatically dismiss the possibility that the dead sometimes communicate with the living, that there is reincarnation, and that some persons perceive events before they actually happen. He incorporated many of these ideas in his book, *A Critical Examination of the Belief in a Life After Death*, published in 1961.

"The history of science is strewn with the corpses of things scientists of the day thought impossible," he once said. "There appear to be certain events which indicate that there are forces in the universe which present-day science does not know about and often pretends to ignore. The evidence for the possibility of some kind of continued existence after death and of some other things now generally regarded as supernatural is sometimes difficult to laugh off. They may be clues to nature as yet unknown and unexplored."

Ducasse often deplored the fact that we live in an era of common sense, which assumes unexplainable occurrences to be paradoxical and incredible. "People tend to reject what they do not understand," he told Robert D. Stein '59 of the *Brown Daily Herald* in a 1957 interview. "This could very well be our reason for rejecting paranormal experiences. But through the medium of scientific investigation we are able to gather evidence and facts and make judgments accordingly. My work is as intriguing as the exploration of any new frontier. My interest is purely scientific. I have no great desire to communicate with the spirits. They don't bother me, and I don't bother them."

Well, Ducasse may have had no great desire to communicate with ghosts, but he would never rule out the possibility of their existence. There was something of the little boy in Ducasse – the little boy who doesn't want to believe in ghosts, yet is fascinated by the subject. But the possibility of the existence of spirits was just one of the seven or eight areas of paranormal phenomena in which Ducasse had more than a modicum of interest.

Whenever he spoke on the subject of ghosts, the professor would lead with the following quotation: "La Rochefoucauld declares that, of true love as of the apparition of ghosts, every man speaks but few have seen it." In the next breath, Ducasse would say that he had personally seen ghosts or, at any rate, what purported to be apparitions of dead persons.

In the mid-1950s, Ducasse had a "spooky" experience at Camp Silver Belle in Ephrata, Pennsylvania, a camp that was a haven for pyschic experiences in the form of materializations. During a long seance, he watched eighteen fully materialized forms emerge from behind the draperies of a cabinet, about eight by four feet, in which a female medium was seated. Prior to the seance, Ducasse had carefully inspected the cabinet and could find no trap doors or other hidden means of entry.

As the spirits (all of whom were dressed in white)

came out of the cabinet they called out the names of people in the audience and were sometimes recognized by them as dead relatives. But the apparition who spoke to Ducasse flubbed her performance.

"She was a beautiful young girl with a shining star on her forehead," he told Selig Greenberg '27, feature writer for the *Providence Journal*. "I asked her who she was and she said she was my mother. But she didn't look or talk like my mother. There was no resemblance whatsoever." Speaking of this incident on another occasion, Ducasse added that the apparition called him "Curt," whereas his mother had always referred to him as "John."

"There is no question," Ducasse told Greenberg, "that people have seen what they thought were ghosts, often resembling some dead relative or friend. Some of these images were probably purely subjective, a sort of walking dream on the part of the beholder. But there have been some other instances where it seems impossible to explain everything away as imaginary. This is especially true of the cases where the apparitions conveyed information which was later established to be authentic and which the persons seeing them had no means of knowing at the time."

And then there are the prankish spirits, not the Marley-type ghost who scared the living daylights out of me on many a boyhood Christmas past, but the spirits (they call themselves poltergeists, to be quite accurate) who cause all sorts of mischief, like dishes flying off the shelves and mysterious knocks in the middle of the night aimed at scaring people out of their houses, not to mention their wits. Ducasse refused to be cornered on these phenomena. "There are some mischievous occurrences without any obvious explanation," he said.

At still another seance at Camp Silver Belle, Ducasse became involved with a mysterious substance known as ectoplasm, a pasty white material that some individuals appear to be able to extrude from their bodies and that is capable of moving objects without support from any other physical force. Ducasse took photos of ectoplasm coming from the nostrils of a man and then touched the substance, which he said felt like dough. He was naturally suspicious and looked around for signs of fakery (of which there apparently was plenty at Camp Silver Belle) but found none.

Another area of interest for Ducasse was levitation. He would tell the story of an Englishman back in the 1870s who, on numerous occasions, rose as high as eighteen inches off the floor, with no visible means of support. Sir William Crookes, an eminent physicist of the day, searched diligently for wires and other signs of a hoax but could find nothing. "While I have never seen levitation, there is no reason to regard it as impossible," said Ducasse.

In the 1950s, a Church of England commission issued a report saying that human illness could sometimes conceivably be caused by demons, leading to a call for exorcism. "If you assume that it is possible for minds to exist without a body," Ducasse told Greenberg of the *Journal*, "then it would be equally possible to assume that some minds are good and some are bad, and the bad ones might be demons."

If Ducasse could not be drawn out of the thickets of qualification on many of the paranormal phenomena, he was more emphatic in stating his belief in the existence of extrasensory perception, including precognition – the ability to perceive an event before it happens.

He cited the abundant evidence of extrasensory perception in the experimental work carried on for years by Dr. J. B. Rhine and his colleagues at Duke University and by others at the University of London. Much of Dr. Rhine's work centered on experiments with cards, in which certain individuals have consistently displayed an ability to guess the design printed on the cards at a far greater rate than chance could account for.

Ducasse had ample experience with still another paranormal phenomenon – mental telepathy. He told Greenberg that one of his earliest experiences with thought transference took place when he was living in Mexico City as a young man and involved a fellow worker with whom he shared a room. His friend had gone to bed and was lying on his right side, facing the wall. Ducasse was reading at a table some twenty feet away.

"Suddenly," he said, "the idea occurred to me to make him turn around. So I looked at him fixedly and imagined that I was grasping his hand with my right hand and twisting it around. I actually made the gesture. Whereupon he jumped up as if he had been stung. 'You're looking at me,' he said. 'Don't do it again.' My roommate later said that he had seen two burning eyes staring at him."

Ducasse also had faith in precognitive experiences, in which people have a dream that something is going to happen and sooner or later it does. In one of his books he noted the documented case of the wife of a bishop of England who awoke in the middle of the night and told her husband that there was a pig in the parlor. The bishop walked downstairs – and there *was* a pig in the parlor. Ducasse was impressed by this. "After all," he wrote, "the bishop was a perfectly respectable old man. Why would he lie?"

Professor Tomas maintains that Ducasse believed strongly in reincarnation. "All his life he was interested in immortality," Tomas says, "and he was always on the lookout for scientific evidence that the mind of the person survives the death of the body. He thought that the evidence, if any at all, would come from psychical research. In his book, *A Critical Examination of the Belief in a Life After Death*, Ducasse concluded that the evidence is slight, but that there is some evidence that persons survive.

"What's more," Tomas continues, "he was convinced that he, himself, had a reincarnation. I recall that he once got a reading from Edgar Cayce, an astrologer who had psychic powers, and Cayce said that two thousand years ago Ducasse had been a powerful minister to one of the pharoahs of Alexandria in Egypt."

As he grew older, Ducasse took steps to see if the dead really could communicate with the living. According to Professor Archambault, who was a student under Ducasse before becoming a colleague, the professor made a pact that would put this issue to the true test. The pact was with Arthur E. Murphy, who served in the philosophy department at Brown under Ducasse before moving to the University of Illinois. The terms were that the one who died first would make a special effort to communicate with the other. The honors went to Murphy, but Ducasse waited in vain for any word from his old friend.

"Later," Archambault says, "Ducasse sealed the same pact with his wife, Mabel. This time, Ducasse went first. Two people couldn't have been closer, but Mabel admitted shortly before she died that there had been no communication. This isn't really surprising," Archambault confirms. "Some days at the office I have trouble getting through to Central Falls."

For many students of Ducasse, probably the greatest surprise was to find so critical a mind not only devoting much time and energy to the investigation of "spiritualism," but accepting many of its startling hypotheses. Brand Blanshard, professor of philosophy at Yale, comments: "Believe me, this took more than unconventionality; it took moral courage. The climate of opinion in this country regarding psychical research is frigid enough to freeze into numb discouragement any stirrings of interest that a young scientist might feel.

"Ducasse, with his fastidiousness of mind and taste, was no doubt often affronted by the dreary twaddle and fraudulence that seems to surround so many mediums. But he did not think they were all dupes and frauds. He was clear that if just one of them was genuine, the repercussions might be revolutionary. For him, that made the inquiry worthwhile. And for his students and readers, his inquiry has put the whole controversial business of psychical research into true philosophical perspective."

One of the "happenings" on campus during my college years was a talk by Professor Ducasse at a fraternity house. These were always very informal affairs, with the professor usually slouched on a table in a corner of the room, legs crossed, spinning tales of paranormal phenomena to students sitting in chairs and lounges or on the floor. A black briefcase was always at his side, from which he would occasionally pull material to illustrate his talk. Even the most sophisticated of students, along with the war-hardened veterans in their early to mid-twenties, sat spellbound before Ducasse on these occasions.

One fall afternoon in either 1948 or 1949, Ducasse spoke at the Sigma Chi House, which was then located on Waterman Street in the building now occupied by the Brown Credit Union. The front room was crowded long before Ducasse arrived, a tribute not only to the speaker but also the ample supply of cookies Mrs. Blackhall baked for just such occasions. I have absolutely no recollection of what the professor said that afternoon, but there is still a vivid memory of the sun streaming through the bay window and creating images that danced crazily on the east wall and the ceiling of the old fraternity house, creating an appropriate setting for the subject of the speaker's talk – ghosts!

The popularity of Ducasse continued into the classroom, although he was known as a stern disciplinarian. "He wouldn't stand for any conversation while he was lecturing," Professor Archambault says. "He would rap on the desk for quiet, which was unusual at the college level."

When Archambault was trying to decide on his major, he attended a Ducasse open house in Rhode Island Hall, then the home of the philosophy department. "As I walked in," Archambault recalls, "there was Ducasse, the chairman of the department, sitting on the floor, legs tucked under him, Indian style, talking to a large group of students who encircled him. The students were asking questions and he was selling philosophy. He spoke not about what philosophy was, but what it was *to do* philosophy, which is the right way to put it because that's what happens. And, as he talked about some of the things one does when one does philosophy, the enthusiasm began to well in him. You could see that intensity, that involvement, that real love of the subject shining through. As a result of that experience, I decided to major in philosophy."

Ducasse was extraordinarily well organized in the classroom, and his lectures were clear and precise. He was a sensuous man who was not about to let the beauties of color, sound, touch, smell, and taste become trampled by the practical pressures of life. He was constantly fascinated by what his senses brought him, and students would often notice that while he lectured he would sniff at a sprig of mint or a bit of flower that he had pulled from his garden earlier in the day.

Ducasse possessed one other sense – the sense to stay one step ahead of his students. "I took a one-semester course with him," says Professor Elmer M. Blistein '42, a member of the Brown English department. "When he took a section, we students, asses that we were, tried to bait him. He returned better than he received. Ducasse was a man of great dignity and compelling knowledge, one I loved to disagree with, especially about educational theory."

Papers and final exams were read personally by Ducasse, who would make extensive comments in the margins. In some cases these precise comments became collector's items with his students. If one could find a fault with Ducasse it would be that he was strictly a lecturer at the undergraduate level. Oh, he would entertain a question once in a while, but he was authoritarian and engaged in little give-and-take with

his students while he was addressing large groups.

This was not the case at the graduate level, where his style was to sit at a seminar table in Rhode Island Hall and in an intimate and friendly fashion relate himself to his students. His standards were extremely high and no favoritism or partiality was shown. If a graduate student could not produce, Ducasse would gently urge that person not to go on in his philosophical studies. For those who seemed able and motivated, however, he would fairly parcel out the few assistantships and fellowships available.

Ducasse was unstinting in his support of his graduate students, even to the extent of accepting full responsibility for getting them a job. One who remembers that well is Frederick C. Dommeyer, who took his master's from Brown in 1935 and his doctorate two years later. He subsequently was chairman of the philosophy department at St. Lawrence University and then San Jose State.

"As I neared the end of my stay at Brown," he writes, "Ducasse sent out 125 letters in my behalf in an effort to find me a position. He was equally helpful at the end of my first year in grad school when he knew there would be no financial aid for me the next year and went out of his way to get me an English-Speaking Union Fellowship for a year at Oxford. If Ducasse had not had the kindness to negotiate that fellowship and then to find an assistantship for me upon my return from England, my budding career as a professor would have been over before it had really had a chance to begin.

"Ducasse did many kind things such as this through his career," Dommeyer continues. "But they were always done in a seemingly disinterested manner, as though they were just part of a day's work. There was never any indication on his part that anyone owed him anything or that there was anything special about his actions. I suspect that for him there *was* nothing special, since his actions simply emanated from a wonderfully moral and kind nature."

During his long tenure (1930-51) as department chairman, Ducasse was known as an authoritarian figure. Professor Roderick Chisholm recently referred to him as "a benevolent despot" and added: "In those days the chairman didn't have to consult with anyone else. He made all the decisions himself. However, I'd say he handled things quite efficiently. We met every Thursday noon at the Minden Hotel when I first joined the department. We would discuss things and then he would inform us of his decisions, most of which he probably had made before the meeting started."

Ducasse took the powers of the chairmanship quite seriously but was never overly impressed with the title. "The only reason for being chairman is to prevent some other son-of-a-bitch from being chairman," he once said.

"Impressive to me was the fact that Ducasse never wanted to hold center stage within the department," says Professor Dommeyer. "He gathered about him a most able staff during my years at Brown. There was Arthur E. Murphy, a man who wrote a great many articles and who, like Ducasse, was a Carus lecturer. Murphy was very popular as a classroom teacher. There was also Ralph Blake and Charles Baylis. Blake read both Greek and Latin fluently and as a result was an excellent teacher of both ancient and medieval philosophy. Baylis was the logician of the staff and taught symbolic logic and logical theory to graduate students in those areas. After World War II, Ducasse pulled together another strong staff, including Roderick Chisholm, Vincent Tomas, and John Ladd.

"The key point," Dommeyer continues, "is that at no point was Ducasse ever envious of their success in teaching or publishing. In fact, he was delighted with their accomplishments. Let it be said that in my forty years of teaching I have not found this to be a universal trait of department chairmen."

Vince Tomas felt that Ducasse did have one flaw in his running of the department: He took the administration point of view more often than was necessary. "Personally, I always considered it the duty of the chairman to fight the administration," Tomas says, "but Ducasse gave his loyalty to the University rather than the department. He would rather save $200 for Brown than give a guy a raise. There was nothing mean about him. It was just his style. When I was chairman, I felt like a union leader. Ducasse was strictly management."

There is some evidence that Ducasse was extremely cautious in other ways. Through most of his years at Brown, the Department of Philosophy was housed in the lower level and the first floor of Rhode Island Hall. Geology was on the second floor of this 1840 building.

"Whenever Ducasse was working on a manuscript," Professor Tomas says, "he'd have extra copies made and located with people off campus as a protection for his work. 'Those bastards up above have big rocks,' he'd say. 'The ceiling might fall in on us at any moment.'"

Ducasse took pride in being a letter-writer of some repute. He corresponded daily with his wife when he was traveling and used letters as a means of communicating with his students as well as members of the department.

"When I was an undergraduate," Rod Chisholm says, "I'd go to see Ducasse and he'd say, 'I think you probably could make that point better in writing, and I could perhaps deal with it in writing.' So, I'd go back to my room and put my thoughts on paper for him. He'd write me in return. We kept on doing that."

The Ducasse file in the John Hay Library also includes a precise but not polite letter from Ducasse to Sears Roebuck complaining that the underwear he had ordered didn't fit properly. This letter particularly amused Martha Mitchell, University archivist. "When people thought of Ducasse," she says, "they had a vision of this brilliant man sitting in his office trying to solve the great philosophical problems of the age whereas, in reality, he was dashing off angry notes to Sears about his underwear problems."

From his early days at Brown, Ducasse was interested in the philosophy of education. In 1943, he served on a five-member committee established by the Rockefeller Foundation and charged with studying the function of philosophy in a liberal education. The committee made a philosophical pilgrimage of 7,000 miles and attended twenty-two conferences in all parts of the country, meeting with college professors, deans, and presidents. They also talked with journalists, scientists, businessmen, and other philosophers. One of the points discussed at each stop was whether or not college students should be made to study philosophy if they have no interest in the subject. From this, the group branched out into a discussion of the wisdom of allowing students to select their own courses.

This five-member group was made up of members of the American Philosophical Association and was chaired by Professor Arthur Murphy of Brown. Yale's Professor Blanshard also served. "Ducasse was senior member of that group," Blanshard wrote recently. "I recall that his conversation was spiced with references to a past that, for a philosopher, was surprisingly varied. Here, his wealth of practical experience and human contacts served him in good stead. He was a lively raconteur, with a ready sense of humor, and when he and his junior colleague, Arthur Murphy (who called him 'Jack Oakie'), felt in a jocular mood one wished the room were bugged so that we could have heard that crackling banter again."

Service on this committee was a valuable experience for Professor Ducasse. Thoughts that had been dancing in his brain for many years were brought into sharper focus. The one-year study under the Rockefeller grant had convinced him that it was time for education to return to the job of turning out the "educated man," which to him meant a shift from the freedom of choice in course selection that students had been enjoying to a more structured curriculum containing a series of distribution requirements.

In 1945, when Brown decided to revise its curriculum, President Wriston named Ducasse to head the key subcommittee on distribution requirements. Professors Phil Taft of economics and Charles Smiley of astronomy also served. In his report to the president, Ducasse wrote of the "endless and whimsically diverse" sets of courses being taken outside their field of concentration by students in American colleges and cited numerous advantages that would result from establishing distribution requirements in five fields: natural sciences, physical sciences, social studies, humanities, and philosophy or mathematics.

The report of the Ducasse subcommittee was adopted by the faculty and put into effect in the fall of 1947. This curriculum, with minor modifications, survived until the decision in the late 1960s to do away with the distribution requirements and swing 180 degrees to allow undergraduates complete freedom of choice in selecting their courses and creating their majors.

One of the things for which Ducasse will long be remembered is the exuberance he brought to whatever he tackled, be it as important as a new curriculum for his university or as ephemeral as looking into the rumor of ghosts in a haunted house. This exuberance was noted by his colleagues overseas, scholars such as Professor R. H. Thouless of Cambridge University in England.

"The freshness and vigor of the articles of C. J. Ducasse led me to suppose that their author was a young man. Later I met him in the flesh and was astonished to find that he was considerably older than myself. The astonishment lessened later as I got to know him better and realized that this lasting freshness of mind was a characteristic element of his personality."

Professor Antony Flew of the University of Keele in England writes of his first meeting with Ducasse in 1954 at a parapsychology conference at Le Piol in the south of France. "My clearest and strongest impression was of freshness and vitality," he writes. "Ducasse just naturally gravitated toward the liveliest members of any group. And these, equally naturally – even when the liveliest happened to be the youngest – accepted him as another of themselves."

Professor Flew remembers the first occasion when Ducasse met Professor Henry H. Price, an eminent British philosopher who also delved into paranormal phenomena: "They found themselves at the same breakfast table at Le Piol, looking toward the Mediterranean, and quickly delighted one another, and everyone else present, by discovering that they shared not only an interest in philosophy and psychical research, but also a liking for owls, for cats, and for mice. What I cannot now remember is whether it was Price or Ducasse who was the first to apologize that this combination of animals was in a way almost self-contradictory."

Although Professor Ducasse traveled to all parts of the world in connection with his job, his wife never accompanied him. The principal reason was that Mabel was at home taking care of the succession of family cats.

When one cat died, Curt and Mabel would quickly get another. Notes Curt Ducasse wrote to his wife while he was traveling were addressed "Dear Cat" or "Dear Pussycat" and were filled with questions about their "son's" appetite and his health. And Professor Ducasse would add pen-and-ink drawings of cats in the margins of his letters.

By far the most famous of the Ducasse cats was Chichibu, a Siamese who was named after the brother of Emperor Hirohito of Japan. Chichibu lived twenty-one years, two months, and four days. Ducasse was sometimes invited to women's clubs to explain what he did to keep the cat alive so long, and he would tell them that the remedy was plenty of affection. Chichibu and Ducasse were particularly close. The cat would wrap himself around his master's neck, and Ducasse would walk around the neighborhood looking very much as if he were wearing a fur collar.

When Chichibu finally died, Mabel, who was a professional painter, did a portrait of the corpse, and then the couple buried the cat in their back yard. A stone with letters engraved in blue (the color of Chichibu's eyes) marks the spot.

There were no more cats after Chichibu's death, basically because the Ducasses felt that a new pet might outlive them. But there were other animals that soon multiplied in the large and beautiful garden behind the white clapboard house at 48 Aberdeen Road in Riverside. Ducasse had a park bench installed in his yard, and when he sat there chipmunks would come out of their holes, run up his leg, and mosey over to the pocket where he kept a generous supply of peanuts and sunflower seeds. For company, there were also squirrels, rabbits, shrews, and either a woodchuck or a skunk that burrowed a tunnel under the house. And then there was Conrad.

Conrad was a field mouse who wasn't content with his station in life. Slightly larger than his peers and quickly identified by a kink in his tail, Conrad built a home for himself in the Ducasse cellar. No living out in the garden for that fellow. During the breakfast hour, Conrad would establish position far enough away from the lord and lady of the household to beat a hasty retreat if that course of action seemed advisable but near enough to snatch up any small morsel of food that fell to the floor. One bright and sunny morning, Ducasse awoke to find Conrad sitting on the bureau peering at him intently.

Ducasse had built a special device in which he could trap the field mice without hurting them. He and Mabel would watch them perform and then turn the mice loose. "By actual count, we caught Conrad 176 times in the trap in our cellar," Ducasse once said. "Several times I walked him a block or two from the house and tossed him into a grassy field, only to find him back in the cellar when I got home. Finally, we took Conrad

for a ride of several miles and set him loose in a large field. But, Mabel and I soon missed him and kept hoping that he would show up for breakfast some morning. He never did."

Mabel Lisle, a native of LaPorte, Colorado, met Curt Ducasse when she was a student at the University of Washington and took one of his courses in the philosophy of aesthetics. They were married in 1921. She earned a master's in fine arts at her alma mater and did further study in New York City. A gifted painter, Mabel Ducasse exhibited at the Providence Art Club and in Boston. She also served as art critic for the *Providence Journal* in the 1920s and 1930s. Their home was designed by her in 1932 and was later featured in the "Home" section of the *Sunday Journal*.

Marge Tomas, former wife of Professor Tomas, was a long-time friend of the Ducasses. She recalls that the couple did not encourage the younger generation, even when they became colleagues, to call them by their first names. "'Mr.' or 'Professor and Mrs.' was more respectful," she says. "They wanted to keep their distance.

"Neither of them ever threw anything away. As a result, the house became cluttered with so many things. My impression is that Mrs. Ducasse did not really enjoy housework or cooking. Whenever it was their duty to entertain, she'd put on a very fine meal. But

Conrad was caught in this trap 176 times.

Ducasse with his favorite cat, Chichibu.

this was not one of her strong points.

"Perhaps Mrs. Ducasse was a little ahead of her time. Although by nature she was a quiet and retiring woman, she was also a bit eccentric and sometimes would come out with unusual remarks. When someone once suggested that she seemed to like cats better than people, Mrs. Ducasse replied, 'Naturally. I only like people insofar as they resemble cats.' She had a certain sense of independence and was inclined to be blunt to the extreme."

Professor Ducasse could be equally blunt. If legend is correct, President Wriston stopped him on the Front Campus one day and asked how Ducasse liked being acting dean of the Graduate School. "Not very much," the professor shot back. "I'm called upon to give speeches more often than I have anything to say."

Neither of the partners ate meat. Usually, nuts and natural foods comprised their diet. "This was partly for moral reasons," Professor Chisholm says. "They thought it was wicked to eat animals just as most people in the world think it is wicked to eat humans. If they went out to dinner and meat was on the menu, they would try to get an omelet or soup instead. On a few occasions, however, they did eat meat rather than make a show."

Professor Chisholm remembers them as a close couple, although each had an existence independent of the other. "Curt traveled all over the country," he said, "but Mabel seldom went with him. This was partly because of their cats. But, also, I think she was happy to stay home and paint. I always thought they were ideally suited for each other."

Professor Tomas agrees. "He and Mabel loved to

walk along Barrington Beach in the evenings, especially at sundown," he says. "I'd frequently see them there, a gray-haired couple, both a bit arthritic, but holding hands like young lovers. Theirs was a hell of a love affair for nearly fifty years. Oh, sure, they'd laugh at each other now and then. Each always claimed that the other was a bit screwy. But underneath it all was a profound love and respect."

When Curt Ducasse reached the mandatory retirement age of seventy in 1951, he gave up the departmental chairmanship – but he didn't retire. Because of his popularity with the students and because the other members of the department were all quite young, President Wriston allowed Ducasse to continue teaching on a part-time basis. "Technically I was retired, but not in practice," he would say.

Then in June of 1958, Ducasse retired again, and this time the Brown Corporation marked the occasion by voting to establish the Curt John Ducasse Premium in Metaphysics. For his part, Ducasse marked the occasion by speaking at a conference on the philosophy of education at Northwestern University a few days later. He also lined up a fall agenda that included three lectures before the Georgia Philosophical Association at the University of Georgia and a once-a-week course on the theory of knowledge at New York University. He also mapped plans for several books and a series of articles. Some retirement!

After 1958, however, Professor Ducasse began to spend more and more time at his Riverside home, which he called his "Athens on the Seekonk" because of the fact that four members of Brown's philosophy department – Blake, Murphy, Baylis, and Ducasse – once lived on the same small side street located not too far from the Providence River. He found time to design and make rings and other jewelry, a skill he had picked up in Mexico City fifty years earlier. He also enjoyed puttering around in his cellar, using his lathe, bandsaw, and drill-press to turn out some fine furniture, including a large desk for his wife's studio that featured a series of secret compartments. There was also time now for reading historical romances and mystery stories.

As he grew older, Ducasse spoke freely of death, but not in the religious sense. Although he was raised in a Protestant family, he broke away from the faith. "Whatever religious feelings I had came from nature and meditation," he said not too long before his death. It followed then that his interest in some form of survival after death was a scientific interest.

He told his friend, Selig Greenberg, that his study of the paranormal had broadened his horizon of the potentialities of human nature and of the universe. "So many people," he said, "are hemmed in by tacit beliefs and disbeliefs, by conformities and the things they take for granted, that they shut their eyes to the fact that the material world is not the whole of this world and that there are apparently dimensions of nature as yet unknown and unexplored. I face the prospect of dying as an interesting adventure, as a sort of laboratory experiment. I shall then find out the truth for myself."

The truth was revealed to Professor Ducasse on September 3, 1969. It was not an easy death. The advanced stages of diabetes ate away at one part of his body after another for more than a year. Mabel, who had a fear of nursing homes, cared for him night and day at 48 Aberdeen Road. Ducasse was cremated at Swan Point Cemetery and his ashes were buried in the backyard next to Chichibu. Now, on the other side of the much-beloved Siamese cat are the ashes of Mabel Ducasse, who died in a nursing home on October 18, 1976, seven years after her husband.

How good a philosopher was Ducasse? His peers rate him highly. History is likely to support that opinion. Professor Dommeyer, who knew him intimately for more than thirty years, calls Ducasse "one of the best of the American and European philosophers of this century."

I t is a fact that Ducasse was far ahead of most of his contemporaries in his receptivity to the possibility that much remains to be discovered about the human mind. Where others might propose one or two explanations for a specific case, Ducasse might consider six or seven.

"This openness was not emptiness or a passive welcoming of any interpretation, as if all had equal merit," Dr. Ian Stevenson, division of psychology at the University of Virginia, recently wrote: "He had sound understanding of the strengths and weaknesses of different kinds of evidence in our field and knew how to weigh and discard worthless material.

"Through his long career, Ducasse considered philosophical activity not so much a closing of doors to wrong conclusions as an opening of doors to lines of thought that one might not previously have considered. This open-mindedness made him deeply sympathetic to psychical research and enabled him to provide his own valuable contribution to para-psychological thought."

Dr. Stevenson spoke of Ducasse as "one of the most kindly and thoroughly benign" persons he had ever known, and added: "He sometimes laughed gently at his opponents but he never seemed to scorn or despise them. He was not a lover of fools, but not their hater either. He was so tactful and constructive that differences rarely amounted to disagreements; he nearly always found some common ground of understanding that averted this." Stevenson noted that if a disagreement did arise, Ducasse would seek some means of compromise, but always without sacrificing the standards of high quality that he set for himself and others. "In any controversy," he concluded, "one still saw that extraordinary courtesy and perhaps Gallic charm that pervaded all his letters and conversations."

Perhaps most of all, Ducasse was an individualist, both in his private life and his profession. Professor Blanshard of Yale felt that this trait gave Ducasse an edge on most of his peers.

"An individualist is often an irritant to his associates," Blanshard wrote, "but as far as I know Ducasse never was, for he was sedulously considerate of those around him. If he differed from others in dress, it was not in the direction so popular today of emulating skid row, but in that of an extra aesthetic fastidiousness. If a practice did not injure others, the fact that it was unconventional was no deterent to him. His friends will remember the green eyeshade he often wore in public and his unique relationship with his Siamese, who used to sit on his shoulders and contemplate his master adoringly while his master contemplated the sum of things.

"What is more important is that Ducasse was an individualist in his thought. You could not, as with many other professors, predict with confidence where he would come out on a given issue, for early in his philosophical career he had abjured the metaphysical system with which he had started in favor of his own special relativism, a skeptical conviction that all the standards of truth, beauty, and goodness are logically arbitrary. He held that the basic insights which separate philosophers are incapable of rational groundings;

they are matters of preference rather than proof. That theory did give him a certain freedom to follow his preference where others would have been bound by system; and the result is that one met with sharp surprises in his thinking."

Although Ducasse turned his interests more and more to psychical research late in his professional life, Professor Chisholm points out that he will be best remembered nationally for his writings on causation and the philosophy of art. His greatest work is a work on metaphysics, *Nature, Mind, and Death*, which *The Encyclopedia Britannica* of 1952 described as the most important publication in its field in 1951.

"Ducasse had few peers as a philosophical craftsman," Chisholm adds. "The best of his writings are paradigmatic of what philosophy ought to be: penetrating, lucid, precise, and objective."

This, however, is not the end of our story. Since the death of Curt and Mabel Ducasse, some strange things have been happening. Marge Tomas, for example, awoke one morning aware that she had been dreaming of the Ducasses. "All of the dream faded except for Dr. Ducasse, whom I could sort of feel or see," Mrs. Tomas says. "In the dream he told me that there were some very important papers in a file cabinet. I woke from the dream with this sense of urgency – that I *must* get these extremely important papers.

"Only three days later Professor Chisholm called to tell me that the American Philosophical Association was having a dispute with Brown over a section of the Ducasse will. Certain papers were needed, he said, and did I know where they were. Well, the papers were in the University Hall office of Deputy Treasurer Larry Robinson. And these were the same papers Professor Ducasse spoke to me about in the dream. It makes one wonder."

Unusual occurrences also have been taking place on lower Aberdeen Road, a short dead-end street of only six houses that ends with the dense and foreboding Squantum Woods. Have there been ghosts at work here? Well, perhaps. You be the judge.

After being vacant for a long spell following the death of Mrs. Ducasse, the Ducasse home was purchased in 1978 by Albert Van Nostrand, professor of English at Brown. Prior to that purchase, Van would have laughed heartily if you had dared to ask if he believed in ghosts. Today, he's no longer sure where he stands on the subject. And he's no longer laughing.

"The neighbors warned me about odd things happening in the Ducasse home," Van Nostrand says. "They were right on target. For example, there is the problem with the three French windows, which are closed and latched tightly when we leave each morning. The problem is that when I come home at night the windows are often open. All the latches appear to fit tightly. I really can't explain it. The things that disturbs me most is that when I tell my neighbors, they just smile and nod knowingly."

There are other strange occurrences, such as the hot water faucet in the bathroom sink, shut off tightly in the morning but bubbling and wheezing by the time people return in the evening. New washers don't stop the bubble or the wheeze. It's also said that three pictures have dropped to the floor from walls in three different rooms – each picture secured into the paneling with large ten-penny nails.

"At first, I was inclined to scoff at these shenanigans," Van Nostrand says, "but my kids, Amy ('75), Jillian ('76), and Christie took me to task. Now, I've adopted a blasé attitude. After all, I knew Curt Ducasse. He was a hell of a nice guy. So, if he wants to come back and visit his old house once in a while, it's all right with me."

It has to be. Van doesn't stand a ghost of a chance of stopping him.

Index